JOHN MILTON

PARADISE LOST
and
PARADISE REGAINED

AIRMONT BOOKS

401 LAFAYETTE ST. • NEW YORK, N. Y. 10003

THE SPECIAL CONTENTS OF THIS EDITION
©, Copyright, 1968, by
Airmont Publishing Company, Inc.

ISBN: 0-8049-0173-2

JOHN MILTON
PARADISE LOST
and
PARADISE REGAINED

INTRODUCTION

One of the best ways to approach John Milton's remarkable poetry is through a consideration of a few salient aspects of his equally remarkable life. Milton was born in 1608, the son of a prosperous scrivener (scriveners drew up wills and other legal documents) who was also an outstanding musician. The combination of his father's money and his own diligence provided for young Milton the best education available in seventeenth-century England. After spending a number of years at a private preparatory school in London, he was admitted to Cambridge University, where he received his B.A. in 1629 and his M.A. in 1632. Then, as now, a good education required far more than simply attending good schools; Milton's academic success was due to his great talent and his unflagging energy. His remark that after the age of twelve he scarcely ever quit studying before midnight indicates his thirst for knowledge (and, incidentally, also helps to explain why he went almost totally blind at the age of forty-four).

One of the reasons why Milton was so diligent a schoolboy was that, even at an early age, he began to prepare himself for the vocation of poetry. The Poet was frequently accorded an exalted position in the Renaissance; if, as it was widely believed, man differs from the animals because of his unique capacity for rational discourse, then it follows that the Poet, the molder of speech, is a leader

3

and teacher of men. In the terms of Horace's well-known dictum, poetry should teach by pleasing. This conception placed responsibility upon the Poet's shoulders for he had to be (so it was felt) a master of all knowledge.

Milton was perhaps the last of the great Renaissance Humanists in England. Humanism can be characterized as an intellectual movement of the Renaissance which sought to rediscover and revitalize the literature of Greece and Rome. No mere antiquarian, Milton delighted in the heritage of the ancient world and did everything he could to make it his own. One Humanist doctrine which especially influenced his writing was the idea of *literary imitation*. Just as Virgil had imitated many aspects of Homer's epics, so it was felt that modern poets could profitably pattern their poems after Classical models. Almost every line of Milton's verse evidences his wide reading and capacious memory; he is the most learned of English poets. Echoes of the *Odyssey*, the *Iliad*, and especially the *Aeneid* permeate his two epics. It should be remarked, however, that his imitation of Virgil, Homer, and many others is neither servile nor gratuitous. Milton wished to call these poets to the reader's mind so that his own poems would gain resonance and depth; his use of his predecessors' work is, in short, creative and artistic.

But to speak of Milton only as a Humanist is seriously to distort his mind and his poetry. Although he treasured the pagan literature of Greece and Rome, his deepest commitment was to Christianity. Like many other Renaissance Humanists, Milton was able to reconcile the apparently conflicting voices of Athens and Jerusalem. His literary imagination was nurtured by the Bible as well as the ancient poets, and his two epics represent his attempt to write epics in the Classical fashion about what is essentially Biblical history.

The greatest historical event in England during Milton's lifetime was the Puritan Revolution, which split the nation into two warring camps—the Church of England and the King on one side against religious dissenters and the Parliament on the other. Milton had long opposed what he felt were the empty ceremonies and hypocrisy of the Church of England, and throughout his life he was a passionate advocate of religious and political liberty. Naturally, when the crisis came he cast his lot with the revolutionary forces. The Puritan leaders recognized

Milton's talents and contracted him to write a number of polemical treatises against opponents of the revolution (mainly 1641–1649). In 1649 he was appointed Secretary of Foreign Tongues to the Council of State, an important position which involved composing the government's Latin correspondence with foreign courts. During these middle years of his life, the pressure of his official duties kept Milton from writing very ambitious poetry (he metaphorically spoke of being able to write only with his left hand at the time). During the final twenty years of his life the house of Stuart re-established itself on the English throne, his own political activities ceased, and he finally found the time to write his two great epics—*Paradise Lost* (1667) and *Paradise Regained* (1671).

Although the twofold basis of Milton's epics—Christian theology and Humanist learning—is being forgotten at an alarming rate in modern society, his epics are not therefore "monuments to dead ideas." Of course, we will never respond to, say, Classical mythology with the same enthusiasm which Milton showed, nor do most of us literally believe in the creation of the world as it is set forth in *Genesis* and in Book Seven of *Paradise Lost*. But these changes in the climate of belief do not make Milton's epics obsolete. Unlike washing machines and automobiles, poems are not superceded by newer models; unlike the quantitative sciences, there is no such thing as progress in art. Milton's epics are not, after all, theological or philosophical treatises which can be refuted—they are poems.

A critical reader, however, must exercise his mind as well as his imagination. One cannot accurately read Milton's epics without knowing some of the ideas which are their conceptual framework. As their titles indicate, the first epic is about the loss of Paradise, the second about its being regained. By eating the fatal apple Adam destroyed Paradise and brought Sin and Death into the world; by dying upon the cross Christ (the "one greater Man" mentioned at the beginning of *Paradise Lost*) redeemed the sin of our first father and regained Paradise. God the Father represents Justice, while the Son of God represents Mercy. The Son of God atones for the sin of man by sacrificing His own life so that the justice of His Father can be fulfilled.

This brings us to a second important idea; what Adam's

sin was. To answer the question we must first begin with Milton's conception of the universe. He saw the world as being hierarchically ordered. That is, the order and goodness of the universe depends upon creatures being in their proper places in a gradated ladder which stretches from God the Creator at the top to brute animals at the bottom. Man's place on this ladder is important, for it is between the angels immediately above and the animals immediately below. Since man was created in the image of God, he has a rational mind; but he also is subject to animalistic and irrational passions. Man, then, is a kind of battleground for these opposing forces. Depending on whether his reason or passions gets the upper hand, man will be either godlike or bestial.

Given this hierarchical view of the universe, obedience becomes one of the greatest human virtues. To be obedient to God is to uphold His perfect order; disobedience brings about chaos and destruction. Disobedience and pride are closely related for Milton. If a person disobeys God, then he is assuming a position which is not his own, and hence he is proud and ambitious. As every Renaissance schoolboy knew, Adam and Eve fell because of pride. Milton, however, was careful to distinguish the fall of Adam from that of Eve.

Eve makes her own fall possible by willfully separating herself from Adam in the Garden (an action which is in itself a violation of God's hierarchy since Man was created superior to Woman). Satan, who has taken the form of a snake to avoid detection, does not physically overpower Eve, but rather insinuates ideas into her mind which cause her to eat the apple of her own free will. The main technique he uses is flattery, which appeals to Eve's greatest weakness—personal vanity. He speaks, for instance, of her "Celestial Beauty" and says she is pretty enough to be "A Goddess among Gods." When her pride finally leads her to eat the Forbidden Fruit, she violates the only commandment God has given her, and she purchases knowledge of Good and Evil only at the expense of her own life.

Adam's motives for eating the apple are quite different from Eve's. As soon as she tells him what she has done, he is terrified. But he immediately decides to share her crime with her. Adam's sin is almost heroic, for we are moved by his devotion to Eve: "from thy State / Mine never shall be parted, bliss or woe." But his love for Eve does not exonerate him from the guilt of having disobeyed God. As the Son of God pointedly asks him, "Was she thy God?" In other words, Adam owed his primary allegiance to his Creator and not to Eve.

Adam and Eve immediately show the effects of their sin, for they burn with lust and then hatefully blame each other for the guilt which they share. Their sin affects nature as well as themselves; the earth shudders, and animals which used to play together now prey on one another. After a period of intense despair, Adam and Eve accept the responsibility for their sin (the first step on the way to penance) and vow to support each other in the harsh world beyond the green walls of Paradise. The last four lines of the poem indicate a degree of ambiguity about the fortunes of our first parents. Although they are weeping as they leave Paradise, they quickly wipe their tears away. Although they have been forever exiled from the joys of Paradise, yet "the world was all before them." If they are being exiled from the old, then, they are also seeking out the new. The archangel Michael tells them as they leave the Garden that, if they practise the Christian virtues, they will have a "Paradise within" themselves and will even be "happier far" than they were in Eden. God's infinite goodness has even brought good out of man's sin; Milton has effectively "justified the ways of God to man."

One of the most interesting characters in *Paradise Lost* is Satan. We should remember, however, that, although Milton made him interesting, Satan is not necessarily the "epic hero" of the poem. From the first time we see him in Book One, Satan undergoes a progressive deterioration in the poem. He does indeed have traces of heroic grandeur in the beginning: he lies on the sea of burning marl as huge as Leviathan. His shield is as vast as the moon, and his towering spear would make a ship's mast look like a fairy's wand. But as the poem progresses, his light becomes dimmer, his size more diminutive, and his nature more base. For example, in Book Four Milton likens Satan to a prowling wolf, a common burglar, a comorant, and finally he is discovered "squat like a toad" at the ear of sleeping Eve. This series of Satanic metamorphoses ends when he adopts the form of a serpent, an animal whose sliminess and cunning equal his own. God ironically punishes Satan in Book Ten, when He transforms him and the rest of the fallen angels into serpents.

Paradise Regained is in many ways different from *Paradise Lost.* It is only about one-third as long as Milton's earlier epic, and it also lacks most of the complexity and drama of *Paradise Lost.* The cast of characters in *Paradise Regained* has been narrowed down to two—the Son of God and Satan. The two epics dramatize the dual nature of the Son of God; we see His divine aspect in *Paradise Lost* and His human aspect in the later epic. The central concern of Milton's epic is again temptation. In *Paradise Lost* Satan tempts Adam and succeeds (although God turns this success to His own purpose), but in the second epic the Son of God resists Satan's guiles.

When the Son of God is wandering in the wilderness, Satan unsuccessfully tempts him on three occasions (the closest Biblical account to Milton's poem is in Luke 4:1-12). Satan's three temptations are as follows: first, he asks the hungry Son of God to turn a stone into bread; second, he offers Him the kingdoms of the world; and last, he tries to talk the Son of God into throwing Himself off a pinnacle to see if His Father will save Him. Of course, the Son of God resists all these temptations, and, ironically, at the end of the poem it is Satan who falls from the pinnacle.

FREDERIC B. TROMLY
Grinnell College

SUGGESTED READING

Genesis and *Luke* (They contain most of the Biblical history in Milton's epics.)

Marjorie Nicolson, *John Milton: A Reader's Guide to His Poetry* (New York, 1963). (This paperback is the best introduction to Milton's verse.)

C. S. Lewis, *A Preface to 'Paradise Lost'* (London, 1942). (Another good introduction to Milton, also available in paperback edition.)

Merritt Y. Hughes, ed., *John Milton: Complete Poems and Major Prose* (New York, 1957). (This is the best one volume edition of Milton's works; it contains very full notes and helpful bibliographies.)

Paradise Lost

THE VERSE OF "PARADISE LOST"

"The measure is English Heroic Verse without Rime, as that of Homer in Greek, and of Virgil in Latin; Rime being no necessary Adjunct or true Ornament of Poem or good Verse, in longer Works especially, but the Invention of a barbarous Age, to set off wretched matter and lame Meeter; grac't indeed since by the use of some famous modern Poets, carried away by Custom, but much to thir own vexation, hindrance, and constraint, to express many things otherwise, and for the most part worse than else they would have exprest them. Not without cause, therefore, some both Italian and Spanish Poets of prime note, have rejected Rime both in longer and shorter Works, as have also, long since, our best English Tragedies, as a thing of itself, to all judicious eares, triveal and of no true musical delight; which consists only in apt Numbers, fit quantity of Syllables, and the sense variously drawn out from one verse into another, not in the jingling sound of like endings, a fault avoyded by the learned Ancients both in Poetry and all good Oratory. This neglect then of Rime, so little is to be taken for a defect, though it may seem so perhaps to vulgar readers, that it rather is to be esteem'd an example set, the first in English, of ancient liberty recover'd to Heroic Poem from the troublesom and modern bondage of Rimeing."

From Milton's own Edition, 1669.

BOOK I

The Argument

This First Book proposes, first in brief, the whole subject, Man's disobedience, and the loss thereupon of Paradise, wherein he was placed. Then touches the prime cause of his fall, the serpent, or rather Satan in the serpent; who, revolting from God, and drawing to his side many legions of Angels, was by the command of God driven out of heaven with all his crew into the great deep. Which action passed over, the Poem hastes into the midst of things, presenting Satan with his Angels now fallen into hell, described here, not in the centre, for heaven and earth may be supposed as yet not made, certainly not yet accursed, but in a place of utter darkness, fitliest called Chaos. Here Satan with his Angels lying on the burning lake, thunderstruck and astonished, after a certain space recovers, as from confusion, calls up him who next in order and dignity lay by him: they confer of their miserable fall. Satan awakens all his legions, who lay till then in the same manner confounded; they rise; their numbers, array of battle, their chief leaders named, according to the idols known afterwards in Canaan and the countries adjoining. To these Satan directs his speech, comforts them with hope yet of regaining heaven, but tells them lastly of a new world and new kind of creature to be created, according to an ancient prophecy or report in heaven; for that Angels were long before this visible creation, was the opinion of many ancient Fathers. To find out the truth of this prophecy, and what to determine thereon, he refers to a full council. What his associates thence attempt. Pandæmonium, the palace of Satan, rises, suddenly built out of the deep: the infernal Peers there sit in council.

Of Man's first disobedience and the fruit
Of that forbidden tree, whose mortal taste
Brought death into the world and all our woe,
With loss of Eden, till one greater Man
Restore us and regain the blissful seat,
Sing heav'nly Muse, that on the secret top
Of Oreb, or of Sinai, didst inspire
That shepherd,[1] who first taught the chosen seed,

[1] Moses.

In the beginning how the heav'ns and earth
Rose out of Chaos; or if Sion hill
Delight thee more, and Siloa's brook[1] that flow'd
Past by the oracle of God; I thence
Invoke thy aid to my advent'rous song,
That with no middle flight intends to soar
Above th' Aonian mount,[2] while it pursues
Things unattempted yet in prose or rhyme.

And chiefly thou, O Spirit, that dost prefer
Before all temples th' upright heart and pure,
Instruct me, for thou know'st; thou from the first
Wast present, and with mighty wings outspread
Dove-like sat'st brooding on the vast abyss,[3]
And mad'st it pregnant: what in me is dark
Illumine, what is low raise and support;
That to the height of this great argument
I may assert eternal Providence,
And justify the ways of God to men.

Say first, for heav'n hides nothing from thy view,
Nor the deep tract of hell—say first, what cause
Moved our grand Parents in that happy state,
Favour'd of heaven so highly, to fall off
From their Creator, and transgress his will
For one restraint, lords of the world besides?
Who first seduced them to that foul revolt?
Th' infernal serpent; he it was, whose guile,
Stirr'd up with envy and revenge, deceived
The mother of mankind, what time his pride
Had cast him out from heav'n, with all his host
Of rebel Angels, by whose aid aspiring
To set himself in glory above his peers,
He trusted to have equall'd the Most High,[4]
If he opposed; and with ambitious aim
Against the throne and monarchy of God
Raised impious war in heav'n, and battle proud,
With vain attempt. Him the almighty Power
Hurl'd headlong flaming from th' ethereal sky,

[1] A small brook that flowed near the Temple of Jerusalem.
[2] A mountain in Bœotia. In mythology, the Muses were said to dwell on it.
[3] Gen. i. 2.
[4] Isaiah xiv. 13–15.

With hideous ruin and combustion, down
To bottomless perdition, there to dwell
In adamantine chains and penal fire,
Who durst defy th' Omnipotent to arms.
Nine times the space that measures day and night
To mortal men, he with his horrid crew
Lay vanquish'd, rolling in the fiery gulf,
Confounded though immortal: but his doom
Reserved him to more wrath; for now the thought
Both of lost happiness and lasting pain
Torments him; round he throws his baleful eyes,
That witness'd huge affliction and dismay,
Mix'd with obdurate pride and stedfast hate.
At once, as far as angels ken, he views
The dismal situation waste and wild;
A dungeon horrible, on all sides round,
As one great furnace, flamed; yet from those flames
No light, but rather darkness visible
Served only to discover sights of woe,
Regions of sorrow, doleful shades, where peace
And rest can never dwell, hope never comes,[1]
That comes to all; but torture without end
Still urges, and a fiery deluge, fed
With ever-burning sulphur unconsumed.
Such place eternal justice had prepared
For those rebellious; here their prison ordain'd
In utter darkness, and their portion set
As far removed from God and light of heav'n,
As from the centre thrice to th' utmost pole.
O how unlike the place from whence they fell!
There the companions of his fall, o'erwhelm'd
With floods and whirlwinds of tempestuous fire,
He soon discerns, and welt'ring by his side
One next himself in power, and next in crime,
Long after known in Palestine, and named
Beëlzebub:[2] To whom th' arch-enemy,

[1] "Lasciate ogni speranza voi ch' intrate," was the inscription placed by Dante over the gates of his "Inferno."

[2] The god of flies, worshipped by the Philistines (2 Kings i. 2). The Jews considered Beelzebub the greatest of the devils. See their accusation of our Lord, St. Matt. xii. 24–27; where it appears that with them Beelzebub and "Satan" were synonymous names. Milton makes them two different fallen angels.

And thence in heav'n call'd Satan,[1] with bold words
Breaking the horrid silence, thus began.

If thou beest he—But O how fall'n! how changed
From him, who in the happy realms of light,
Clothed with transcendent brightness, didst outshine
Myriads, though bright! If he, whom mutual league,
United thoughts and counsels, equal hope
And hazard in the glorious enterprise,
Join'd with me once, now misery hath join'd
In equal ruin: into what pit thou seest
From what height fall'n, so much the stronger proved
He with his thunder; and till then who knew
The force of those dire arms? yet not for those,
Nor what the potent victor in his rage
Can else inflict, do I repent, or change,
Though changed in outward lustre, that fix'd mind
And high disdain from sense of injured merit,
That with the Mightiest raised me to contend,
And to the fierce contention brought along
Innumerable force of Spirits arm'd,
That durst dislike his reign; and, me preferring,
His utmost power with adverse power opposed
In dubious battle on the plains of heav'n,
And shook his throne. What though the field be lost?
All is not lost; th' unconquerable will,
And study of revenge, immortal hate
And courage never to submit or yield,
And what is else not to be overcome;
That glory never shall his wrath or might
Extort from me: to bow and sue for grace
With suppliant knee, and deify his power.
Who from the terror of this arm so late
Doubted his empire, that were low indeed,
That were an ignominy and shame beneath
This downfall; since by fate the strength of Gods
And this empyreal substance cannot fail;
Since through experience of this great event,
In arms not worse, in foresight much advanced,
We may with more successful hope resolve
To wage by force or guile eternal war,

[1] Satan is a Hebrew word, signifying "enemy." *The* enemy both
of God and man.

Irreconcileable to our grand foe,
Who now triumphs, and in th' excess of joy
Sole reigning holds the tyranny of heav'n.

  So spake th' apostate Angel, though in pain,
Vaunting aloud, but rack'd with deep despair:
And him thus answer'd soon his bold compeer.

  O Prince, O Chief of many thronèd Powers,
That led th' imbattell'd Seraphim to war
Under thy conduct, and, in dreadful deeds
Fearless, endanger'd heav'n's perpetual King,
And put to proof his high supremacy;
Whether upheld by strength, or chance, or fate,
Too well I see and rue the dire event,
That with sad overthrow and foul defeat
Hath lost us heav'n, and all this mighty host
In horrible destruction laid thus low,
As far as Gods and heavenly essences
Can perish: for the mind and spirit remains
Invincible, and vigor soon returns,
Though all our glory extinct, and happy state
Here swallow'd up in endless misery.
But what if he our conqueror, whom I now
Of force believe almighty, since no less
Than such could have o'erpower'd such force as ours,
Has left us this our spirit and strength entire,
Strongly to suffer and support our pains,
That we may so suffice his vengeful ire,
Or do him mightier service, as his thralls
By right of war, whate'er his business be,
Here in the heart of hell to work in fire,
Or do his errands in the gloomy deep:
What can it then avail, though yet we feel
Strength undiminish'd, or eternal being
To undergo eternal punishment?
Whereto with speedy words th' Arch-fiend replied.

  Fall'n Cherub, to be weak is miserable,
Doing or suffering: but of this be sure,
To do ought good never will be our task,
But ever to do ill our sole delight;
As being the contrary to his high will,
Whom we resist. If then his providence
Out of our evil seek to bring forth good,

Our labor must be to pervert that end,
And out of good still to find means of evil;
Which oft-times may succeed, so as perhaps
Shall grieve him, if I fail not, and disturb
His inmost counsels from their destined aim.
But see! the angry victor hath recall'd
His ministers of vengeance and pursuit
Back to the gates of heav'n: the sulphurous hail,
Shot after us in storm, o'erblown hath laid
The fiery surge, that from the precipice
Of heav'n received us falling, and the thunder,
Wing'd with red lightning and impetuous rage,
Perhaps hath spent his shafts, and ceases now
To bellow through the vast and boundless deep.
Let us not slip th' occasion, whether scorn
Or satiate fury yield it from our foe.
Seest thou yon dreary plain, forlorn and wild,
The seat of desolation, void of light,
Save what the glimmering of these livid flames
Casts pale and dreadful? thither let us tend
From off the tossing of these fiery waves,
There rest, if any rest can harbor there,
And, reassembling our afflicted powers,
Consult how we may henceforth most offend
Our enemy, our own loss how repair,
How overcome this dire calamity,
What reinforcement we may gain from hope,
If not, what resolution from despair.
    Thus Satan talking to his nearest mate,
With head up-lift above the wave, and eyes
That sparkling blazed; his other parts besides
Prone on the flood, extended long and large,
Lay floating many a rood, in bulk as huge
As whom the fables name of monstrous size,
Titanian, or Earth-born, that warred on Jove,[1]
Briareus, or Typhon, whom the den
By ancient Tarsus held, or that sea-beast
Leviathan, which GOD of all his works

[1] The Titans were monstrous giants, said to have made war
against the gods. Briareus had a hundred hands. Typhon was the
same as Typhœus, who was imprisoned by Jupiter in a cave near
Tarsus, in Cilicia.

Created hugest that swim th' ocean stream;
Him haply slumbering on the Norway foam
The pilot of some small night-founder'd skiff
Deeming some island, oft, as seamen tell,
With fixèd anchor in his scaly rind
Moors by his side under the lee, while night
Invests the sea, and wishèd morn delays[1]
So stretched out huge in length the Arch-fiend lay,
Chain'd on the burning lake, nor ever thence
Had risen or heaved his head, but that the will
And high permission of all-ruling heaven
Left him at large to his own dark designs;
That with reiterated crimes he might
Heap on himself damnation, while he sought
Evil to others, and enraged might see
How all his malice served but to bring forth
Infinite goodness, grace, and mercy shown
On man by him seduced; but on himself
Treble confusion, wrath, and vengeance pour'd.
Forthwith upright he rears from off the pool
His mighty stature; on each hand the flames
Driven backward slope their pointing spires, and roll'd
In billows leave i' th' midst a horrid vale.
Then with expanded wings he steers his flight
Aloft, incumbent on the dusky air,
That felt unusual weight, till on dry land
He lights, if it were land that ever burn'd
With solid, as the lake with liquid, fire;
And such appear'd in hue, as when the force
Of subterranean wind transports a hill
Torn from Pelorus,[2] or the shatter'd side
Of thund'ring Ætna, whose combustible
And fuel'd entrails thence conceiving fire,
Sublimed with mineral fury, aid the winds,
And leave a singèd bottom, all involved
With stench and smoke: such resting found the sole
Of unbless'd feet. Him follow'd his next mate,
Both glorying to have 'scaped the Stygian flood,
As Gods, and by their own recover'd strength,

[1] The whale is evidently here intended.
[2] Capo di Faro, in Sicily.

Not by the sufferance of supernal power.
 Is this the region, this the soil, the clime
Said then the lost Arch-Angel, this the seat
That we must change for heav'n, this mournful gloom
For that celestial light? be it so, since he,
Who now is Sov'reign, can dispose and bid
What shall be right: farthest from him is best,
Whom reason hath equall'd, force hath made supreme
Above his equals. Farewell happy fields,
Where joy for ever dwells: hail horrors; hail
Infernal world; and thou profoundest hell
Receive thy new possessor; one who brings
A mind not to be changed by place or time.
The mind is its own place, and in itself
Can make a heav'n of hell, a hell of heav'n,[1]
What matter where, if I be still the same,
And what I should be, all but less than he
Whom thunder hath made greater? here at least
We shall be free; th' Almighty hath not built
Here for his envy, will not drive us hence:
Here we may reign secure, and in my choice
To reign is worth ambition, though in hell:
Better to reign in hell, than serve in heav'n.
But wherefore let we then our faithful friends,
Th' associates and copartners of our loss,
Lie thus astonish'd on th' oblivious pool,
And call them not to share with us their part
In this unhappy mansion; or once more
With rallied arms to try what may be yet
Regain'd in heav'n, or what more lost in hell?
 So Satan spake, and him Beëlzebub
Thus answer'd: Leader of those armies bright,
Which but th' Omnipotent none could have foil'd,
If once they hear that voice, their liveliest pledge
Of hope in fears and dangers, heard so oft
In worst extremes, and on the perilous edge
Of battle when it raged, in all assaults
Their surest signal, they will soon resume

---

[1] "There's nothing either good or bad, but Thinking makes it so."—SHAKESPEARE.

New courage and revive, though now they lie
Grov'ling and prostrate on yon lake of fire,
As we erewhile, astounded and amazed,
No wonder, fall'n such a pernicious highth.[1]

He scarce had ceased, when the superior fiend
Was moving toward the shore; his ponderous shield,
Ethereal temper, massy, large, and round,
Behind him cast; the broad circumference
Hung on his shoulders like the moon, whose orb
Through optic glass the Tuscan artist[2] views
At ev'ning, from the top of Fesole
Or in Valdarno, to descry new lands,
Rivers or mountains in her spotty globe.
His spear, to equal which the tallest pine,
Hewn on Norwegian hills to be the mast
Of some great Ammiral, were but a wand,
He walk'd with to support uneasy steps
Over the burning marle, not like those steps
On heaven's azure, and the torrid clime
Smote on him sore besides, vaulted with fire.
Nathless he so endured, till on the beach
Of that inflamèd sea he stood and call'd
His legions, Angel forms, who lay entranced,
Thick as autumnal leaves that strow the brooks
In Vallombrosa,[3] where th' Etrurian shades
High overarch'd embower; or scatter'd sedge
Afloat, when with fierce winds Orion arm'd [4]
Hath vex'd the Red-sea coast, whose waves o'erthrew
Busiris[5] and his Memphian chivalry,
While with perfidious hatred they pursued
The sojourners of Goshen, who beheld
From the safe shore their floating carcases
And broken chariot wheels: so thick bestrown

[1] Height.

[2] Galileo. Milton became acquainted with the great astronomer when travelling in Italy. Optic-glass was the name given then and some time after to the telescope.

[3] In Tuscany.

[4] Orion is the constellation representing an armed warrior. "It was supposed to be attended with stormy weather. 'Assurgens fluctu nimbosus Orion.' VIR. *Æn.* I. 539."—NEWTON.

[5] The Pharaoh of Exodus xiv.

Abject and lost lay these, covering the flood,
Under amazement of their hideous change.
He called so loud, that all the hollow deep
Of hell resounded: Princes, Potentates,
Warriors, the flow'r of heav'n, once yours, now lost,
If such astonishment as this can seize
Eternal spirits; or have ye chosen this place
After the toil of battle to repose
Your wearied virtue, for the ease you find
To slumber here, as in the vales of heav'n?
Or in this abject posture have ye sworn
To adore the conqueror? who now beholds
Cherub and Seraph rolling in the flood
With scatter'd arms and ensigns, till anon
His swift pursuers from heav'n gates discern
Th' advantage, and descending tread us down
Thus drooping, or with linkèd thunderbolts
Transfix us to the bottom of this gulf.
Awake, arise, or be for ever fall'n.

 They heard, and were abash'd, and up they sprung
Upon the wing, as when men wont to watch
On duty, sleeping found by whom they dread,
Rouse and bestir themselves ere well awake.
Nor did they not perceive the evil plight
In which they were, or the fierce pains not feel;
Yet to their General's voice they soon obey'd,
Innumerable. As when the potent rod
Of Amram's Son, in Ægypt's evil day,
Waved round the coast up call'd a pitchy cloud
Of locusts, warping on the eastern wind,
That o'er the realm of impious Pharaoh hung
Like night, and darken'd all the land of Nile:[1]
So numberless were those bad angels seen
Hovering on wing under the cope of hell,
'Twixt upper, nether, and surrounding fires;
Till, as a signal given, th' uplifted spear
Of their great Sultan waving to direct
Their course, in even balance down they light
On the firm brimstone, and fill all the plain;

[1] Exodus x. 15.

A multitude like which the populous north[1]
Pour'd never from her frozen loins, to pass
Rhene or the Danaw,[2] when her barbarous sons[3]
Came like a deluge on the south, and spread
Beneath Gibraltar to the Libyan sands.
Forthwith from ev'ry squadron and each band
The heads and leaders thither haste, where stood
Their great Commander; God-like shapes and forms
Excelling human, Princely Dignities,
And powers, that erst in heaven sat on thrones;
Though of their names in heavenly records now
Be no memorial, blotted out and razed
By their rebellion from the books of life.[4]
Nor had they yet among the sons of Eve
Got them new names; till wand'ring o'er the earth,
Through God's high sufferance for the trial of man,
By falsities and lies the greatest part
Of mankind they corrupted to forsake
God their creator, and th' invisible
Glory of him that made them to transform
Oft to the image of a brute, adorn'd

[1] The "populous north," as the northern parts of the world are observed to be more fruitful of people than the hotter countries. Sir William Temple calls it "the northern hive." "Poured never;" a very proper word to express the inundations of these northern nations. "From her frozen loins;" it is the Scripture expression of children and descendants "coming out of the loins," as Gen. xxxv. 11, "Kings shall come out of thy loins;" and these are called *frozen loins* only on account of the coldness of the climate.—NEWTON.

[2] "To pass Rhene or the Danaw." He might have said, consistently with his verse, the Rhine or Danube, but he chose the more uncommon names, Rhene, of the Latin, and Danaw, of the German, both which words are used too, in Spenser.—NEWTON.

[3] "When her barbarous sons," &c. They were truly barbarous; for besides exercising several cruelties, they destroyed all the monuments of learning and politeness wherever they came. "Came like a deluge." Spenser, describing the same people, has the same simile, "Faërie Queen, B. II. cant. 1st. 15:—

"And overflowed all countries far away,
    Like Noye's great flood, with their importune sway."

They were the Goths and Huns, and Vandals, who overran all the southern provinces of Europe, and, crossing the Mediterranean beneath Gibraltar, landed in Africa, and spread themselves as far as Libya. *Beneath* Gibraltar means more southward.—NEWTON.

[4] Psalm ix. 5, 6. Rev. iii. 5.

With gay religions full of pomp and gold,
And Devils to adore for Deities:[1]
Then were they known to men by various names,
And various idols through the heathen world.
  Say, Muse, their names then known, who first, who last,
Roused from the slumber on that fiery couch
At their great Emp'ror's call, as next in worth,
Came singly where he stood on the bare strand,
While the promiscuous crowd stood yet aloof?
The chief were those, who, from the pit of hell
Roaming to seek their prey on earth, durst fix
Their seats long after next the seat of God,
Their altars by his altar, Gods adored
Among the nations round, and durst abide
Jehovah thund'ring out of Sion, throned
Between the Cherubim; yea, often placed
Within his sanctuary itself their shrines,
Abominations;[2] and with cursèd things
His holy rites and solemn feasts profaned,
And with their darkness durst affront his light.
First Moloch, horrid King,[3] besmear'd with blood
Of human sacrifice, and parents' tears,
Though for the noise of drums and timbrels loud
Their children's cries unheard, that past through fire[4]
To his grim idol. Him the Ammonite
Worshipp'd in Rabba and her wat'ry plain,
In Argob, and in Basan, to the stream
Of utmost Arnon. Nor content with such
Audacious neighborhood, the wisest heart
Of Solomon he led by fraud to build
His temple right against the temple of God,
On that opprobrious hill,[5] and made his grove
The pleasant valley of Hinnom, Tophet thence

---

[1] Levit. xvii. 7. Psalm cvi. 37.

[2] Ezek. viii. 15, 16.

[3] The word *Moloch* means *King*. He is styled *horrid* on account of the awful human sacrifices offered to him.

[4] Moloch was represented by an idol of brass sitting on a throne, crowned. Before him was a furnace. His extended arms sloped down to it. Infants placed in his arms fell into the furnace and were consumed.

[5] 1 Kings xi. 7.

And black Gehenna call'd,[1] the type of hell.[2]
Next Chemos,[3] th' óbscene dread of Moab's sons,
From Aroer to Nebo, and the wild
Of southmost Abarim; in Hesebon
And Heronaim, Seon's realm, beyond
The flow'ry dale of Sibma clad with vines,
And Eleale, to the Asphaltic pool:
Peor his other name, when he enticed
Israel in Sittim, on their march from Nile,
To do him wanton rites, which cost them woe.
Yet thence his lustful orgies he enlarged
Even to that hill of scandal, by the grove
Of Moloch homicide, lust hard by hate;
Till good Josiah[4] drove them thence to hell.
With these came they, who, from the bord'ring flood
Of old Euphrates to the brook that parts
Ægypt from Syrian ground, had general names
Of Baalim and Ashtaroth,[5] those male,
These feminine: for spirits when they please
Can either sex assume, or both; so soft
And uncompounded is their essence pure;
Nor tied or manacled with joint or limb,
Nor founded on the brittle strength of bones,
Like cumbrous flesh; but in what shape they choose,
Dilated or condensed, bright or obscure,
Can execute their airy purposes,
And works of love or enmity fulfil.
For those the race of Israel oft forsook
Their living strength, and unfrequented left
His righteous altar, bowing lowly down
To bestial gods; for which their heads as low
Bow'd down in battle, sunk before the spear
Of despicable foes. With these in troop
Came Astoreth, whom the Phœnicians called

[1] It was called *Tophet* from *toph*, a drum, the noise of drums being employed to drown the cries of the poor babes offered to the idol.

[2] So used by our Lord.

[3] 1 Kings xi. 7.

[4] 2 Kings xxiii.

[5] Frequently named together in Scripture. They were the sun, Baal; the moon, Astoreth; and the stars; *im* being the plural termination of the name Baal.

Astarte, queen of heaven, with crescent horns;
To whose bright image nightly by the moon
Sidonian virgins paid their vows and songs,
In Sion also not unsung, where stood
Her temple on th' offensive mountain, built
By that uxorious king,[1] whose heart though large,
Beguiled by fair idolatresses, fell
To idols foul. Thammuz[2] came next behind,
Whose annual wound in Lebanon allured
The Syrian damsels to lament his fate
In amorous ditties all a summer's day,
While smooth Adonis from his native rock
Ran purple to the sea, supposed with blood
Of Thammuz yearly wounded: the love-tale
Infected Sion's daughters with like heat,
Whose wanton passions in the sacred porch
Ezekiel saw,[3] when by the vision led
His eyes survey'd the dark idolatries
Of alienated Judah. Next came one
Who mourn'd in earnest, when the captive ark
Maim'd his brute image, head and hands lopt off
In his own temple, on the grunsel [4] edge,
Where he fell flat, and shamed his worshippers:
Dagon his name;[5] sea monster, upward man
And downward fish: yet had his temple high
Rear'd in Azotus, dreaded through the coast
Of Palestine, in Gath, and Ascalon,

[1] Solomon; who built a temple to Astoreth, the moon, on the Mount of Olives.

[2] Adonis. See Maundrell's "Travels," p. 34. "We had the fortune to see what may be supposed to be the occasion of that opinion which Lucian relates concerning this river (the Adonis; called by the Turks, Ibrahim Bassa), viz., that this stream, at certain seasons of the year, especially about the feast of Adonis, is of a bloody color; which the Heathens looked upon as proceeding from a kind of sympathy in the river for the death of Adonis. Something like this, we saw, actually came to pass; for the water was stained to a surprising redness, and, as we observed in travelling had discolored the sea a great way into a reddish hue, occasioned, doubtless, by a sort of minium, or red earth, washed into the river by the violence of the rain, and not by any stain from Adonis' blood."

[3] Ezek. viii. 12.

[4] Threshold, *groundsel*.

[5] 1 Sam. v. 4.

And Accaron, and Gaza's frontier bounds.
Him follow'd Rimmon,[1] whose delightful seat
Was fair Damascus, on the fertile banks
Of Abbana and Pharphar, lucid streams.
He also against the house of GOD was bold
A leper once he lost,[2] and gain'd a king,
Ahaz his sottish conqueror, whom he drew
GOD's altar to disparage,[3] and displace
For one of Syrian mode, whereon to burn
His odious off'rings, and adore the gods
Whom he had vanquish'd. After these appear'd
A crew, who under names of old renown,
Osiris, Isis, Orus,[4] and their train,
With monstrous shapes and sorceries abused
Fanatic Ægypt and her priests, to seek
Their wand'ring Gods disguised in brutish forms,[5]
Rather than human. Nor did Israel 'scape
Th' infection, when their borrow'd gold composed
The calf in Oreb;[6] and the rebel king
Doubled that sin in Bethel and in Dan,
Lik'ning his Maker to the grazèd ox,[7]
Jehovah, who in one night, when he pass'd
From Ægypt marching, equall'd with one stroke
Both her first-born and all her bleating gods.
Belial [8] came last, than whom a spirit more lewd
Fell not from heaven, or more gross to love
Vice for itself: to him no temple stood
Or altar smoked; yet who more oft than he
In temples and at altars, when the priest
Turns atheist, as did Eli's sons, who fill'd
With lust and violence the house of GOD?
In courts and palaces he also reigns,
And in luxurious cities, where the noise
Of riot ascends above their loftiest towers,

[1] A Syrian god.
[2] Naaman. See 2 Kings v. 17.
[3] 2 Kings xvi. 10. 2 Chron. xxviii. 23.
[4] Orus was the son of Osiris (the sun) and Isis (the moon).
[5] The sacred calf, the ram, &c.
[6] Exod. xxxii.
[7] 1 Kings xii. 28.
[8] The god of lewdness and luxury.

And injury, and outrage: and when night
Darkens the streets, then wander forth the sons
Of Belial, flown with insolence and wine.
Witness the streets of Sodom, and that night
In Gibeah, when the hospitable door
Exposed a matron to avoid worse rape.

These were the prime in order and in might;
The rest were long to tell, though far renown'd
Th' Ionian gods, of Javan's issue,[1] held
Gods, yet confess'd later than heav'n and earth,
Their boasted parents. Titan, heav'n's first-born,[2]
With his enormous brood and birthright seized
By younger Saturn, he from mightier Jove,
His own and Rhea's son, like measure found;
So Jove usurping reign'd: these first in Crete
And Ida known:[3] thence on the snowy top
Of cold Olympus ruled the middle air,
Their highest heaven; or on the Delphian cliff[4]
Or in Dodona,[5] and through all the bounds
Of Doric land;[6] or who with Saturn old
Fled over Adria to th' Hesperian fields,[7]
And o'er the Celtic roam'd the utmost isles.[8]

All these and more came flocking; but with looks
Down-cast and damp, yet such wherein appear'd
Obscure some glimpse of joy, to have found their chief
Not in despair, to have found themselves not lost
In loss itself; which on his countenance cast

---

[1] Javan, the fourth son of Japhet, was supposed to have settled
Ionia, in the south-west part of Asia Minor. The gods of the Greek
mythology are here meant.

[2] Titan, supposed to be the son of Heaven and Earth, was the
father of the giants. Saturn, his younger brother, seized his empire,
and was, in his turn, deposed by his son Jupiter.

[3] Jupiter was said to have been born on Mount Ida, in the island
of Crete (now Candia). He and the other Greek gods then passed
to Greece, and Jupiter reigned on Mount Olympus, in Thessaly.

[4] Mount Parnassus, where the city of Delphi, famous for its
Oracle, was situated.

[5] A city and wood sacred to Jupiter, famous also for its Oracle.

[6] "Doric land," Greece.

[7] Italy.

[8] France, the abode of the Celts. "Utmost isles," Great Britain,
&c., &c.: *Ultima Thule*.

Like doubtful hue: but he, his wonted pride
Soon recollecting, with high words, that bore
Semblance of worth not substance, gently raised
Their fainted courage, and dispell'd their fears.
Then straight commands, that at the warlike sound
Of trumpets loud and clarions be uprear'd
His mighty standard: that proud honor claim'd
Azazel [1] as his right, a cherub tall;
Who forthwith from the glittering staff unfurl'd
Th' imperial ensign, which, full high advanced,
Shone like a meteor, streaming to the wind,
With gems and golden lustre rich emblazed,
Seraphic arms and trophies; all the while
Sonorous metal blowing martial sounds:
At which the universal host up sent
A shout that tore hell's concave, and beyond
Frighted the reign of Chaos and old Night.
All in a moment through the gloom were seen
Ten thousand banners rise into the air
With orient colors waving: with them rose
A forest huge of spears; and thronging helms
Appear'd, and serried shields in thick array
Of depth immeasurable: anon they move
In perfect phalanx to the Dorian mood [2]
Of flutes and soft recorders;[3] such as raised
To highth of noblest temper heroes old
Arming to battle; and instead of rage
Deliberate valor breath'd, firm, and unmoved
With dread of death to flight or foul retreat;
Nor wanting power to mitigate and swage
With solemn touches troubled thoughts, and chase
Anguish, and doubt, and fear, and sorrow, and pain,
From mortal or immortal minds. Thus they,
Breathing united force, with fixèd thought,
Moved on in silence to soft pipes, that charm'd

---

[1] This name is used for some demon or devil by several ancient authors, Jewish and Christian.—NEWTON.

[2] A solemn style of music, exciting to cool and deliberate courage.—NEWTON. The ancients had three different styles of music: the Lydian, soft and languishing; the Phrygian, gay and animated; the Dorian, solemn and majestic.

[3] A species of flute or flageolet.

Their painful steps o'er the burnt soil; and now
Advanced in view they stand, a horrid front
Of dreadful length and dazzling arms, in guise
Of warriors old with order'd spear and shield,
Awaiting what command their mighty chief
Had to impose: he through the armèd files
Darts his experienced eye, and soon traverse
The whole batallion views; their order due,
Their visages and stature as of Gods;
Their number last he sums. And now his heart
Distends with pride, and hard'ning in his strength
Glories; for never, since created man,
Met such embodied force, as named with these
Could merit more than that small infantry[1]
Warr'd on by cranes; though all the giant brood
Of Phlegra[2] with th' heroic race were join'd
That fought at Thebes[3] and Ilium,[4] on each side
Mix'd with auxiliar Gods; and what resounds
In fable or romance of Uther's son,[5]
Begirt with British and Armoric knights;
And all who since, baptized or infidel
Jousted in Aspramont or Montalban,[6]
Damasco, or Marocco, or Trebisond,
Or whom Biserta sent from Afric shore,
When Charlemain with all his peerage fell
By Fontarabia. Thus far these beyond
Compare of mortal prowess, yet observed
Their dread commander: he, above the rest
In shape and gesture proudly eminent,
Stood like a tow'r; his form had yet not lost
All her original brightness, nor appear'd
Less than Arch angel ruin'd, and th' excess

[1] The Pigmies. See "Basilides Athenæi," IX. 43.
[2] Phlegra, a city of Macedonia, where the Titans, or giants, dwelt who made war against the gods.
[3] Thebes, a city of Bœotia, famous for the war between the sons of Œdipus, Eteocles and Polynices. The subject of Statius's "Thebaïd."
[4] Troy, the siege of which is the subject of Homer's "Iliad." The gods took different sides in this war.
[5] Arthur. Armoric knights were knights of Armorica, or Brittany.
[6] Romantic names of places mentioned in Ariosto's poem, "Orlando Furioso," and in the old romances.

Of glory obscured: as when the sun new-risen
Looks through the horizontal misty air,
Shorn of his beams; or from behind the moon,
In dim eclipse, disastrous twilight sheds
On half the nations, and with fear of change
Perplexes monarchs:[1] darken'd so, yet shone
Above them all th' Arch angel: but his face
Deep scars of thunder had intrench'd, and care
Sat on his faded cheek, but under brows
Of dauntless courage, and considerate pride
Waiting revenge: cruel his eye, but cast
Signs of remorse and passion to behold
The fellows of his crime, the followers rather,
Far other once beheld in bliss, condemn'd
For ever now to have their lot in pain,
Millions of spirits for his fault amerced [2]
Of heav'n, and from eternal splendors flung.
For his revolt, yet faithful how they stood,
Their glory wither'd: as when heaven's fire
Hath scath'd the forest oaks or mountain pines,
With singèd top their stately growth, though bare,
Stands on the blasted heath. He now prepared
To speak; whereat their doubled ranks they bend
From wing to wing, and half enclose him round
With all his peers: attention held them mute.
Thrice he assay'd, and thrice in spite of scorn
Tears, such as angels weep, burst forth; at last
Words interwove with sighs found out their way.
   O myriads of immortal spirits, O Powers
Matchless, but with th' Almighty, and that strife
Was not inglorious, though th' event was dire,
As this place testifies, and this dire change
Hateful to utter: but what power of mind,
Foreseeing or presaging, from the depth
Of knowledge past or present, could have fear'd,
How such united force of Gods, how such
As stood like these, could ever know repulse?
For who can yet believe, though after loss,
That all these puissant legions, whose exile

   [1] Alluding to the superstition that an eclipse or comet foretold
the disturbance of nations.
   [2] Deprived of by forfeiture. See Quarles's "Divine Poems," p. 18.

Hath emptied heav'n,[1] shall fail to reascend
Self-raised, and repossess their native seat?
For me, be witness all the host of heav'n,
If counsels different or danger shunn'd
By me have lost our hopes: but he, who reigns
Monarch in heav'n, till then as one secure
Sat on his throne, upheld by old repute,
Consent, or custom, and his regal state
Put forth at full, but still his strength conceal'd,
Which tempted our attempt, and wrought our fall.
Henceforth his might we know, and know our own,
So as not either to provoke, or dread
New war, provoked; our better part remains
To work in close design, by fraud or guile,
What force effected not; that he no less
At length from us may find, who overcomes
By force, hath overcome but half his foe.
Space may produce new worlds, whereof so rife
There went a fame in heav'n, that he ere long
Intended to create, and therein plant
A generation, whom his choice regard
Should favor equal to the sons of heaven:
Thither, if but to pry, shall be perhaps
Our first eruption, thither or elsewhere;
For this infernal pit shall never hold
Celestial spirits in bondage, nor th' Abyss
Long under darkness cover. But these thoughts
Full counsel must mature: peace is despair'd;
For who can think submission? war then, war
Open or understood, must be resolved.
　　He spake: and to confirm his words outflew
Millions of flaming swords, drawn from the thighs
Of mighty Cherubim; the sudden blaze
Far round illumined hell: highly they raged
Against the highest, and fierce with grasped arms
Clash'd on their sounding shields the din of war,
Hurling defiance toward the vault of heav'n.
　　There stood a hill not far, whose grisly top
Belch'd fire and rolling smoke; the rest entire
Shone with a glossy scurf, undoubted sign
That in his womb was hid metallic ore,

[1] Rev. xii. 4.

The work of sulphur. Thither, wing'd with speed,
A numerous brigade hasten'd; as when bands
Of pioneers, with spade and pickaxe arm'd,
Forerun the royal camp, to trench a field,
Or cast a rampart. Mammon[1] led them on,
Mammon, the least erected spirit that fell
From heav'n; for ev'n in heav'n his looks and thoughts
Were always downward bent, admiring more
The riches of heav'n's pavement, trodden gold,
Than aught divine or holy else enjoy'd
In vision beatific. By him first
Men also, and by his suggestion taught,
Ransack'd the centre, and with impious hands
Rifled the bowels of their mother earth
For treasures better hid. Soon had his crew
Open'd into the hill a spacious wound,
And digg'd out ribs of gold. Let none admire
That riches grow in hell; that soil may best
Deserve the precious bane. And here let those
Who boast in mortal things, and wond'ring tell
Of Babel and the works of Memphian kings,
Learn how their greatest monuments of fame
And strength and art are easily outdone
By spirits reprobate, and in an hour
What in an age they with incessant toil
And hands innumerable scarce perform.
Nigh on the plain in many cells prepared,
That underneath had veins of liquid fire
Sluiced from the lake, a second multitude
With wond'rous art founded the massy ore,
Severing each kind, and scumm'd the bullion dross.
A third as soon had formed within the ground
A various mould, and from the boiling cells
By strange conveyance fill'd each hollow nook:
As in an organ from one blast of wind
To many a row of pipes the sound-board breathes.
Anon out of the earth a fabric huge
Rose, like an exhalation, with the sound
Of dulcet symphonies and voices sweet,
Built like a temple, where pilasters round

[1] The word Mammon is Syriac for riches (Matt. vi. 24); personified also by Spenser.

Were set, and Doric pillars overlaid
With golden architrave; nor did there want
Cornice or frieze with bossy sculptures graven;
The roof was fretted gold. Not Babylon,
Nor great Alcairo[1] such magnificence
Equall'd in all their glories, to inshrine
Belus or Serapis their Gods, or seat
Their kings, when Ægypt with Assyria strove
In wealth and luxury. Th' ascending pile
Stood fixt her stately highth, and straight the doors
Op'ning their brazen folds, discover, wide
Within, her ample spaces, o'er the smooth
And level pavement: from the archèd roof,
Pendant by subtle magic, many a row
Of starry lamps and blazing cressets, fed
With Naphtha and Asphaltus, yielded light
As from a sky. The hasty multitude
Admiring enter'd, and the work some praise,
And some the architect: his hand was known
In heav'n by many a towered structure high,
Where sceptered angels held their residence,
And sat as princes; whom the supreme King
Exalted to such power, and gave to rule,
Each in his hierarchy, the orders bright.
Nor was his name unheard or unadored
In ancient Greece; and in Ausonian land
Men call'd him Mulciber;[2] and how he fell
From heav'n they fabled, thrown by angry Jove
Sheer o'er the crystal battlements; from morn
To noon he fell, from noon to dewy eve,
A summer's day; and with the setting sun
Dropt from the Zenith like a falling star,
On Lemnos, th' Ægean isle; thus they relate,
Erring; for he with this rebellious rout
Fell long before; nor aught avail'd him now
To have built in heav'n high towers; nor did he 'scape
By all his engines, but was headlong sent
With his industrious crew to build in hell.
    Meanwhile the wingèd heralds by command
Of sov'reign power, with awful ceremony

[1] Cairo, in Egypt.
[2] Vulcan. See Homer, "Iliad," 1–590.

And trumpets sound, throughout the host proclaim
A solemn council forthwith to be held
At Pandæmonium, the high capital
Of Satan and his peers: their summons call'd
From every band and squarèd regiment
By place or choice the worthiest; they anon
With hundreds and with thousands trooping came
Attended: all access was throng'd, the gates
And porches wide, but chief the spacious hall,
Though like a cover'd field, where champions bold
Wont ride in arm'd, and at the Soldan's chair
Defied the best of Panim chivalry
To mortal combat or career with lance,
Thick swarm'd both on the ground and in the air,
Brush'd with the hiss of rustling wings. As bees
In spring time, when the sun with Taurus rides,
Pour forth their populous youth about the hive
In clusters; they among fresh dews and flowers
Fly to and fro, or on the smoothèd plank,
The suburb of their straw-built citadel,
New rubb'd with balm, expatiate, and confer
Their state affairs: So thick the aery crowd
Swarm'd and were straiten'd; till, the signal giv'n,
Behold a wonder! they, but now who seem'd
In bigness to surpass earth's giant sons,
Now less than smallest dwarfs, in narrow room
Throng numberless, like that Pygmean race
Beyond the Indian mount, or Fairy Elves,
Whose midnight revels, by a forest side,
Or fountain, some belated peasant sees,
Or dreams he sees, while over head the moon
Sits arbitress,[1] and nearer to the earth
Wheels her pale course; they, on their mirth and dance
Intent, with jocund music charm his ear;
At once with joy and fear his heart rebounds.
Thus incorporeal spirits to smallest forms
Reduced their shapes immense, and were at large
Though without number still, amidst the hall
Of that infernal court. But far within,
And in their own dimensions like themselves,
The great Seraphic lords and Cherubim

[1] Spectatress.—Hor. *Ep.* V. 49.

In close recess and secret conclave sat,
A thousand Demi-gods on golden seats,
Frequent and full. After short silence then
And summons read, the great consult began.

BOOK II

The Argument

The consultation begun, Satan debates whether another battle be to be hazarded for the recovery of heaven: some advise it, others dissuade. A third proposal is preferred, mentioned before by Satan, to search the truth of that prophecy or tradition in heaven concerning another world, and another kind of creature, equal, or not much inferior to themselves, about this time to be created: their doubt who shall be sent on this difficult search: Satan their chief undertakes alone the voyage, is honored and applauded. The council thus ended, the rest betake them several ways, and to several employments, as their inclinations lead them, to entertain the time till Satan return. He passes on his journey to hell gates, finds them shut, and who sat there to guard them, by whom at length they are opened, and discover to him the great gulf between hell and heaven: with what difficulty he passes through, directed by Chaos, the Power of that place, to the sight of this new world which he sought.

HIGH on a throne of royal state, which far
Outshone the wealth of Ormus[1] and of Ind,
Or where the gorgeous east with richest hand
Show'rs on her kings Barbaric pearl and gold,[2]
Satan exalted sat, by merit raised
To that bad eminence; and, from despair
Thus high uplifted beyond hope, aspires
Beyond thus high, insatiate to pursue
Vain war with heav'n, and by success untaught
His proud imaginations thus display'd.
    Powers and dominions, Deities of heav'n,[3]
For since no deep within her gulf can hold
Immortal vigor, though oppress'd and fall'n,

---

[1] In the Persian Gulf.

[2] It was the Eastern custom for the princes of the blood royal and the emirs to sprinkle gold dust and seed pearl on the head of the monarch at his coronation. See "Vie de Tamerlane" (translated by M. Petit de la Croix), B. II. c. 1.

[3] Colos. i. 16.

34

I give not heav'n for lost: from this descent
Celestial virtues rising will appear
More glorious and more dread, than from no fall,
And trust themselves to fear no second fate.
Me though just right and the fix'd laws of heav'n
Did first create your leader, next free choice,
With what besides, in council or in fight,
Hath been achieved of merit; yet this loss,
Thus far at least recover'd, hath much more
Establish'd in a safe unenvied throne,
Yielded with full consent. The happier state
In heav'n, which follows dignity, might draw
Envy from each inferior; but who here
Will envy whom the highest place exposes
Foremost to stand against the Thund'rer's aim
Your bulwark, and condemns to greatest share
Of endless pain? Where there is then no good
For which to strive, no strife can grow up there
From faction; for none sure will claim in hell
Precedence, none, whose portion is so small
Of present pain, that with ambitious mind
Will covet more. With this advantage then
To union, and firm faith, and firm accord,
More than can be in heav'n, we now return
To claim our just inheritance of old,
Surer to prosper than prosperity
Could have assured us; and by what best way,
Whether of open war or covert guile,
We now debate; who can advise, may speak.
    He ceased; and next him Moloch, scepter'd king,
Stood up, the strongest and the fiercest spirit
That fought in heav'n, now fiercer by despair:
His trust was with th' Eternal to be deem'd
Equal in strength, and rather than be less
Cared not to be at all; with that care lost
Went all his fear: of God, or hell, or worse,
He reck'd not; and these words thereafter spake:
    My sentence is for open war: of wiles,
More unexpert, I boast not: them let those
Contrive who need, or when they need, not now:
For while they sit contriving, shall the rest,
Millions that stand in arms and longing wait

The signal to ascend, sit ling'ring here
Heav'n's fugitives, and for their dwelling-place
Accept this dark opprobrious den of shame,
The prison of his tyranny who reigns
By our delay? no, let us rather choose,
Arm'd with hell flames and fury, all at once
O'er heav'n's high towers to force resistless way,
Turning our tortures into horrid arms
Against the torturer; when to meet the noise
Of his almighty engine he shall hear
Infernal thunder, and for lightning see
Black fire and horror shot with equal rage
Among his angels; and his throne itself
Mixt with Tartarean sulphur and strange fire,
His own invented torments. But perhaps
The way seems difficult and steep to scale
With upright wing against a higher foe.
Let such bethink them, if the sleepy drench
Of that forgetful lake benumb not still,
That in our proper motion we ascend
Up to our native seat: descent and fall
To us is adverse. Who but felt of late,
When the fierce foe hung on our broken rear
Insulting, and pursued us through the deep,
With what compulsion and laborious flight
We sunk thus low? th' ascent is easy then;
Th' event is fear'd; should we again provoke
Our stronger, some worse way his wrath may find
To our destruction: if there be in hell
Fear to be worse destroy'd: what can be worse
Than to dwell here, driv'n out from bliss, condemn'd
In this abhorrèd deep to utter woe;
Where pain of unextinguishable fire
Must exercise us without hope of end,
The vassals of his anger, when the scourge
Inexorably, and the torturing hour
Calls us to penance? more destroy'd than thus
We should be quite abolish'd and expire.
What fear we then? what doubt we to incense
His utmost ire? which, to the highth enraged,
Will either quite consume us, and reduce
To nothing this essential; happier far,

Than miserable to have eternal being.
Or if our substance be indeed divine,
And cannot cease to be, we are at worst
On this side nothing; and by proof we feel
Our power sufficient to disturb his heav'n,
And with perpetual inroads to alarm,
Though inaccessible, his fatal throne:[1]
Which, if not victory, is yet revenge.

   He ended frowning, and his look denounced
Desperate revenge and battle dangerous
To less than Gods. On th' other side up rose
Belial, in act more graceful and humane;
A fairer person lost not heav'n; he seem'd
For dignity composed and high exploit:
But all was false and hollow; though his tongue
Dropp'd Manna, and could make the worse appear
The better reason, to perplex and dash
Maturest counsels; for his thoughts were low;
To vice industrious, but to nobler deeds
Timorous and slothful: yet he pleased the ear,
And with persuasive accent thus began.

   I should be much for open war, O Peers,
As not behind in hate, if what was urged,
Main reason to persuade immediate war,
Did not dissuade me most, and seem to cast
Ominous conjecture on the whole success;
When he, who most excels in fact of arms,
In what he counsels and in what excels
Mistrustful, grounds his courage on despair
And utter dissolution, as the scope
Of all his aim, after some dire revenge.
First, what revenge? the towers of heav'n are filled
With armèd watch, that render all access
Impregnable; oft on the bordering deep
Encamp their legions, or with obscure wing
Scout far and wide into the realm of night,
Scorning surprise. Or could we break our way
By force, and at our heels all hell should rise,
With blackest insurrection to confound
Heav'n's purest light, yet our great enemy
All incorruptible would on his throne

[1] Upheld by fate.—Newton.

Sit unpolluted; and th' ethereal mould
Incapable of stain would soon expel
Her mischief, and purge off the baser fire,
Victorious. Thus repulsed, our final hope
Is flat despair: we must exasperate
Th' almighty Victor to spend all his rage,
And that must end us, that must be our cure,
To be no more: sad cure; for who would lose,
Though full of pain, this intellectual being,
Those thoughts that wander through eternity,
To perish rather, swallowed up and lost
In the wide womb of uncreated night,
Devoid of sense and motion? and who knows,
Let this be good, whether our angry foe
Can give it, or will ever? how he can,
Is doubtful; that he never will, is sure.
Will he, so wise, let loose at once his ire,
Belike through impotence or unaware,
To give his enemies their wish, and end
Them in his anger, whom his anger saves
To punish endless? Wherefore cease we then?
Say they who counsel war;—We are decreed.
Reserved, and destined to eternal woe;
Whatever doing, what can we suffer more,
What can we suffer worse?—Is this then worst,
Thus sitting, thus consulting, thus in arms?
What, when we fled amain, pursued and struck
With heav'n's afflicting thunder, and besought
The deep to shelter us? this hell then seem'd
A refuge from those wounds. Or when we lay
Chain'd on the burning lake? that sure was worse.
What if the breath that kindled those grim fires[1]
Awaked should blow them into sevenfold rage,
And plunge us in the flames? or from above
Should intermitted vengeance arm again
His red right hand to plague us? what, if all
Her stores were open'd and this firmament
Of hell should spout her cataracts of fire,
Impendent horrors, threatening hideous fall
One day upon our heads; while we, perhaps
Designing or exhorting glorious war,

[1] Isaiah xxx. 33.

Caught in a fiery tempest shall be hurl'd
Each on his rock transfix'd, the sport and prey
Of racking whirlwinds; or for ever sunk
Under yon boiling ocean, wrapt in chains,
There to converse with everlasting groans,
Unrespited, unpitied, unreprieved,
Ages of hopeless end? this would be worse.
War therefore open or conceal'd, alike
My voice dissuades; for what can force or guile
With him, or who deceive his mind, whose eye
Views all things at one view? He from heav'n's highth
All these our motions vain sees and derides;
Not more almighty to resist our might,
Than wise to frustrate all our plots and wiles.
Shall we then live thus vile, th' race of heav'n
Thus trampled, thus expell'd, to suffer here
Chains and these torments? better these than worse
By my advice; since fate inevitable
Subdues us, and omnipotent decree,
The victor's will. To suffer, as to do,
Our strength is equal, nor the law unjust
That so ordains: this was at first resolved,
If we were wise, against so great a foe
Contending, and so doubtful what might fall.
I laugh, when those, who at the spear are bold
And vent'rous, if that fail them, shrink and fear
What yet they know must follow, to endure
Exile, or ignominy, or bonds, or pain,
The sentence of their conqueror: this is now
Our doom; which if we can sustain and bear,
Our supreme foe in time may much remit
His anger, and perhaps thus far removed
Not mind us not offending, satisfied
With what is punish'd: whence these raging fires
Will slacken, if his breath stir not their flames.
Our purer essence then will overcome
Their noxious vapor, or enured not feel;
Or changed at length, and to the place conform'd
In temper and in nature, will receive
Familiar the fierce heat, and void of pain;
This horror will grow mild, this darkness light:
Besides what hope the never ending flight

Of future days may bring, what chance, what change
Worth waiting, since our present lot appears
For happy though but ill, for ill not worst,
If we procure not to ourselves more woe.

    Thus Belial with words cloth'd in reason's garb
Counsell'd ignoble ease, and peaceful sloth,
Not peace: and after him thus Mammon spake.

    Either to disenthrone the King of heav'n
We war, if war be best, or to regain
Our own right lost: Him to unthrone we then
May hope, when everlasting Fate shall yield
To fickle Chance, and Chaos judge the strife:
The former vain to hope argues as vain
The latter: for what place can be for us
Within heav'n's bound, unless heav'n's Lord supreme
We overpower? suppose He should relent
And publish grace to all, on promise made
Of new subjection; with what eyes could we
Stand in his presence humble, and receive
Strict laws imposed, to celebrate his throne
With warbled hymns, and to his Godhead sing
Forced hallelujahs; while he lordly sits
Our envied Sov'reign, and his altar breathes
Ambrosial odors and ambrosial flowers,
Our servile offerings? This must be our task
In heav'n, this our delight; how wearisome
Eternity so spent in worship paid
To whom we hate! Let us not then pursue
By force impossible, by leave obtain'd
Unacceptable, though in heav'n, our state
Of splendid vassalage, but rather seek
Our own good from ourselves, and from our own
Live to our selves, though in this vast recess,
Free, and to none accountable, preferring
Hard liberty before the easy yoke
Of servile pomp. Our greatness will appear
Then most conspicuous, when great things of small,
Useful of hurtful, prosperous of adverse,
We can create; and in what place so e'er
Thrive under evil, and work ease out of pain
Through labor and endurance. This deep world
Of darkness do we dread? how oft amidst

Thick clouds and dark doth heav'n's all-ruling Sire
Choose to reside, his glory unobscured,
And with the majesty of darkness round
Covers his throne;[1] from whence deep thunders roar
Must'ring their rage, and heav'n resembles hell?
As he our darkness, cannot we His light
Imitate when we please? this desert soil
Wants not her hidden lustre, gems and gold;
Nor want we skill or art, from whence to raise
Magnificence; and what can heav'n shew more?
Our torments also may in length of time
Become our elements, these piercing fires
As soft as now severe, our temper changed
Into their temper; which must needs remove
The sensible of pain. All things invite
To peaceful counsels, and the settled state
Of order, how in safety best we may
Compose our present evils, with regard
Of what we are and were, dismissing quite
All thoughts of war. Ye have what I advise.
    He scarce had finish'd, when such murmur fill'd
Th' assembly, as when hollow rocks retain
The sound of blustering winds, which all night long
Had roused the sea, now with hoarse cadence lull
Sea-faring men o'er watch'd, whose bark by chance
Or pinnace anchors in a craggy bay
After the tempest: such applause was heard
As Mammon ended, and his sentence pleased,
Advising peace: for such another field
They dreaded worse than hell: so much the fear
Of thunder and the sword of Michael
Wrought still within them; and no less desire
To found this nether empire, which might rise,
By policy and long process of time,
In emulation opposite to heav'n.
Which when Beëlzebub perceived, than whom,
Satan except, none higher sat, with grave
Aspect he rose, and in his rising seem'd
A pillar of state: deep on his front engraven
Deliberation sat and public care;
And princely counsel in his face yet shone,

[1] Psalm xviii. 11–13; xcvii. 2.

Majestic though in ruin: sage he stood,
With Atlantean[1] shoulders fit to bear
The weight of mightiest monarchies; his look
Drew audience and attention still as night
Or summer's noon-tide air, while thus he spake.
    Thrones and imperial Powers, offspring of heav'n,
Ethereal Virtues; or these titles now
Must we renounce, and changing style be call'd
Princes of hell? for so the popular vote
Inclines, here to continue, and build up here
A growing empire. Doubtless; while we dream,
And know not that the King of heav'n hath doom'd
This place our dungeon, not our safe retreat
Beyond his potent arm, to live exempt
From heav'n's high jurisdiction, in new league
Banded against his throne, but to remain
In strictest bondage, though thus far removed,
Under the inevitable curb, reserv'd
His captive multitude: for he, be sure,
In highth or depth, still first and last will reign
Sole King, and of his kingdom lose no part
By our revolt, but over hell extend
His empire, and with iron sceptre rule,[2]
Us here, as with his golden those in heav'n.
What sit we then projecting peace and war?
War hath determined us, and foil'd with loss
Irreparable; terms of peace yet none
Vouchsafed or sought; for what peace will be giv'n
To us enslaved, but custody severe,
And stripes, and arbitrary punishment
Inflicted? and what peace can we return,
But to our power hostility and hate,
Untamed reluctance, and revenge, though slow,
Yet ever plotting how the conqueror least
May reap his conquest, and may least rejoice
In doing what we most in suffering feel?
Nor will occasion want, nor shall we need
With dangerous expedition to invade
Heav'n, whose high walls fear no assault, or siege,
Or ambush from the deep. What if we find

[1] Atlas was fabled to have held the heavens on his shoulders.
[2] Psalm ii. 9.

Some easier enterprize? There is a place,
(If ancient and prophetic fame in heav'n
Err not,) another world, the happy seat
Of some new race call'd Man, about this time
To be created like to us, though less
In power and excellence, but favor'd more
Of Him who rules above; so was His will
Pronounced among the Gods, and by an oath,
That shook heav'n's whole circumference, confirm'd.
Thither let us bend all our thoughts, to learn
What creatures there inhabit, of what mould
Or substance, how endued, and what their power,
And where their weakness, how attempted best,
By force or subtilty. Though heav'n be shut,
And heav'n's high Arbitrator sit secure
In his own strength, this place may lie exposed,
The utmost border of his kingdom, left
To their defence who hold it: here perhaps
Some advantageous act may be achieved
By sudden onset, either with hell fire
To waste his whole creation, or possess
All as our own, and drive as we were driven
The puny habitants; or if not drive,
Seduce them to our party, that their God
May prove their foe, and with repenting hand
Abolish his own works. This would surpass
Common revenge, and interrupt his joy
In our confusion, and our joy upraise
In his disturbance; when his darling sons,
Hurl'd headlong to partake with us, shall curse
Their frail original, and faded bliss,
Faded so soon. Advise if this be worth
Attempting, or to sit in darkness here
Hatching vain empires.—Thus Beëlzebub
Pleaded his devilish counsel, first devised
By Satan, and in part proposed; for whence,
But from the author of all ill, could spring
So deep a malice, to confound the race
Of mankind in one root, and earth with hell
To mingle and involve, done all to spite
The great Creator? but their spite still serves
His glory to augment. The bold design

Pleased highly those infernal states, and joy
Sparkled in all their eyes; with full assent
They vote: whereat his speech he thus renews.

　　Well have ye judged, well ended long debate,
Synod of Gods, and, like to what ye are,
Great things resolved; which from the lowest deep
Will once more lift us up, in spite of fate,
Nearer our ancient seat; perhaps in view
Of those bright confines, whence with neighboring arms
And opportune excursion we may chance
Re-enter heav'n: or else in some mild zone
Dwell, not unvisited of heav'n's fair light,
Secure, and at the brigt'ning orient beam
Purge off this gloom; the soft delicious air
To heal the scar of these corrosive fires
Shall breathe her balm. But first whom shall we send
In search of this new world? whom shall we find
Sufficient? who shall tempt with wand'ring feet
The dark unbottom'd infinite abyss,
And through the palpable obscure find out
His uncouth way, or spread his airy flight,
Upborne with indefatigable wings,
Over the vast abrupt, ere he arrive[1]
The happy isle? [2] what strength, what art can then
Suffice, or what evasion bear him safe
Through the strict sentries and stations thick
Of angels watching round? here he had need
All circumspection, and we now no less
Choice in our suffrage; for on whom we send
The weight of all, and our last hope, relies.

　　This said, he sat; and expectation held
His look suspense, awaiting who appear'd
To second, or oppose, or undertake
The perilous attempt: but all sat mute,
Pondering the danger with deep thoughts; and each
In others' count'nance read his own dismay
Astonish'd; none among the choice and prime
Of those heav'n-warring champions could be found
So hardy, as to proffer or accept

[1] An old English idiom.—See Shakespeare's *Henry VI.* Part iii.
Act v.
[2] The earth surrounded by air.

Alone the dreadful voyage; till at last
Satan, whom now transcendent glory raised
Above his fellows, with monarchal pride,
Conscious of highest worth, unmoved thus spake.

O Progeny of heav'n, empyreal Thrones,
With reason hath deep silence and demur
Seized us, though undismay'd: long is the way
And hard, that out of hell leads up to light;
Our prison strong; this huge convex of fire,
Outrageous to devour, immures us round
Ninefold, and gates of burning adamant
Barr'd over us prohibit all egress.
These pass'd, if any pass, the void profound
Of unessential [1] night receives him next
Wide gaping, and with utter loss of being
Threatens him, plunged in that abortive gulf.
If thence he 'scape into whatever world,
Or unknown region, what remains him less
Than unknown dangers and as hard escape?
But I should ill become this throne, O Peers,
And this imperial sov'reignty, adorn'd
With splendor, arm'd with power, if aught proposed
And judged of public moment, in the shape
Of difficulty or danger, could deter
Me from attempting. Wherefore do I assume
These royalties, and not refuse to reign,
Refusing to accept as great a share
Of hazard as of honor, due alike
To him who reigns, and so much to him due
Of hazard more, as he above the rest
High honor'd sits? Go, therefore, mighty Powers,
Terror of heav'n though fall'n! intend at home,
While here shall be our home, what best may ease
The present misery, and render hell
More tolerable; if there be cure or charm
To respite, or deceive, or slack the pain
Of this ill mansion. Intermit no watch
Against a wakeful foe, while I abroad
Through all the coasts of dark destruction seek
Deliverance for us all: this enterprize
None shall partake with me. Thus saying

[1] Void of being.

Rose the monarch and prevented all reply;
Prudent, lest from his resolution raised
Others among the chief might offer now,
Certain to be refused, what erst they fear'd;
And so refused might in opinion stand
His rivals, winning cheap the high repute,
Which he through hazard huge must earn. But they
Dreaded not more the adventure, than his voice
Forbidding; and at once with him they rose:
Their rising all at once was as the sound
Of thunder heard remote. Towards him they bend
With awful reverence prone; and as a God
Extol him equal to the highest in heav'n:
Nor failed they to express how much they praised,
That for the general safety he despised
His own; for neither do the spirits damn'd
Lose all their virtue, lest bad men should boast
Their specious deeds on earth, which glory excites,
Or close ambition varnish'd o'er with zeal.
Thus they their doubtful consultations dark
Ended, rejoicing in their matchless chief:
As when from mountain tops the dusky clouds
Ascending, while the north wind sleeps, o'erspread
Heav'n's cheerful face, the low'ring element
Scowls o'er the darken'd landscape snow, or shower;
If chance the radiant sun with farewell sweet
Extend his ev'ning beam, the fields revive,
The birds their notes renew, and bleating herds
Attest their joy, that hill and valley rings.
O shame to men! devil with devil damn'd
Firm concord holds, men only disagree
Of creatures rational, though under hope
Of heav'nly grace; and God proclaiming peace,
Yet live in hatred, enmity, and strife
Among themselves, and levy cruel wars,
Wasting the earth, each other to destroy:[1]
As if, which might induce us to accord,
Man had not hellish foes enow besides,
That day and night for his destruction wait.

[1] An allusion to the age of civil strife and controversies in which Milton's lot was cast.

The Stygian council thus dissolved; and forth
In order came the grand infernal peers;
Midst came their mighty paramount, and seem'd
Alone the antagonist of heav'n, nor less
Than hell's dread emperor, with pomp supreme
And God-like imitated state: him round
A globe of fiery Seraphim inclosed
With bright emblazonry and horrent[1] arms
Then of their session ended they bid cry
With trumpets regal sound the great result:
Toward the four winds four speedy Cherubim
Put to their mouths the sounding alchymy,[2]
By heralds' voice explain'd: the hollow abyss
Heard far and wide, and all the host of hell
With deaf'ning shout returned them loud acclaim.

Thence more at ease their minds, and somewhat raised
By false presumptuous hope, the rangèd Powers
Disband, and wand'ring each his several way
Pursues, as inclination or sad choice
Leads him perplex'd, where he may likeliest find
Truce to his restless thoughts, and entertain
The irksome hours, till his great chief return.
Part, on the plain or in the air sublime,
Upon the wing or in swift race contend,
As at the Olympian games, or Pythian fields:
Part curb their fiery steeds, or shun the goal
With rapid wheels, or fronted brigades form.
As when to warn proud cities war appears
Waged in the troubled sky,[3] and armies rush
To battle in the clouds, before each van
Prick forth the aery knights, and couch their spears
Till thickest legions close; with feats of arms
From either end of heav'n the welkin burns.
Others with vast Typhœan rage more fell

[1] Bristling.
[2] Gold or silver trumpets. Herald's alchemy would be "or and argent."
[3] These appearances in the clouds have been frequently recorded. On the Mont d'Or, the night before the battle in which Philip von Arteveldt was killed, an armed host was seen contending in the sky.

Rend up both rocks and hills, and ride the air
In whirlwind:[1] hell scarce holds the wild uproar.
As when Alcides[2] from Œchalia crown'd
With conquest felt th' envenom'd robe, and tore
Through pain up by the roots Thessalian pines.
And Lichas from the top of Œta threw
Into th' Euboic sea. Others more mild,
Retreated in a silent valley, sing
With notes angelical to many a harp
Their own heroic deeds and hapless fall
By doom of battle; and complain that fate
Free virtue should enthral to force or chance.
Their song was partial; but the harmony,
What could it less when spirits immortal sing?
Suspended hell, and took with ravishment
The thronging audience. In discourse more sweet,
For eloquence the soul, song charms the sense,
Others apart sat on a hill retired,
In thoughts more elevate, and reason'd high
Of providence, foreknowledge, will, and fate,
Fix'd fate, free will, foreknowledge absolute;
And found no end, in wand'ring mazes lost.
Of good and evil much they argued then,
Of happiness and final misery,
Passion and apathy, and glory and shame,
Vain wisdom all, and false philosophy:
Yet with a pleasing sorcery could charm
Pain for a while or anguish, and excite
Fallacious hope, or arm th' obdured breast
With stubborn patience as with triple steel.
Another part in squadrons and gross bands,
On bold adventure to discover wide
That dismal world, if any clime perhaps,
Might yield them easier habitation, bend

---

[1] Alluding to the war of the Titans.

[2] Hercules, named Alcides after his grandfather, Alceus. On his
return from the conquest of Œchalia, a city of Bœotia, he re-
ceived from his wife the envenomed robe of the Centaur. It clung
to him and could only be removed with the flesh. In his agony the
demigod tore up pines by the roots, and threw Lichas, the mes-
senger who had brought him the robe, from the top of Mount
Œta into the Eubean Sea.

Four ways their flying march, along the banks
Of four infernal rivers, that disgorge
Into the burning lake their baleful streams;
Abhorrèd Styx,[1] the flood of deadly hate;
Sad Acheron of sorrow, black and deep;
Cocytus, named of lamentation loud
Heard on the rueful stream; fierce Phlegethon,
Whose waves of torrent fire inflame with rage.
Far off from these a slow and silent stream,
Lethe the river of oblivion, rolls
Her wat'ry labyrinth, whereof who drinks,
Forthwith his former state and being forgets,
Forgets both joy and grief, pleasure and pain.
Beyond this flood a frozen continent
Lies, dark and wild, beat with perpetual storms
Of whirlwind and dire hail; which on firm land
Thaws not, but gathers heap, and ruin seems
Of ancient pile; all else deep snow and ice;
A gulf profound as that Serbonian[2] bog
Betwixt Damiata and mount Casius old,
Where armies whole have sunk: the parching air
Burns frore,[3] and cold performs th' effect of fire,
Thither by harpy-footed Furies haled
At certain revolutions all the damn'd
Are brought; and feel by turns the bitter change
Of fierce extremes, extremes by change more fierce,
From beds of raging fire to starve in ice
Their soft ethereal warmth, and there to pine
Immovable, infix'd, and frozen round,
Periods of time; thence hurried back to fire.
They ferry over this Lethean sound
Both to and fro, their sorrow to augment,
And wish and struggle, as they pass to reach
The tempting stream, with one small drop to lose
In sweet forgetfulness all pain and woe,

[1] The names and qualities of these rivers are all taken from the Greek mythology.

[2] Serbonis was a huge bog in Egypt, sometimes so covered with sand as to be indistinguishable from the land. It was 200 furlongs long, and 1,000 round. Damietta was a city on one of the eastern mouths of the Nile.

[3] Frostily. See Eccles. xlii. 20, 21.

All in one moment, and so near the brink:
But fate withstands, and to oppose th' attempt
Medusa,[1] with Gorgonian terror guards
The ford, and of itself the water flies
All taste of living wight, as once it fled
The lip of Tantalus. Thus roving on
In confused march forlorn, th' advent'rous bands,
With shudd'ring horror pale, and eyes aghast,
Viewed first their lamentable lot, and found
No rest: through many a dark and dreary vale
They pass'd, and many a region dolorous,
O'er many a frozen, many a fiery Alp,
Rocks, caves, lakes, fens, bogs, dens, and shades of death,
A universe of death, which God by curse
Created evil, for evil only good,
Where all life dies, death lives, and nature breeds,
Perverse, all monstrous, all prodigious things,
Abominable, inutterable, and worse
Than fables yet have feign'd, or fear conceived,
Gorgons, and Hydras, and Chimæras[2] dire.

  Meanwhile the adversary of GOD and man,
Satan, with thoughts inflamed of highest design,
Puts on swift wings, and toward the gates of hell
Explores his solitary flight; sometimes
He scours the right-hand coast, sometimes the left;
Now shaves with level wing the deep, then soars
Up to the fiery concave towering high.
As when far off at sea a fleet descried
Hangs in the clouds, by equinoctial winds
Close sailing from Bengala, or the isles
Of Ternate and Tidore,[3] whence merchants bring
Their spicy drugs: they on the trading flood
Through the wide Æthiopian to the Cape
Ply, stemming nightly toward the pole: so seem'd
Far off the flying fiend. At last appear
Hell bounds, high reaching to the horrid roof;
And thrice threefold the gates; three folds were brass,

[1] Medusa was a Gorgon of horrid beauty, who had the power of turning those who gazed on her into stone. Forgetfullness could never be permitted to the lost spirits.
[2] Monsters of the heathen mythology.
[3] Two of the Molucca islands.

Three iron, three of adamantine rock,
Impenetrable, impaled with circling fire,
Yet unconsumed. Before the gates there sat
On either side a formidable shape;[1]
The one seem'd woman to the waist, and fair,
But ended foul in many a scaly fold,
Voluminous and vast, a serpent arm'd
With mortal sting: about her middle round
A cry of hell hounds never ceasing bark'd
With wide Cerberean[2] mouths full loud, and rung
A hideous peel: yet, when they list, would creep,
If aught disturb'd their noise, into her womb,
And kennel there; yet there still bark'd and howl'd
Within unseen. Far less abhorr'd than these
Vex'd Scylla bathing in the sea that parts
Calabria from the hoarse Trinacrian shore:[3]
Nor uglier follow the Night-hag, when call'd
In secret riding through the air she comes,
Lured with the smell of infant blood, to dance
With Lapland witches, while the laboring moon
Eclipses at their charms. The other shape,
If shape it might be call'd, that shape had none
Distinguishable in member, joint, or limb,
Or substance might be call'd that shadow seem'd,
For each seem'd either; black it stood as night,
Fierce as ten furies, terrible as hell
And shook a dreadful dart; what seem'd his head
The likeness of a kingly crown had on.
Satan was now at hand, and from his seat
The monster moving onward came as fast,
With horrid strides; hell trembled as he strode.
The undaunted fiend what this might be admired;
Admired, not fear'd; GOD and his SON except,
Created thing naught valued he, nor shunn'd;
And with disdainful look thus first began.

[1] Here begins the famous allegory of Milton, which is a sort of
paraphrase of St. James i. 15: "Then when lust hath conceived, it
bringeth forth sin; and sin, when it is finished, bringeth forth
death."

[2] Like those of Cerberus, the dog with three heads, supposed to
keep the gate of hell.

[3] Trinacria was the ancient name for Sicily. Scylla Charybdis
were the whirlpools between it and Italy.

Whence and what art thou, execrable shape,
That dar'st, though grim and terrible, advance
Thy miscreated front athwart my way
To yonder gates? through them I mean to pass,
That be assured without leave ask'd of thee.
Retire, or taste thy folly, and learn by proof,
Hell-born, not to contend with spirits of heav'n.

To whom the goblin full of wrath replied,
Art thou that traitor angel, art thou he,
Who first broke peace in heav'n and faith, till then
Unbroken, and in proud rebellious arms
Drew after him the third part of heav'n's sons
Conjured [1] against the Highest; for which both thou
And they, outcast from GOD, are here condemn'd
To waste eternal days in woe and pain?
And reckon'st thou thyself with spirits of heav'n,
Hell-doom'd, and breath'st defiance here and scorn,
Where I reign king, and, to enrage thee more,
Thy king and lord? Back to thy punishment,
False fugitive, and to thy speed add wings,
Lest with a whip of scorpions I pursue
Thy lingering, or with one stroke of this dart
Strange horror seize thee, and pangs unfelt before.

So spake the grisly terror, and in shape,
So speaking and so threat'ning, grew tenfold
More dreadful and deform: on the other side
Incensed with indignation Satan stood
Unterrified, and like a comet burn'd,
That fires the length of Ophiucus[2] huge
In th' arctic sky, and from his horrid hair
Shakes pestilence and war. Each at the head
Levell'd his deadly aim; their fatal hands
No second stroke intend, and such a frown
Each cast at the other, as when two black clouds,
With heav'n's artillery fraught, come rattling on
Over the Caspian;[3] then stand front to front
Hov'ring a space, till winds the signal blow

---

[1] Conspired.

[2] Serpentarius, a northern constellation. Its length would be about
forty degrees. Comets were supposed to threaten "pestilence and
war."

[3] The Caspian is a remarkably tempestuous sea.

To join their dark encounter in mid air:
So frown'd the mighty combatants, that hell
Grew darker at their frown, so match'd they stood;
For never but once more[1] was either like
To meet so great a foe: and now great deeds
Had been achieved, whereof all hell had rung,
Had not the snaky sorceress that sat
Fast by hell gate, and kept the fatal key,
Ris'n, and with hideous outcry rush'd between.

O father, what intends thy hand, she cried,
Against thy only son? What fury, O son,
Possesses thee to bend that mortal dart
Against thy father's head? and know'st for whom?
For Him who sits above, and laughs the while
At thee ordained His drudge, to execute
Whate'er His wrath, which He calls justice, bids;
His wrath, which one day will destroy ye both.

She spake, and at her words the hellish pest
Forbore; then these to her Satan return'd:

So strange thy outcry, and thy words so strange
Thou interposest, that my sudden hand
Prevented spares to tell thee yet by deeds
What it intends; till first I know of thee,
What thing thou art, thus double form'd, and why,
In this infernal vale first met, thou call'st
Me father, and that phantasm call'st my son:
I know thee not, nor ever saw till now
Sight more detestable than him and thee.
To whom thus the portress of hell gate replied.

Hast thou forgot me then, and do I seem
Now in thine eye so foul, once deem'd so fair
In heav'n? when at th' assembly, and in sight
Of all the seraphim with thee combined
In bold conspiracy against heav'n's King,
All on a sudden miserable pain
Surprized thee, dim thine eyes, and dizzy swum
In darkness, while thy head flames thick and fast
Threw forth, till on the left side op'ning wide,
Likest to thee in shape and countenance bright,
Then shining heav'nly fair, a Goddess arm'd,

[1] Jesus Christ is here intimated, who was to destroy death, and
him that has the power of death (Heb. ii. 14).

Out of thy head I sprung:[1] amazement seized
All the host of heav'n; back they recoil'd afraid
At first, and call'd me Sin, and for a sign
Portentous held me: but familiar grown,
I pleased, and with attractive graces won
The most averse, thee chiefly, who full oft
Thyself in me thy perfect image viewing
Becam'st enamour'd, and such joy thou took'st
With me in secret, that my womb conceived
A growing burthen. Meanwhile war arose,
And fields were fought in heaven; wherein remain'd
(For what could else?) to our almighty foe
Clear victory, to our part loss and rout
Through all the empyrean: down they fell
Driv'n headlong from the pitch of heav'n,'down
Into this deep, and in the general fall
I also; at which time this powerful key
Into my hand was giv'n, with charge to keep
These gates for ever shut, which none can pass
Without my op'ning. Pensive here I sat
Alone, but long I sat not, till my womb,
Pregnant by thee, and now excessive grown,
Prodigious motion felt and rueful throes.
At last this odious offspring whom thou seest,
Thine own begotten, breaking violent way,
Tore through my entrails, that with fear and pain
Distorted all my nether shape thus grew
Transform'd: but he my inbred enemy
Forth issued, brandishing his fatal dart
Made to destroy.[2] I fled, and cried out Death;
Hell trembled at the hideous name, and sigh'd
From all her caves, and back resounded Death.
I fled, but he pursued, though more, it seems,
Inflamed with lust than rage, and swifter far
Me overtook his mother all dismay'd,
And, in embraces forcible and foul,
Ingend'ring with me, of that rape begot
These yelling monsters that with ceaseless cry

[1] The allegory here follows the Greek fable of the birth of
Minerva—*Wisdom*—said to have sprung from the head of Jupiter;
as *Sin* is here figured to have sprung from the head of Satan.
[2] St. James i. 15.

Surround me, as thou saw'st, hourly conceived
And hourly born, with sorrow infinite
To me: for when they list into the womb
That bred them they return, and howl and gnaw
My bowels, their repast; then bursting forth
Afresh with conscious terrors vex me round,
That rest or intermission none I find.
Before mine eyes in opposition sits
Grim Death my son and foe, who sets them on,
And me his parent would full soon devour
For want of other prey, but that he knows
His end with mine involved; and knows that I
Should prove a bitter morsel, and his bane,
Whenever that shall be; so Fate pronounced.
But thou, O father, I forewarn thee, shun
His deadly arrow; neither vainly hope
To be invulnerable in those bright arms,
Though temper'd heavenly; for that mortal dint,
Save he who reigns above, none can resist.
  She finish'd, and the subtle fiend his lore
Soon learn'd now milder, and thus answer'd smooth.
Dear daughter, since thou claim'st me for thy sire,
And my fair son here show'st me, the dear pledge
Of dalliance had with thee in heaven, and joys
Then sweet, now sad to mention, through dire change
Befall'n us, unforeseen, unthought of, know
I come no enemy, but to set free
From out this dark and dismal house of pain,
Both him and thee, and all the heav'nly host
Of spirits that, in our just pretences arm'd,
Fell with us from on high: from them I go
This uncouth errand sole, and one for all
Myself expose, with lonely steps to tread
Th' unfounded deep, and through the void immense
To search with wandering quest a place foretold
Should be, and, by concurring signs, ere now
Created, vast and round, a place of bliss
In the purlieus of heaven, and therein placed
A race of upstart creatures, to supply
Perhaps our vacant room, though more removed,
Lest heav'n surcharged with potent multitude
Might hap to move new broils. Be this, or aught

Than this more secret, now designed, I haste
To know, and, this once known, shall soon return,
And bring ye to the place where thou and Death
Shall dwell at ease, and up and down unseen
Wing silently the buxom air, imbalm'd
With odors; there ye shall be fed and fill'd
Immeasurably, all things shall be your prey.
   He ceased, for both seem'd highly pleased, and Death
Grinn'd horrible a ghastly smile, to hear
His famine should be fill'd, and blest his maw
Destined to that good hour: no less rejoiced
His mother bad, and thus bespake her sire:
   The key of this infernal pit by due,
And by command of heav'n's all-powerful King,
I keep, by him forbidden to unlock
These adamantine gates; against all force
Death ready stands to interpose his dart,
Fearless to be o'ermatch'd by living might.
But what owe I to his commands above,
Who hates me, and hath hither thrust me down
Into this gloom of Tartarus profound,
To sit in hateful office, here confined,
Inhabitant of heav'n, and heav'nly-born,
Here, in perpetual agony and pain,
With terrors and with clamors compass'd round
Of mine own brood, that on my bowels feed?
Thou art my father, thou my author, thou
My being gav'st me; whom should I obey
But thee? whom follow? thou wilt bring me soon
To that new world of light and bliss, among
The Gods who live at ease, where I shall reign
At thy right hand voluptuous, as beseems
Thy daughter and thy darling, without end.
   Thus saying, from her side the fatal key,
Sad instrument of all our woe, she took;
And towards the gate rolling her bestial train,
Forthwith the huge portcullis high up drew,
Which but herself not all the Stygian powers
Could once have moved; then in the keyhole turns
Th' intricate wards, and every bolt and bar
Of massy iron or solid rock with ease
Unfastens: on a sudden open fly

With impetuous recoil and jarring sound
Th' infernal doors, and on their hinges grate
Harsh thunder, that the lowest bottom shook
Of Erebus. She open'd, but to shut
Excell'd her power; the gates wide open stood,
That with extended wings a banner'd host
Under spread ensigns marching might pass through
With horse and chariots rank'd in loose array;
So wide they stood, and like a furnace mouth
Cast forth redounding smoke and ruddy flame.
Before their eyes in sudden view appear
The secrets of the hoary deep, a dark
Illimitable ocean, without bound,
Without dimension, where length, breadth, and highth,
And time and place are lost; where eldest Night
And Chaos, ancestors of Nature,[1] hold
Eternal anarchy amidst the noise
Of endless wars, and by confusion stand:
For hot, cold, moist, and dry, four champions fierce,
Strive here, for mast'ry, and to battle bring
Their embryon atoms; they around the flag
Of each his faction, in their several clans,
Light-arm'd or heavy, sharp, smooth, swift, or slow,
Swarm populous, unnumber'd as the sands
Of Barca or Cyrene's[2] torrid soil,
Levied to side with warring winds, and poise
Their lighter wings. To whom these most adhere,
He rules a moment; Chaos umpire sits,
And by decision more imbroils the fray
By which he reigns: next him high arbiter
Chance governs all. Into this wild abyss,
The womb of nature and perhaps her grave,
Of neither sea, nor shore, nor air, nor fire,
But all these in their pregnant causes mix'd
Confus'dly, and which thus must ever fight,
Unless th' almighty Maker them ordain
His dark materials to create more worlds;
Into this wild abyss the wary fiend

---

[1] All the ancients believed that Night (or darkness) existed from
the beginning, and that Chaos (or confusion) was the origin of all
things.
[2] A city and province of Libya.

Stood on the brink of hell, and look'd a while,
Pondering his voyage; for no narrow frith
He had to cross. Nor was his ear less peal'd
With noises loud and ruinous, to compare
Great things with small, than when Bellona storms,
With all her battering engines bent to rase
Some capital city; or less than if this frame
Of heav'n were falling, and these elements
In mutiny had from her axle torn
The stedfast earth. At last his sail-broad vans
He spreads for flight, and in the surging smoke
Uplifted spurns the ground; thence many a league
As in a clouded chair ascending rides
Audacious; but, that seat soon failing, meets
A vast vacuity: all unawares
Flutt'ring his pennons vain plumb down he drops
Ten thousand fathom deep, and to this hour
Down had been falling, had not by ill chance
The strong rebuff of some tumultuous cloud
Instinct with fire and nitre hurried him
As many miles aloft: that fury stay'd,
Quenched in a boggy syrtis, neither sea,
Nor good dry land: nigh foundered on he fares,
Treading the crude consistence, half on foot,
Half flying; behoves him now both oar and sail.
As when a gryphon[1] through the wilderness
With wingèd course o'er hill or moory dale
Pursues the Arimaspian,[2] who by stealth
Had from his wakeful custody purloin'd
The guarded gold: so eagerly the fiend
O'er bog or steep, through strait, rough, dense, or rare,
With head, hands, wings, or feet, pursues his way,
And swims, or sinks, or wades, or creeps, or flies.
At length a universal hubbub wild
Of stunning sounds and voices all confused,
Borne through the hollow dark, assaults his ear
With loudest vehemence: thither he plies,

[1] Gryphon, a fabulous creature; a lion with an eagle's head, said to guard gold mines.
[2] The Arimaspians were a one-eyed people of Scythia, who took gold, when they could get it, from the gryphons who guarded it. See Pliny's "Natural History," lib. vii. c. 2.

Undaunted to meet there whatever power
Or spirit of the nethermost abyss
Might in that noise reside, of whom to ask
Which way the nearest coast of darkness lies,
Bordering on light; when straight behold the throne
Of Chaos, and his dark pavilion spread
Wide on the wasteful Deep: with him enthroned
Sat sable-vested Night, eldest of things,
The consort of his reign; and by them stood
Orcus and Ades,[1] and the dreaded name
Of Demogorgon;[2] Rumor next, and Chance,
And Tumult, and Confusion, all imbroil'd,
And Discord with a thousand various mouths.
To whom Satan turning boldly, thus.—Ye Powers,
And Spirits of this nethermost abyss,
Chaos and ancient Night, I come no spy,
With purpose to explore or to disturb
The secrets of your realm; but by constraint,
Wand'ring this darksome desert, as my way
Lies through your spacious empire up to light,
Alone, and without guide, half lost, I seek
What readiest path leads where your gloomy bounds
Confine with heav'n; or if some other place,
From your dominion won, th' ethereal King
Possesses lately, thither to arrive
I travel this profound; direct my course;
Directed, no mean recompense it brings
To your behoof, if I that region lost,
All usurpation thence expell'd, reduce
To her original darkness and your sway,
Which is my present journey, and once more
Erect the standard there of ancient Night;
Yours be th' advantage all, mine the revenge.

    Thus Satan; and him thus the Anarch old,
With falt'ring speech and visage incomposed,
Answer'd. I know thee, stranger, who thou art,
That mighty leading angel, who of late
Made head against heav'n's King, though overthrown,
I saw and heard; for such a numerous host

[1] Orcus, Pluto; Ades, a personification, any dark place.—
RICHARDSON.
[2] A fiend, whose very name the heathen feared to pronounce.

Fled not in silence through the frighted deep,
With ruin upon ruin, rout on rout,
Confusion worse confounded; and heav'n gates
Pour'd out by millions her victorious bands
Pursuing. I upon my frontiers here
Keep residence; if all I can will serve,
That little which is left so to defend,
Encroach'd on still through your intestine broils
Weak'ning the sceptre of old Night: first hell,
Your dungeon, stretching far and wide beneath;
Now lately heaven and earth, another world,
Hung o'er my realm, link'd in a golden chain
To that side heav'n from whence your legions fell:
If that way be your walk, you have not far;
So much the nearer danger: go and speed;
Havock, and spoil, and ruin are my gain.

He ceased; and Satan stay'd not to reply,
But glad that now his sea should find a shore,
With fresh alacrity and force renew'd
Springs upward, like a pyramid of fire,
Into the wild expanse, and through the shock
Of fighting elements, on all sides round
Environ'd, wins his way; harder beset
And more endanger'd, than when Argo[1] pass'd
Through Bosphorus betwixt the justling rocks:
Or when Ulysses on the larboard shunned
Charybdis, and by th' other whirlpool steer'd,
So he with difficulty and labor hard
Moved on, with difficulty and labor he;
But he once past, soon after when man fell,
Strange alteration! Sin and death amain
Following his track, such was the will of Heav'n,
Paved after him a broad and beaten way
Over the dark abyss, whose boiling gulf
Tamely endured a bridge of wond'rous length,
From hell continued, reaching th' utmost orb
Of this frail world; by which the spirits perverse
With easy intercourse pass to and fro
To tempt or punish mortals, except whom
God and good angels guard by special grace.

[1] The ship in which Jason and his companions sailed to fetch the golden fleece from Colchis, in the Black Sea.

But now at last the sacred influence
Of light appears, and from the walls of heav'n
Shoots far into the bosom of dim Night
A glimmering dawn: here Nature first begins
Her farthest verge, and Chaos to retire
As from her outmost works, a broken foe,
With tumult less and with less hostile din,
That Satan with less toil and now with ease
Wafts on the calmer wave by dubious light,
And like a weather-beaten vessel holds
Gladly the port, though shrouds and tackle torn;
Or in the emptier waste, resembling air,
Weighs his spread wings, at leisure to behold
Far off th' empyreal heav'n, extended wide
In circuit, undetermined square or round,
With opal towers and battlements adorn'd
Of living sapphire, once his native seat;
And fast by hanging in a golden chain
This pendant world,[1] in bigness as a star
Of smallest magnitude close by the moon.
Thither full fraught with mischievous revenge,
Accursed, and in a cursèd hour, he hies.

[1] See *Measure for Measure*, Act iii. Sc. 1.

BOOK III

THE ARGUMENT

God sitting on his throne sees Satan flying towards this world, then newly created; shows him to the Son, who sat at his right hand; foretells the success of Satan in perverting mankind; clears his own justice and wisdom from all imputation, having created Man free, and able enough to have withstood his tempter; yet declares his purpose of grace towards him, in regard he fell not of his own malice, as did Satan, but by him seduced. The Son of God renders praises to his Father for the manifestation of his gracious purpose towards Man; but God again declares, that grace cannot be extended towards Man without the satisfaction of divine justice; Man hath offended the majesty of God by aspiring to Godhead, and therefore with all his progeny devoted to death must die, unless some one can be found sufficient to answer for his offence, and undergo his punishment. The Son of God freely offers himself a ransom for Man; the Father accepts him, ordains his incarnation, pronounces his exaltation above all names in heaven and earth; commands all the Angels to adore him; they obey, and, hymning to their harps in full choir, celebrate the Father and the Son. Meanwhile Satan alights upon the bare convex of this world's outermost orb; where wandering he first finds a place, since called the Limbo of Vanity; what persons and things fly up thither; thence comes to the gate of heaven, described ascending by stairs, and the waters above the firmament that flow about it: his passage thence to the orb of the sun; he finds there Uriel the regent of that orb; but first changes himself into the shape of a meaner angel; and pretending a zealous desire to behold the new creation, and Man whom God had placed here, inquires of him the place of his habitation, and is directed; alights first on Mount Niphates.

HAIL holy light, offspring of heav'n first-born
Or of th' Eternal co-eternal beam
May I express thee unblamed? since GOD is light,[1]
And never but in unapproachèd light
Dwelt from eternity, dwelt then in thee,

[1] 1 St. John i. 5. 1 Tim. vi. 16.

Bright effluence of bright essence increate.
Or hear'st thou rather pure ethereal stream,
Whose fountain who shall tell? [1] before the sun,
Before the heavens thou wert, and at the voice
Of GOD, as with a mantle, didst invest
The rising world of waters dark and deep,
Won from the void and formless infinite.
Thee I revisit now with bolder wing,
Escaped the Stygian pool, though long detain'd
In that obscure sojourn, while in my flight
Through utter and through middle darkness borne,
With other notes, than to th' Orphean lyre,[2]
I sung of Chaos and eternal Night,
Taught by the heav'nly Muse to venture down
The dark descent, and up to reascend,
Though hard and rare: thee I revisit safe,
And feel thy sov'reign vital lamp; but thou
Revisit'st not these eyes, that roll in vain
To find thy piercing ray, and find no dawn;
So thick a drop serene[3] hath quench'd their orbs,
Or dim suffusion veil'd. Yet not the more
Cease I to wander where the Muses haunt
Clear spring, or shady grove, or sunny hill,
Smit with the love of sacred song; but chief
Thee Sion, and the flowery brooks beneath,
That wash thy hallow'd feet, and warbling flow,
Nightly I visit; nor sometimes forget
Those other two equall'd with me in fate,
So were I equall'd with them in renown,
Blind Thamyris[4] and blind Mæonides,[5]
And Tiresias[6] and Phineus[7] prophets old.
Then feed on thoughts, that voluntary move
Harmonious numbers; as the wakeful bird
Sings darkling, and in shadiest covert hid

[1] Job xxxviii. 19.
[2] Orpheus wrote a hymn to Night, addressing her as "Mother of gods and men."
[3] Milton's blindness was caused by *gutta serena*.
[4] A Thracian who invented the Doric measure.—NEWTON.
[5] Homer.
[6] A blind Theban prophet.—NEWTON.
[7] King of Arcadia.—NEWTON.

Tunes her nocturnal note: thus with the year
Seasons return, but not to me returns
Day, or the sweet approach of even or morn,
Or sight of vernal bloom, or summer's rose,
Or flocks, or herds, or human face divine;
But cloud instead, and ever-during dark
Surrounds me, from the cheerful ways of men
Cut off, and for the book of knowledge fair
Presented with a universal blank
Of nature's works to me expunged and rased,
And wisdom at one entrance quite shut out.
So much the rather thou celestial Light
Shine inward, and the mind through all her powers
Irradiate, there plant eyes, all mist from thence
Purge and disperse, that I may see and tell
Of things invisible to mortal sight.
　　Now had the Almighty Father from above,
From the pure empyrean where he sits
High throned above all highth, bent down his eye.
His own works and their works at once to view:
About him all the sanctities of heaven
Stood thick as stars, and from his sight received
Beatitude past utterance; on his right
The radiant image of his glory sat,
His only Son: on earth He first beheld
Our two first parents, yet the only two
Of mankind, in the happy garden placed,
Reaping immortal fruits of joy and love,
Uninterrupted joy, unrivall'd love,
In blissful solitude: He then survey'd
Hell and the gulf between, and Satan there
Coasting the wall of heav'n on this side night
In the dun air sublime, and ready now
To stoop with wearied wings, and willing feet
On the bare outside of this world, that seem'd
Firm land imbosom'd without firmament,
Uncertain which, in ocean or in air.
Him GOD beholding from His prospect high,
Wherein past, present, future, He beholds,
Thus to His only Son foreseeing spake.
　　Only begotten Son, seest thou what rage
Transports our adversary, whom no bounds

Prescribed, no bars of hell, nor all the chains
Heap'd on him there, not yet the main abyss
Wide interrupt, can hold, so bent he seems
On desperate revenge, that shall redound
Upon his own rebellious head. And now
Through all restraint broke loose he wings his way
Not far off heav'n, in the precincts of light,
Directly towards the new created world,
And man there placed, with purpose to assay
If him by force he can destroy, or worse,
By some false guile pervert; and shall pervert;
For man will hearken to his glozing lies,
And easily trangress the sole command,
Sole pledge of his obedience: so will fall
He and his faithless progeny. Whose fault?
Whose but his own? ingrate, he had of me
All he could have: I made him just and right,
Sufficient to have stood, though free to fall.
Such I created all th' ethereal Powers
And Spirits, both them who stood and them who fail'd:
Freely they stood who stood, and fell who fell.
Not free, what proof could they have given sincere
Of true allegiance, constant faith, or love,
Where only, what they needs must do, appear'd,
Not what they would? what praise could they receive?
What pleasure I from such obedience paid,
When will and reason (reason also is choice,)
Useless and vain, of freedom both despoil'd,
Made passive both, had served necessity,
Not me? They therefore, as to right belong'd,
So were created, nor can justly accuse
Their Maker, or their making, or their fate;
As if predestination over-ruled
Their will, disposed by absolute decree
Or high foreknowledge: they themselves decreed
Their own revolt, not I: if I foreknew,
Foreknowledge had no influence on their fault,
Which had no less proved certain unforeknown.
So without least impulse or shadow of fate,
Or aught by me immutably foreseen,
They trespass, authors to themselves in all,
Both what they judge and what they choose; for so

I form'd them free, and free they must remain,
Till they enthrall themselves; I else must change
Their nature, and revoke the high decree,
Unchangeable, eternal, which ordain'd
Their freedom; they themselves ordain'd their fall.
The first sort by their own suggestion fell,
Self-tempted, self-depraved: man falls deceived
By the other first: man therefore shall find grace,
The other none: in mercy and justice both,
Through heav'n and earth, so shall my glory excel;
But mercy first and last shall brightest shine.

    Thus while GOD spake, ambrosial fragrance fill'd
All heav'n, and in the blessèd spirits elect
Sense of new joy ineffable diffused.
Beyond compare the Son of GOD was seen
Most glorious, in him all his father shone
Substantially express'd,[1] and in his face
Divine compassion visibly appear'd,
Love without end, and without measure grace;
Which uttering thus he to his father spake.

    O Father, gracious was that word which closed
Thy sov'reign sentence, that man should find grace;
For which both heav'n and earth shall high extol
Thy praises, with th' innumerable sound
Of hymns and sacred songs, wherewith thy throne
Encompass'd shall resound thee ever blest.
For should man finally be lost, should man
Thy creature late so loved, thy youngest son,
Fall circumvented thus by fraud, though join'd
With his own folly? that be from thee far,
That far be from thee, Father, who art judge
Of all things made, and judgest only right.
Or shall the adversary thus obtain
His end, and frustrate thine? shall he fulfil
His malice, and thy goodness bring to naught,
Or proud return though to his heavier doom,
Yet with revenge accomplish'd, and to hell
Draw after him the whole race of mankind,
By him corrupted? or wilt thou thyself
Abolish thy creation, and unmake,
For him, what for thy glory thou hast made?

[1] Heb. i. 3.—HUME.

So should thy goodness and thy greatness both
Be question'd and blasphemed without defence.
   To whom the great Creator thus replied.
O Son, in whom my soul hath chief delight,
Son of my bosom, Son who art alone
My word, my wisdom, and effectual might,
All hast thou spoken as my thoughts are, all
As my eternal purpose hath decreed:
Man shall not quite be lost, but saved who will,
Yet not of will in him, but grace in me
Freely vouchsafed: once more I will renew
His lapsèd powers, though forfeit and enthrall'd
By sin to foul exorbitant desires:
Upheld by me, yet once more he shall stand
On even ground against his mortal foe,
By me upheld, that he may know how frail
His fall'n condition is, and to me owe
All his deliv'rance, and to none but me.
Some I have chosen of peculiar grace
Elect above the rest; so is my will:
The rest shall hear me call, and oft be warn'd
Their sinful state, and to appease betimes
Th' incensèd Deity, while offer'd grace
Invites; for I will clear their senses dark.
What may suffice, and soften stony hearts[1]
To pray, repent, and bring obedience due.
To prayer, repentance, and obedience due.
Though but endeavor'd with sincere intent,
Mine ear shall not be slow, mine eye not shut.
And I will place within them as a guide
My umpire Conscience, whom if they will hear,
Light after light well used they shall attain,
And to the end persisting safe arrive.
This my long sufferance and my day of grace
They who neglect and scorn shall never taste;
But hard be harden'd, blind be blinded more,
That they may stumble on, and deeper fall;
And none but such from mercy I exclude.
But yet all is not done; man disobeying
Disloyal breaks his fealty, and sins
Against the high supremacy of heav'n,

[1] Ezek. xxxvi. 26.

Affecting Godhead, and so losing all,
To expiate his treason hath naught left,
But to destruction sacred and devote.
He with his whole posterity must die;
Die he or justice must; unless for him
Some other able, and as willing, pay
The rigid satisfaction, death for death.
Say, heav'nly Powers, where shall we find such love?
Which of you will be mortal to redeem
Man's mortal crime, and just th' unjust to save? [1]
Dwells in all heaven charity so dear?

He ask'd, but all the heav'nly choir stood mute,
And silence was in heav'n: on man's behalf
Patron or intercessor none appear'd,
Much less that durst upon his own head draw
The deadly forfeiture, and ransom set.
And now without redemption all mankind
Must have been lost, adjudged to death and hell
By doom severe, had not the Son of God,
In whom the fulness dwells of love divine,
His dearest mediation thus renew'd.

Father, thy word is pass'd, man shall find grace;
And shall grace not find means, that finds her way,
The speediest of thy wing'd messengers,
To visit all thy creatures, and to all
Comes unprevented, unimplored, unsought?
Happy for man, so coming; he her aid
Can never seek, once dead in sins and lost;
Atonement for himself or offering meet,
Indebted and undone, hath none to bring.
Behold me then, me for him, life for life,
I offer, on me let thine anger fall;
Account me man; I for his sake will leave
Thy bosom, and this glory next to thee
Freely put off, and for him lastly die
Well pleased; on me let Death wreak all his rage;
Under his gloomy power I shall not long
Lie vanquish'd; thou hast given me to possess
Life in myself for ever, by thee I live, [2]
Though now to Death I yield, and am his due

[1] 1 Peter iii. 18.
[2] John v. 26.

All that of me can die; yet that debt paid,
Thou wilt not leave me in the loathsome grave
His prey, nor suffer my unspotted soul
For ever with corruption there to dwell:[1]
But I shall rise victorious, and subdue
My vanquisher, spoil'd of his vaunted spoil;
Death his death's wound shall then receive, and stoop
Inglorious, of his mortal sting disarm'd.
I through the ample air in triumph high
Shall lead hell captive[2] maugre hell, and show
The powers of darkness bound. Thou, at the sight
Pleased, out of heaven shalt look down and smile,
While by thee raised I ruin all my foes,
Death last, and with his carcase glut the grave:[3]
Then with the multitude of my redeem'd
Shall enter heaven long absent, and return,
Father, to see thy face, wherein no cloud
Of anger shall remain, but peace assured
And reconcilement: wrath shall be no more
Thenceforth, but in thy presence joy entire.
  His words here ended, but his meek aspect
Silent yet spake, and breathed immortal love
To mortal men, above which only shone
Filial obedience: as a sacrifice
Glad to be offer'd, he attends the will
Of his great Father. Admiration seized
All heav'n, what this might mean and whither tend
Wond'ring; but soon th' Almighty thus reply'd:
  O thou in heav'n and earth the only peace
Found out for mankind under wrath, O thou
My sole complacence! well thou know'st how dear
To me are all my works, nor man the least,
Though last created, that for him I spar
Thee from my bosom and right hand, to save,
By losing thee awhile, the whole race lost.
Thou therefore whom thou only canst redeem
Their nature also to thy nature join;
And be thyself man among men on earth,
Made flesh, when time shall be, of virgin seed,

[1] Psalm xvi. 10.
[2] Psalm lxviii. 18. Col. ii. 15.
[3] 1 Cor. xv. 26.

By wondrous birth: be thou in Adam's room
The head of all mankind, though Adam's son.
As in him perish all men, so in thee,
As from a second root, shall be restored,[1]
As many as are restored, without thee none.
His crime makes guilty all his sons; thy merit
Imputed shall absolve them who renounce
Their own both righteous and unrighteous deeds,
And live in thee transplanted, and from thee
Receive new life. So man, as is most just,
Shall satisfy for man, be judged and die;
And dying rise, and rising with him raise
His brethren, ransom'd with his own dear life.
So heav'nly love shall outdo hellish hate,
Giving to death, and dying to redeem;
So dearly to redeem what hellish hate
So easily destroy'd, and still destroys
In those who, when they may, accept not grace.
Nor shalt thou by descending to assume
Man's nature lessen or degrade thine own.
Because thou hast, though throned in highest bliss
Equal to God, and equally enjoying
God-like fruition, quitted all to save
A world from utter loss, and hast been found
By merit more than birthright Son of God,
Found worthiest to be so by being good,
Far more than great or high; because in thee
Love hath abounded more than glory abounds;
Therefore thy humiliation shall exalt
With thee thy manhood also to this throne;
Here shalt thou sit incarnate, here shalt reign
Both God and Man, Son both of God and Man,
Anointed universal king; all power
I give thee, reign for ever, and assume
Thy merits; under thee as head supreme
Thrones, Princedoms, Powers, Dominions, I reduce:
All knees to thee shall bow, of them that bide[2]
In heav'n, or earth, or under earth in hell;
When thou attended gloriously from heav'n
Shalt in the sky appear, and from thee send

[1] 1 Cor. xv. 22.
[2] Phil. ii. 10.

The summoning archangels to proclaim
Thy dread tribunal: forthwith from all winds
The living, and forthwith the cited dead
Of all past ages, to the general doom
Shall hasten, such a peal shall rouse their sleep.
Then, all thy saints assembled, thou shalt judge
Bad men and angels; they arraign'd shall sink
Beneath thy sentence; hell, her numbers full,
Thenceforth shall be for ever shut. Meanwhile
The world shall burn, and from her ashes spring
New heav'n and earth,[1] wherein the just shall dwell,
And after all their tribulations long
See golden days, fruitful of golden deeds,
With joy and love triumphing, and fair truth:
Then thou thy regal sceptre shalt lay by,[2]
For regal sceptre then no more shall need,
GOD shall be all in all.[3] But all ye Gods
Adore him, who to compass all this dies,
Adore the Son, and honor him as me.

No sooner had th' Almighty ceased, but all
The multitude of angels with a shout,
Loud as from numbers without number, sweet
As from blest voices, uttering joy, heav'n rung
With jubilee, and loud hosannas fill'd
Th' eternal regions. Lowly reverent
Towards either throne they bow, and to the ground
With solemn adoration down they cast[4]
Their crowns inwove with amarant and gold
Immortal amarant,[5] a flow'r which once
In Paradise fast by the Tree of Life
Began to bloom, but soon for man's offence
To heav'n removed, where first it grew, there grows,
And flow'rs aloft shading the fount of life,
And where the river of bliss through midst of heav'n
Rolls o'er Elysian flowers her amber stream;

[1] 2 Peter iii. 12, 13.
[2] Heb. i. 6.
[3] 1 Cor. xv. 24.
[4] Rev. iv. 10.
[5] A flower of a purple velvet color. It was supposed not to die when gathered, but recovered its lustre when sprinkled with water. The name is Greek for "unfading."—HUME.

With these that never fade the spirits elect
Bind their resplendent locks inwreath'd with beams;
Now in loose garlands thick thrown off; the bright
Pavement, that like a sea of jasper shone,
Impurpled with celestial roses smiled.
Then crown'd again their golden harps they took,
Harps ever tuned, that glittering by their side
Like quivers hung, and with preamble sweet
Of charming symphony they introduce
Their sacred song, and waken raptures high;
No voice exempt, no voice but well could join
Melodious part, such concord is in heav'n.
    Thee Father first they sung, Omnipotent,
Immutable, Immortal, Infinite,
Eternal King; Thee author of all being,
Fountain of light, Thyself invisible
Amidst the glorious brightness where Thou sitt'st
Throned inaccessible, but when Thou shad'st
The full blaze of Thy beams, and through a cloud
Draw round about Thee like a radiant shrine,
Dark with excessive bright Thy skirts appear;
Yet dazzle heav'n, that brightest Seraphim
Approach not, but with both wings veil their eyes.
Thee next they sang of all creation first,
Begotten Son, Divine Similitude,
In whose conspicuous countenance, without cloud
Made visible, the Almighty Father shines,
Whom else no creature can behold: on Thee
Impress'd th' effulgence of His glory abides;
Transfused on Thee his ample Spirit rests.
He heav'n of heavens and all the powers therein
By Thee created, and by Thee threw down
Th' aspiring Dominations. Thou that day
Thy Father's dreadful thunder didst not spare,
Nor stop thy flaming chariot wheels, that shook
Heav'n's everlasting frame, while o'er the necks
Thou drov'st of warring angels disarray'd.
Back from pursuit Thy powers with loud acclaim
Thee only extoll'd, Son of Thy Father's might,
To execute fierce vengeance on his foes;
Not so on man; him thro' their malice fall'n,
Father of mercy and grace, Thou didst not doom

So strictly; but much more to pity incline.
No sooner did Thy dear and only Son
Perceive thee purposed not to doom frail man
So strictly, but much more to pity inclined,
He to appease Thy wrath, and end the strife
Of mercy and justice in Thy face discern'd,
Regardless of the bliss wherein He sat
Second to Thee, offer'd himself to die
For man's offence. O unexampled love,
Love nowhere to be found less than Divine!
Hail Son of GOD, Saviour of men, Thy name
Shall be the copious matter of my song
Henceforth, and never shall my harp thy praise
Forget, nor from thy Father's praise disjoin.
   Thus they in heav'n, above the starry sphere,
Their happy hours in joy and hymning spent.
Meanwhile upon the firm opacous globe
Of this round world, whose first convex divides
The luminous inferior orbs, inclosed
From Chaos and th' inroad of Darkness old,
Satan alighted walks: a globe far off
It seem'd, now seems a boundless continent,
Dark, waste, and wild, under the frown of night
Starless exposed, and ever-threat'ning storms
Of Chaos blust'ring round, inclement sky;
Save on that side which from the wall of heav'n
Though distant far some small reflection gains
Of glimmering air, less vex'd with tempest loud
Here walk'd the fiend at large in spacious field.
As when a vulture on Imaus[1] bred,
Whose snowy ridge the roving Tartar bounds,
Dislodging from a region scarce of prey
To gorge the flesh of lambs or yeanling kids
On hills where flocks are fed, flies towards the springs
Of Ganges or Hydaspes, Indian streams;
But in his way lights on the barren plains
Of Sericana,[2] where Chineses drive
With sails and wind their cany wagons light:

[1] A mountain in Asia. Its name signifies snowy. It is the eastern
boundary of Western Tartary.
[2] Serica lies between China on the east and Imaus on the west.—
NEWTON.

So on this windy sea of land the fiend
Walk'd up and down alone bent on his prey,
Alone, for other creature in this place[1]
Living or lifeless to be found was none,
None yet, but store hereafter from the earth
Up hither like aërial vapors flew
Of all things transitory and vain, when sin
With vanity had fill'd the works of men:
Both all things vain, and all who in vain things
Built their fond hopes of glory or lasting fame,
Or happiness in this or th' other life;
All who have their reward on earth, the fruits
Of painful superstition and blind zeal,
Nought seeking but the praise of men, here find
Fit retribution, empty as their deeds:
All th' unaccomplish'd works of nature's hand,
Abortive, monstrous, or unkindly mix'd,
Dissolved on earth, fleet hither, and in vain,
Till final dissolution, wander here,
Not in the neighb'ring moon, as some have dream'd,[2]
Those argent fields more likely habitants,
Translated saints, or middle spirits hold
Betwixt th' angelical and human kind:
Hither of ill-join'd sons and daughters born[3]
First from the ancient world those giants came
With many a vain exploit, though then renown'd:
The builders next of Babel on the plain
Of Sennaar, and still with vain design
New Babels, had they wherewithal, would build:
Others came single; he who to be deem'd
A God leap'd fondly into Ætna flames,
Empedocles,[4] and he who to enjoy
Plato's Elysium leap'd into the sea,
Cleombrotus,[5] and many more too long,

[1] Limbo.
[2] Ariosto, in the "Orlando Furioso."
[3] The sons of God "ill-joined" with the daughters of "men." See
Gen. vi. 4. Subject of Moore's "Loves of the Angels," and Byron's
"Heaven and Earth."
[4] A Pythagorean philosopher. His attempt at disappearing in an
extraordinary manner from the earth was defeated by the volcano
throwing back his iron patterns.
[5] An Epirot.

Embryoes and idiots, eremites and friars,
White, black, and grey,[1] with all their trumpery.
Here pilgrims roam, that stray'd so far to seek
In Golgotha him dead, who lives in heav'n;
And they who to be sure of paradise
Dying put on the weeds of Dominic,
Or in Franciscan think to pass disguised;[2]
They pass the planets seven, and pass the fix'd,
And that crystalline sphere whose balance weighs
The trepidation talk'd,[3] and that first moved:
And now St. Peter at heav'n's wicket seems
To wait them with his keys, and now at foot
Of heav'n's ascent they lift their feet, when, lo!
A violent cross wind from either coast
Blows them transverse ten thousand leagues awry
Into the devious air: then might ye see
Cowls, hoods, and habits with their wearers tost
And flutter'd into rags; then reliques, beads,
Indulgences, dispenses, pardons, bulls,
The sport of winds: all these upwhirl'd aloft
Fly o'er the back side of the world far off,
Into a limbo large and broad, since call'd
The Paradise of Fools, to few unknown
Long after, now unpeopled, and untrod.
All this dark globe the fiend found as he pass'd,
And long he wander'd, till at last a gleam
Of dawning light turn'd thitherward in haste
His travelled steps; far distant he descries,
Ascending by degrees magnificent
Up to the wall of heav'n a structure high,
At top whereof, but far more rich appear'd
The work as of a kingly palace gate,
With frontispiece of diamond and gold
Imbellish'd; thick with sparkling orient gems
The portal shone, inimitable on earth
By model or by shading pencil drawn.

---

[1] Carmelites, Dominicans, and Franciscans.
[2] In the dark ages, a ridiculous superstition prevailed that a dying sinner who put on the habit of a religious order was sure of salvation. It was frequently done.
[3] Milton speaks here according to Ptolemy's astronomy.—*From* NEWTON.

The stairs were such as whereon Jacob saw[1]
Angels ascending and descending, bands
Of guardians bright, when he from Esau fled
To Padan-Aram in the field of Luz,
Dreaming by night under the open sky,
And waking cried, *This is the gate of heav'n.*
Each stair mysteriously was meant, nor stood
There always, but drawn up to heav'n sometimes
Viewless, and underneath a bright sea flow'd
Of jasper, or of liquid pearl, whereon
Who after came from earth sailing arrived
Wafted by angels, or flew o'er the lake,
Rapt in a chariot drawn by fiery steeds.
The stairs were then let down, whether to dare
The fiend by easy ascent, or aggravate
His sad exclusion from the doors of bliss:
Direct against which open'd from beneath,
Just o'er the blissful seat of paradise,
A passage down to th' earth, a passage wide,
Wider by far than that of after-times
Over mount Sion, and, though that were large,
Over the Promised Land to GOD so dear,
By which, to visit oft those happy tribes,
On high behests his angels to and fro
Pass'd frequent, and his eye with choice regard,
From Paneas, the fount of Jordan's flood,
To Beërsaba, where the Holy Land
Borders on Egypt and the Arabian shore:
So wide the op'ning seem'd, where bounds were set
To darkness, such as bound the ocean wave.
Satan from hence now on the lower stair,
That scaled by steps of gold to heaven gate,
Looks down with wonder at the sudden view
Of all this world at once. As when a scout
Through dark and desert ways with peril gone
All night, at last by break of cheerful dawn
Obtains the brow of some high-climbing hill,
Which to his eye discovers unaware
The goodly prospect of some foreign land
First-seen, or some renown'd metropolis,
With glistering spires and pinnacles adorn'd,

[1] Gen. xxviii. 12, 13.

Which now the rising sun gilds with his beams:
Such wonder seized, though after heaven seen,
The spirit malign; but much more envy seized
At sight of all this world beheld so fair.
Round he surveys, and well might, where he stood
So high above the circling canopy
Of night's extended shade, from eastern point
Of Libra to the fleecy star[1] that bears
Andromeda far off Atlantic seas
Beyond th' horizon; then from pole to pole
He views in breadth, and without longer pause
Down right into the world's first region throws
His flight precipitant, and winds with ease
Through the pure marble air his oblique way
Amongst innumerable stars, that shone
Stars distant, but nigh hand seem'd other worlds,
Or other worlds they seem'd, or happy isles,
Like those Hesperian gardens[2] famed of old,
Fortunate fields, and groves, and flow'ry vales,
Thrice happy isles; but who dwelt happy there
He stay'd not to enquire: above them all
The golden sun in splendor likest heaven
Allured his eye: thither his course he bends
Through the calm firmament; but up or down,
By centre or eccentric, hard to tell,
Or longitude, where the great luminary,
Aloof the vulgar constellations thick,
That from his lordly eye keep distance due,
Dispenses light from far; they as they move
Their starry dance in numbers that compute
Days, months, and years, towards his all-cheering lamp
Turn swift their various motions, or are turn'd
By his magnetic beam, that gently warms
The universe, and to each inward part
With gentle penetration, though unseen,
Shoots invisible virtue even to the deep;
So wond'rously was set his station bright.
There lands the fiend, a spot like which perhaps

[1] Aries, *i.e.*, from one half of the ecliptic to the other, from east to west. The constellation Andromeda is immediately above or over Aries.—NEWTON.

[2] The Cape Verde Islands; the "Fortunate Islands."

Astronomers in the sun's lucent orb
Through his glazed optic tube yet never saw.
The place he found beyond expression bright
Compared with aught on earth, metal or stone;
Not all parts like, but all alike inform'd
With radiant light, as glowing iron with fire;
If metal, part seem'd gold, part silver clear;
If stone, carbuncle most or chrysolite,
Ruby or topaz, to the twelve that shone
In Aaron's breast-plate,[1] and a stone[2] besides
Imagined rather oft than elsewhere seen,
That stone, or like to that which here below
Philosophers in vain so long have sought,
In vain, though by their powerful art they bind
Volatile Hermes,[3] and call up unbound
In various shapes old Proteus from the sea,
Drain'd through a limbeck to his native form.
What wonder then if fields and regions here
Breathe forth elixir pure, and rivers run
Portable gold, when with one virtuous touch
Th' arch-chemic sun so far from us remote
Produces with terrestrial humor mix'd
Here in the dark so many precious things
Of color glorious and effect so rare?
Here matter new to gaze the devil met
Undazzled, far and wide his eye commands,
For sight no obstacle found here, nor shade,
But all sun-shine; as when his beams at noon
Culminate from th' Equator, as they now
Shot upward still direct, whence no way round
Shadow from body opaque can fall, and the air,
Nowhere so clear, sharpen'd his visual ray
To objects distant far, whereby he soon
Saw within ken a glorious angel stand,
The same whom John saw also in the sun:[4]

[1] Exod. xxviii. 15–21.

[2] The philosopher's stone, supposed to have the power (if found) of turning the baser metals into gold.

[3] Quicksilver, called Hermes by the alchemists. The names of heathen gods were applied to the materials of the alchemist's laboratory. Proteus was a sea-god capable of transforming himself into various shapes.

[4] Rev. xix. 17.

His back was turn'd, but not his brightness hid;
Of beaming sunny rays, a golden tiar
Circled his head, nor less his locks behind
Illustrious on his shoulders fledge with wings
Lay waving round; on some great charge employ'd
He seem'd, or fix'd in cogitation deep.
Glad was the spirit impure, as now in hope
To find who might direct his wand'ring flight
To paradise the happy seat of man,
His journey's end, and our beginning woe.
But first he casts to change his proper shape,
Which else might work him danger or delay:
And now a stripling Cherub he appears,
Not of the prime, yet such as in his face
Youth smiled celestial, and to every limb
Suitable grace diffused, so well he feign'd;
Under a coronet his flowing hair
In curls on either cheek play'd; wings he wore
Of many a color'd plume sprinkled with gold;
His habit fit for speed succinct, and held
Before his decent steps a silver wand.
He drew not nigh unheard, the angel bright,
E'er he drew nigh, his radiant visage turn'd,
Admonish'd by his ear, and straight was known
Th' arch-angel Uriel,[1] one of the sev'n
Who in God's presence nearest to his throne
Stand ready at command, and are his eyes
That run through all the heav'ns, or down to th' earth
Bear his swift errands, over moist and dry,
O'er sea and land: him Satan thus accosts.

Uriel, for thou of those sev'n spirits that stand
In sight of God's high throne, gloriously bright,
The first art wont his great authentic will
Interpreter through highest heav'n to bring,
Where all his sons thy embassy attend;
And here art likeliest by supreme decree
Like honor to obtain, and as His eye
To visit oft this new creation round;
Unspeakable desire to see, and know

---

[1] Uriel is derived from two Hebrew words, signifying *God is my light.*—NEWTON. See mention made of him in Apocrypha, 2 Esdras, 4, 5.

All these his wondrous works, but chiefly man,
His chief delight and favor, him for whom
All these his works so wondrous he ordain'd
Hath brought me from the choirs of Cherubim
Alone thus wand'ring. Brightest Seraph, tell
In which of all these shining orbs hath man
His fixèd seat, or fixèd seat hath none,
But all these shining orbs his choice to dwell;
That I may find him, and, with secret gaze
Or open admiration, him behold,
On whom the great Creator hath bestow'd
Worlds, and on whom hath all these graces pour'd;
That both in him and all things, as is meet,
The universal Maker we may praise;
Who justly hath driven out his rebel foes
To deepest hell, and to repair that loss
Created this new happy race of men
To serve him better: wise are all his ways.
 So spake the false dissembler unperceived;
For neither man nor angel can discern
Hypocrisy, the only evil that walks
Invisible, except to GOD alone,
By His permissive will through heav'n and earth:
And oft, though wisdom wake, suspicion sleeps
At wisdom's gate, and to simplicity
Resigns her charge, while goodness thinks no ill
Where no ill seems; which now for once beguiled
Uriel, though regent of the sun, and held
The sharpest-sighted spirit of all in heav'n:
Who to the fraudulent imposter foul
In his uprightness answer thus return'd.
 Fair angel, thy desire which tends to know
The works of GOD, thereby to glorify
The great Work-master, leads to no excess
That reaches blame, but rather merits praise
The more it seems excess, that led thee hither
From thy empyreal mansion thus alone,
To witness with thine eyes what some perhaps
Contented with report hear only in heav'n:
For wonderful indeed are all His works,
Pleasant to know, and worthiest to be all
Had in remembrance always with delight:

But what created mind can comprehend
Their number, or the wisdom infinite
That brought them forth, but hid their causes deep?
I saw, when at his word the formless mass,
This world's material mould, came to a heap:
Confusion heard his voice, and wild uproar
Stood ruled, stood vast infinitude confined;
Till at his second bidding darkness fled,
Light shone, and order from disorder sprung.
Swift to their several quarters hasted then
The cumbrous elements, earth, flood, air, fire,
And this ethereal quintessence of heav'n
Flew upward, spirited with various forms,
That roll'd orbicular, and turn'd to stars
Numberless, as thou seest, and how they move;
Each had his place appointed, each his course,
The rest in circuit walls this universe.
Look downward on that globe whose hither side
With light from hence, though but reflected shines;
That place is earth the seat of man, that light
His day, which else as th' other hemisphere
Night would invade, but there the neighboring moon,
So call that opposite fair star, her aid
Timely interposes, and her monthly round
Still ending, still renewing, through mid heav'n,
With borrow'd light her countenance triform
Hence fills and empties to enlighten th' earth,
And in her pale dominion checks the night.
That spot to which I point is paradise,
Adam's abode, those lofty shades his bower:
Thy way thou canst not miss, me mine requires.

    Thus said, he turn'd, and Satan bowing low,
As to superior spirits is wont in heaven,
Where honor due and reverence none neglects,
Took leave, and toward the coast of earth beneath,
Down from th' ecliptic, sped with hoped success,
Throws his steep flight in many an aery wheel,
Nor stay'd, till on Niphates' top[1] he lights.

---

[1] A mountain bordering on Mesopotamia, near which the earthly
paradise is supposed to have been placed.—*From* HUME.

BOOK IV

The Argument

Satan now in prospect of Eden, and nigh the place where he must now attempt the bold enterprise which he undertook alone against GOD and man, falls into many doubts with himself, and many passions, fear, envy, and despair; but at length confirms himself in evil, journeys on to paradise, whose outward prospect and situation is described, overleaps the bounds, sits in the shape of a cormorant on the Tree of life, as the highest in the garden, to look about him. The garden described; Satan's first sight of Adam and Eve; his wonder at their excellent form and happy state, but with resolution to work their fall: overhears their discourse, thence gathers that the Tree of knowledge was forbidden them to eat of, under penalty of death; and thereon intends to found his temptation, by seducing them to transgress: then leaves them awhile to know further of their state by some other means. Meanwhile Uriel descending on a sunbeam warns Gabriel, who had in charge the gate of paradise, that some evil spirit had escaped the deep, and passed at noon by his sphere in the shape of a good angel down to paradise, discovered afterwards by his furious gestures in the mount. Gabriel promises to find him ere morning. Night coming on, Adam and Eve discourse of going to their rest: their bower described; their evening worship. Gabriel drawing forth his bands of nightwatch to walk the round of paradise, appoints two strong angels to Adam's bower, lest the evil spirit should be there doing some harm to Adam or Eve sleeping; there they find him at the ear of Eve, tempting her in a dream, and bring him, though unwilling, to Gabriel; by whom questioned, he scornfully answers, prepares resistance; but hindered by a sign from heaven flies out of paradise.

O FOR that warning voice, which he,[1] who saw
Th' Apocalypse, heard cry in heaven aloud,

[1] St. John. Rev. xii. 10. "And I heard a loud voice saying in heaven, . . ." and at verse 12, "Woe to the inhabiters of the earth and of the sea! for the devil is come down unto you. . . . ."

Then when the Dragon,[1] put to second rout,
Came furious down to be revenged on men,
"Woe to the inhabitants on earth!" that now,
While time was, our first parents had been warn'd
The coming of their secret foe, and 'scaped,
Happily so 'scaped his mortal snare; for now
Satan, now first inflamed with rage, came down,
The tempter ere th' accuser of mankind,
To wreak on innocent frail man his loss
Of that first battle, and his flight to hell:
Yet not rejoicing in his speed, though bold,
Far off and fearless, nor with cause to boast,
Begins his dire attempt, which, nigh the birth
Now rolling, boils in his tumultuous breast,
And like a devilish engine back recoils
Upon himself; horror and doubt distract
His troubled thoughts, and from the bottom stir
The hell within him, for within him hell
He brings, and round about him, nor from hell
One step, no more than from himself, can fly
By change of place: now conscience wakes despair
That slumber'd, wakes the bitter memory
Of what he was, what is, and what must be,
Worse; of worse deeds worse suffering must ensue.
Sometimes towards Eden, which now in his view
Lay pleasant, his grieved look he fixes sad;
Sometimes towards heav'n and the full-blazing sun,
Which now sat high in his meridian tow'r:
Then, much revolving, thus in sighs began.

O thou that, with surpassing glory crown'd,[2]
Look'st from thy sole dominion like the God
Of this new world, at whose sight all the stars
Hide their diminish'd heads, to thee I call,
But with no friendly voice, and add thy name
O Sun, to tell thee how I hate thy beams,
That bring to my remembrance from what state
I fell, how glorious once above thy sphere;

[1] Devil.
[2] Milton originally designed to write a tragedy on the Fall, and
this grand speech was intended to begin it. This is asserted by
Porson on the authority of Milton's nephew, Edward Philips.

Till pride and worse ambition threw me down,
Warring in heav'n against heav'n's matchless King.
Ah, wherefore! He deserved no such return
From me, whom He created what I was
In that bright eminence, and with His good
Upbraided none; nor was His service hard.
What could be less than to afford Him praise,
The easiest recompense, and pay Him thanks,
How due! yet all His good proved ill in me,
And wrought but malice; lifted up so high
I sdein'd [1] subjection, and thought one step higher
Would set me highest, and in a moment quit
The debt immense of endless gratitude,
So burthensome, still paying, still to owe;
Forgetful what from Him I still received,
And understood not that a grateful mind
By owing, owes not, but still pays, at once
Indebted and discharged; what burden then?
O had his powerful destiny ordain'd
Me some inferior angel, I had stood
Then happy; no unbounded hope had raised
Ambition! Yet why not? some other power
As great might have aspired, and me though mean
Drawn to his part; but other powers as great
Fell not, but stand unshaken, from within
Or from without, to all temptations arm'd.
Hadst thou the same free will and power to stand?
Thou hadst: whom hast thou then or what to accuse,
But heav'n's free love dealt equally to all?
Be then His love accursed, since love or hate,
To me alike, it deals eternal woe:
Nay cursed be thou since against His thy will
Chose freely what it now so justly rues.
Me miserable! which way shall I fly
Infinite wrath, and infinite despair?
Which way I fly is hell; myself am hell;
And in the lowest deep a lower deep
Still threat'ning to devour me opens wide;
To which the hell I suffer seems a heav'n.
O then at last relent: is there no place

[1] Disdained.

Left for repentance, none for pardon left?
None left but my submission; and that word
Disdain forbids me, and my dread of shame
Among the spirits beneath, whom I seduced
With other promises and other vaunts
Than to submit, boasting I could subdue
Th' Omnipotent. Ay me! they little know
How dearly I abide that boast so vain,
Under what torments inwardly I groan;
While they adore me on the throne of hell,
With diadem and sceptre high advanced
The lower still I fall, only supreme
In misery; such joy ambition finds.
But say I could repent, and could obtain
By act of grace my former state; how soon
Would highth recall high thoughts, how soon unsay
What feign'd submission swore: ease would recant
Vows made in pain, as violent and void.
For never can true reconcilement grow
Where wounds of deadly hate have pierced so deep;
Which would but lead me to a worse relapse
And heavier fall: so should I purchase dear
Short intermission bought with double smart.
This knows my Punisher; therefore as far
From granting He, as I from begging peace:
All hope excluded thus, behold in stead
Of us out-cast, exiled, his new delight,
Mankind, created, and for him this world.
So farewell hope, and with hope farewell fear,
Farewell remorse: all good to me is lost;
Evil, be thou my good; by thee at least
Divided empire with heav'n's King I hold,
By thee, and more than half perhaps will reign;
As man ere long and this new world shall know.
　　Thus while he spake, each passion dimm'd his face
Thrice changed with pale ire, envy, and despair,
Which marr'd his borrow'd visage, and betray'd
His counterfeit, if any eye beheld:
For heav'nly minds from such distempers foul
Are ever clear. Whereof he soon aware
Each perturbation smooth'd with outward calm,

Artificer of fraud; and was the first
That practised falsehood under saintly show,
Deep malice to conceal, couch'd with revenge.
Yet not enough had practised to deceive
Uriel once warn'd; whose eye pursued him down
The way he went, and on th' Assyrian mount
Saw him disfigured, more than could befall
Spirit of happy sort: his gestures fierce
He mark'd and mad demeanor, then alone,
As he supposed, all unobserved, unseen.
So on he fares, and to the border comes
Of Eden, where delicious Paradise,
Now nearer, crowns with her enclosure green,
As with a rural mound, the champain head
Of a steep wilderness, whose hairy sides
With thicket overgrown, grotesque and wild,
Access denied; and over head up grew
Insuperable highth of loftiest shade,
Cedar, and pine, and fir, and branching palm,
A sylvan scene, and as the ranks ascend
Shade above shade, a woody theatre
Of stateliest view. Yet higher than their tops
The verdurous wall of Paradise up sprung;
Which to our general sire gave prospect large
Into his nether empire neighboring round.
And higher than that wall a circling row
Of goodliest trees loaden with fairest fruit,
Blossoms and fruits at once of golden hue
Appear'd, with gay enamell'd colors mixt:
On which the sun more glad impress'd his beams,
Than in fair evening cloud, or humid bow,
When God hath shower'd the earth; so lovely seem'd
That landscape: and of pure now purer air
Meets his approach, and to the heart inspires
Vernal delight and joy, able to drive
All sadness but despair: now gentle gales
Fanning their odoriferous wings dispense
Native perfumes, and whisper whence they stole
Those balmy spoils. As when to them who sail
Beyond the Cape of Hope, and now are past
Mozambic, off at sea north-east winds blow

Sabean odors from the spicy shore[1]
Of Araby the blest, with such delay
Well pleased they slack their course and many a league
Cheer'd with the grateful smell old Ocean smiles:
So entertain'd those odorous sweets the fiend
Who came their bane, though with them better pleased
Than Asmodeus[2] with the fishy fume,
That drove him, though enamor'd, from the spouse
Of Tobit's son, and with a vengeance sent
From Media post to Egypt, there fast bound.

Now to th' ascent of that steep savage hill
Satan had journey'd on, pensive and slow;
But further way found none, so thick entwined
As one continued brake, the undergrowth
Of shrubs and tangling brushes had perplex'd
All path of man or beast that past that way.
One gate there only was, and that looked east
On th' other side: which when th' arch-felon saw,
Due entrance he disdain'd, and in contempt
At one slight bound high overleap'd all bound
Of hill or highest wall, and sheer within
Lights on his feet. As when a prowling wolf,

[1] The perfumes from the shores of India and its islands can be
perceived far out at sea, when the wind blows off the land—
        "The spicy breezes
      Blow soft from Ceylon's isle,"
says Bishop Heber in his fine Missionary Hymn; and every one
who has lived in the East will remember how oppressive *on shore*
the scent-ladened air, heavy with perfume, is. How constantly it
recalls to one's mind Byron's exquisite lines in the "Bride of
Abydos"—
      "The light wings of Zephyr, oppress'd with perfume,
        Wax faint o'er the gardens of Gul in her bloom;"
but coming on the briny sea breezes this fragrance is delightful to
the mariner. It is in spring, when the wind blows off the shore,
that the air thus becomes the harbinger of a near haven. Milton is
said to have taken his description from *Diodorus Siculus*, B. III.
40.—*Notes on* GRAY.

[2] An evil spirit, who, loving Sarah, the daughter of Raguel,
would not suffer any of the young men who espoused her to live.
He was exorcised by the fumes arising from the heart and liver
of a fish, which Tobit, by the instruction of an angel, burnt on the
evening of his wedding. See Apocrypha, Tobit, viii.

Whom hunger drives to seek new haunt for prey,
Watching where shepherds pen their flocks at eve
In hurdled cotes amid the field secure,
Leaps o'er the fence with ease into the fold:
Or as a thief bent to unhoard the cash
Of some rich burgher, whose substantial doors,
Cross-barr'd and bolted fast, fear no assault,
In at the window climbs, or o'er the tiles:
So clomb this first grand thief into God's fold;
So since into his church lewd hirelings climb.
Thence up he flew, and on the Tree of Life,
The middle tree and highest[1] there that grew,
Sat like a cormorant; yet not true life
Thereby regain'd, but sat devising death
To them who lived; nor on the virtue thought
Of that life giving plant, but only used
For prospect, what well used had been the pledge
Of immortality. So little knows
Any, but God alone, to value right
The good before him, but perverts best things
To worst abuse, or to their meanest use.
Beneath him with new wonder now he views
To all delight of human sense exposed
In narrow room nature's whole wealth, yea more,
A heav'n on earth: for blissful Paradise
Of God the garden was, by him in the east
Of Eden planted; Eden stretch'd her line
From Auran[2] eastward to the royal tow'rs
Of great Seleucia, built by Grecian kings,
Or where the sons of Eden long before
Dwelt in Telassar.[3] In this pleasant soil
His far more pleasant garden God ordain'd;
Out of the fertile ground he caused to grow
All trees of noblest kind for sight, smell, taste;
And all amid them stood the Tree of Life,
High eminent, blooming ambrosial fruit,
Of vegetable gold, and next to life
Our death, the Tree of Knowledge, grew fast by,

[1] Gen. ii. 9.
[2] Haran.—*From* NEWTON.
[3] Isaiah xxxvii. 12. A province of the children of Eden, placed by Ptolemy in Babylonia.—*From* NEWTON.

Knowledge of good bought dear by knowing ill.
Southward through Eden went a river large,
Nor changed his course, but through the shaggy hill
Pass'd underneath ingulf'd; for God had thrown
That mountain as his garden mould, high raised
Upon the rapid current, which, through veins
Of porous earth with kindly thirst up drawn,
Rose a fresh fountain, and with many a rill
Water'd the garden; thence united fell
Down the steep glade, and met the nether flood,
Which from his darksome passage now appears;
And now divided into four main streams
Runs diverse, wand'ring many a famous realm
And country, whereof here needs no account;
But rather to tell how, if art could tell,
How from that sapphire fount the crispèd brooks,
Rolling on orient pearl and sands of gold,
With mazy error under pendant shades
Ran Nectar, visiting each plant, and fed
Flow'rs worthy of Paradise, which not nice art
In beds and curious knots, but nature boon
Pour'd forth profuse on hill, and dale and plain,
Both where the morning sun first warmly smote
The open field, and where the unpierced shade
Imbrown'd the noontide bow'rs. Thus was this place
A happy rural seat of various view:
Groves whose rich trees wept odorous gums and balm,
Others whose fruit burnish'd with golden rind
Hung amiable, Hesperian fables true,
If true, here only, and of delicious taste.
Betwixt them lawns, or level downs, and flocks
Grazing the tender herb, were interposed,
Or palmy hillock, or the flow'ry lap
Of some irriguous valley spread her store,
Flow'rs of all hue, and without thorn the rose.
Another side umbrageous grots and caves
Of cool recess, o'er which the mantling vine
Lays forth her purple grape, and gently creeps
Luxuriant: meanwhile murmuring waters fall
Down the slope hills, dispers'd, or in a lake,
That to the fringèd bank with myrtle crown'd
Her crystal mirror holds, unite their streams.

The birds their choir apply; airs, vernal airs,
Breathing the smell of field and grove, attune
The trembling leaves, while universal Pan,[1]
Knit with the Graces and the Hours in dance,
Led on th' eternal spring. Not that fair field
Of Enna, where Proserpine gathering flow'rs,
Herself a fairer flower, by gloomy Dis[2]
Was gather'd, which cost Ceres all that pain
To seek her through the world; nor that sweet grove
Of Daphne by Orontes and the inspired
Castalian spring might with this paradise
Of Eden strive: nor that Nyseian isle
Girt with the river Triton, where old Cham,
Whom Gentiles Ammon call and Libyan Jove,
Hid Amalthea and her florid son
Young Bacchus from his stepdame Rhea's eye;
Nor where Abassin kings their issue guard,
Mount Amara,[3] though this by some supposed
True paradise, under the Ethiop line
By Nilus' head, enclosed with shining rock,
A whole day's journey high, but wide remote
From this Assyrian garden, where the fiend
Saw undelighted, all delight, all kind
Of living creatures new to sight and strange.

   Two of far nobler shape erect and tall,
Godlike erect, with native honor clad,
In native majesty, seem'd lords of all,
And worthy seem'd: for in their looks divine
The image of their glorious Maker shone,
Truth, wisdom, sanctitude severe and pure,

[1] Pan was a symbol of Nature. The Graces symbolized Spring,
Summer, and Autumn. The Hours, the time requisite for the pro-
duction and perfection of things.—RICHARDSON.

[2] Pluto. All the loveliest dreams of mythology, and the places re-
markable for natural beauty—the Plains of Enna, in Sicily; the
laurel-grove of Daphne, by the River Orontes; the Castalian
Spring, haunted by the Muses; the Greek Isle, where Bacchus was
nursed; the Happy Valley where the Princes of Abyssinia were
nursed—are here named to exalt the wondrous beauty of the
earthly Paradise by comparison.

[3] High hills in Ethiopia, under the equator; within their circuit
lay the guarded valley where the royal children of Abyssinia
dwelt.—MASSEY. Our readers will be reminded of *Rasselas*.

Severe, but in true filial freedom placed,
Whence true authority in men: though both
Not equal, as their sex not equal, seem'd;
For contemplation he and valour form'd,
For softness she and sweet attractive grace;
He for God only, she for God in him.[1]
His fair large front and eye sublime declared
Absolute rule; and hyacinthine locks
Round from his parted forelock manly hung
Clust'ring, but not beneath his shoulders broad:
She as a veil down to the slender waist
Her unadornèd golden tresses wore
Dishevell'd, but in wanton ringlets waved
As the vine curls her tendrils, which implied
Subjection, but required with gentle sway,
And by her yielded, by him best received,
Yielded with coy submission, modest pride,
And sweet reluctant amorous delay.
Nor those mysterious parts were then conceal'd;
Then was not guilty shame; dishonest shame
Of nature's works, honor dishonorable,
Sin-bred, how have ye troubled all mankind
With shows instead, mere shows of seeming pure.
And banish'd from man's life his happiest life,
Simplicity and spotless innocence!
So pass'd they naked on, nor shunn'd the sight
Of God or Angel, for they thought no ill:
So hand in hand they pass'd, the loveliest pair
That ever since in love's embraces met;
Adam the goodliest man of men since born
His sons, the fairest of her daughters Eve.
Under a tuft of shade, that on a green
Stood whisp'ring soft, by a fresh fountain side
They sat them down; and after no more toil
Of their sweet gard'ning labor than sufficed
To recommend cool Zephyr, and made ease
More easy, wholesome thirst and appetite
More grateful, to their supper fruits they fell,
Nectarine fruits, which the compliant boughs
Yielded them, side-long as they sat recline
On the soft downy bank damask'd with flow'rs.

[1] 1 Cor. xi. 7–9.

The savory pulp they chew, and in the rind,
Still as they thirsted, scoop the brimming stream:
Nor gentle purpose nor endearing smiles
Wanted, nor youthful dalliance, as beseems
Fair couple, link'd in happy nuptial league
Alone as they. About them frisking play'd
All beasts of th' earth, since wild, and of all chase
In wood or wilderness, forest or den;
Sporting the lion ramp'd, and in his paw
Dandled the kid; bears, tigers, ounces, pards,
Gamboll'd before them; th' unwieldly elephant
To make them mirth used all his might, and wreath'd
His lithe proboscis; close the serpent sly
Insinuating wove with Gordian twine
His braided train, and of his fatal guile
Gave proof unheeded; others on the grass
Couch'd and now fill'd with pasture gazing sat,
Or bedward ruminating: for the sun
Declined was hasting now with prone career
To th' ocean isles and in th' ascending scale
Of heav'n the stars that usher evening rose:
When Satan still in gaze, as first he stood,
Scarce thus at length fail'd speech recover'd sad.
    O hell! what do mine eyes with brief behold,
Into our room of bliss thus high advanced
Creatures of other mould, earth-born perhaps,
Not spirits, yet to heav'nly spirits bright
Little inferior; whom my thoughts pursue
With wonder, and could love, so lively shines
In them divine resemblance, and such grace
The hand that form'd them on their shape hath pour'd!
Ah gentle pair, ye little think how nigh
Your change approaches, when all these delights
Will vanish and deliver ye to woe;
More woe, the more your taste is now of joy:
Happy, but for so happy ill secured
Long to continue; and this high seat your heav'n
Ill fenced for heav'n to keep out such a foe
As now is enter'd: yet no purposed foe
To you, whom I could pity thus forlorn,
Though I unpitied. League with you I seek,
And mutual amity, so straight, so close,

That I with you must dwell, or you with me
Henceforth: my dwelling haply may not please,
Like this fair paradise, your sense; yet such
Accept, your Maker's work; He gave it me.
Which I as freely give: hell shall unfold [1]
To entertain you two, her widest gates,
And send forth all her kings: there will be room,
Not like these narrow limits, to receive
Your numerous offspring; if no better place,
Thank him who puts me loth to this revenge
On you, who wrong me not, for Him who wrong'd.
And should I at your harmless innocence
Melt, as I do, yet public reason just,
Honor and empire with revenge enlarged,
By conquering this new world, compels me now
To do what else, though damn'd, I should abhor.

    So spake the fiend, and with necessity,
The tyrant's plea, excused his devilish deeds.
Then from his lofty stand on that high tree
Down he alights among the sportful herd
Of those fourfooted kinds, himself now one,
Now other, as their shape served best his end
Nearer to view his prey, and unespied
To mark what of their state he more might learn
By word or action mark'd: about them round
A lion now he stalks with fiery glare,
Then as a tiger, who by chance had spied
In some purlieu two gentle fawns at play,
Strait couches close, then rising changes oft,
His couchant watch, as one who chose his ground,
Whence rushing he might surest seize them both
Griped in each paw: when Adam first of men,
To first of women Eve thus moving speech,
Turn'd him all ear to hear new utterance flow.

    Sole partner and sole part of all those joys,
Dearer thyself than all, needs must the Power
That made us, and for us this ample world,
Be infinitely good, and of His good
As liberal and free as infinite,
That raised us from the dust and placed us here
In all this happiness, who at His hand

[1] Isaiah xiv. 9.

Have nothing merited, nor can perform
Aught whereof He hath need, He who requires
From us no other service than to keep
This one, this easy charge, of all the trees
In paradise that bear delicious fruit
So various, not to taste that only Tree
Of Knowledge, planted by the Tree of Life;
So near grows death to life; whate'er death is,
Some dreadful thing no doubt; for well thou know'st
God hath pronounced it death to taste that tree,
The only sign of our obedience left
Among so many signs of power and rule
Conferr'd upon us, and dominion given
Over all other creatures that possess
Earth, air and sea. Then let us not think hard
One easy prohibition, who enjoy
Free leave so large to all things else, and choice
Unlimited of manifold delights:
But let us ever praise him and extol
His bounty, following our delightful task
To prune these growing plants, and tend these flowers;
Which were it toilsome, yet with thee were sweet.
    To whom thus Eve replied. O thou, for whom
And from whom I was form'd, flesh of thy flesh,
And without whom am to no end, my guide
And head, what thou hast said is just and right:
For we to him indeed all praises owe,
And daily thanks; I chiefly, who enjoy
So far the happier lot, enjoying thee
Pre-eminent by so much odds, while thou
Like consort to thyself canst nowhere find.
That day I oft remember, when from sleep
I first awaked, and found myself reposed
Under a shade on flowers, much wond'ring where
And what I was, whence thither brought, and how
Not distant far from thence a murmuring sound
Of waters issued from a cave, and spread
Into a liquid plain, then stood unmoved,
Pure as th' expanse of heav'n; I thither went
With unexperienced thought, and laid me down
On the green bank, to look into the clear
Smooth lake, that to me seem'd another sky.

As I bent down to look, just opposite
A shape within the wat'ry gleam appear'd
Bending to look on me: I started back,
It started back; but pleased I soon return'd,
Pleased it return'd as soon with answering looks
Of sympathy and love: there I had fix'd
Mine eyes till now, and pined with vain desire,
Had not a voice thus warn'd me, What thou seest,
What there thou seest, fair creature, is thyself;
With thee it came and goes: but follow me,
And I will bring thee where no shadow stays
Thy coming, and thy soft embraces; he
Whose image thou art, him thou shalt enjoy
Inseparably thine, to him shalt bear
Multitudes like thyself, and thence be call'd
Mother of human race. What could I do,
But follow straight, invisibly thus led?
Till I espied thee, fair indeed and tall,
Under a plantain; yet, methought, less fair,
Less winning soft, less amiably mild,
Than that smooth wat'ry image; back I turn'd,
Thou following criedst aloud, Return, fair Eve,
Whom fliest thou? whom thou fliest, of him thou art,
His flesh, his bone; to give thee being I lent
Out of my side to thee, nearest my heart,
Substantial life, to have thee by my side
Henceforth an individual solace dear:
Part of my soul, I seek thee, and thee claim,
My other half. With that thy gentle hand
Seized mine; I yielded, and from that time see
How beauty is excell'd by manly grace,
And wisdom, which alone is truly fair.
   So spake our general mother, and, with eyes
Of conjugal attraction unreproved
And meek surrender, half embracing lean'd
On our first father; half her swelling breast
Naked met his under the flowing gold
Of her loose tresses hid: he, in delight
Both of her beauty and submissive charms,
Smiled with superior love, as Jupiter
On Juno smiles, when he impregns the clouds
That shed May flowers, and press'd her matron lip

With kisses pure: aside the devil turn'd
For envy, yet with jealous leer malign
Eyed them askance, and to himself thus plain'd.
  Sight hateful, sight tormenting! thus these two
Imparadised in one another's arms,
The happier Eden, shall enjoy their fill
Of bliss on bliss, while I to hell am thrust,
Where neither joy nor love, but fierce desire,
Among our other torments not the least,
Still unfulfill'd with pain of longing pines.
Yet let me not forget what I have gain'd
From their own mouths: all is not theirs it seems;
One fatal tree there stands of Knowledge call'd
Forbidden them to taste: knowledge forbidden?
Suspicious, reasonless. Why should their Lord
Envy them that? can it be sin to know?
Can it be death? and do they only stand
By ignorance? is that their happy state,
The proof of their obedience and their faith?
O fair foundation laid whereon to build
Their ruin! hence I will excite their minds
With more desire to know, and to reject
Envious commands, invented with design
To keep them low, whom knowledge might exalt
Equal with Gods; aspiring to be such,
They taste and die: what likelier can ensue?
But first with narrow search I must walk round
This garden, and no corner leave unspied;
A chance but chance may lead where I may meet
Some wand'ring spirit of heav'n, by fountain side,
Or in thick shade retired, from him to draw
What further would be learn'd. Live while ye may,
Yet happy pair; enjoy, till I return,
Short pleasures, for long woes are to succeed.
  So saying, his proud step he scornful turn'd,
But with sly circumspection, and began
Through wood, through waste, o'er hill, o'er dale, his
    roam.
Meanwhile in utmost longitude, where heav'n
With earth and ocean meets, the setting sun
Slowly descended, and with right aspect
Against the eastern gate of paradise

Levell'd his ev'ning rays: it was a rock
Of alabaster, piled up to the clouds,
Conspicuous far, winding with one ascent
Accessible from earth, one entrance high;
The rest was craggy cliff, that overhung
Still as it rose, impossible to climb.
Betwixt these rocky pillars Gabriel [1] sat,
Chief of the angelic guards, awaiting night;
About him exercised heroic games
Th' unarmèd youth of heav'n; but nigh at hand
Celestial armory, shields, helms, and spears,
Hung high with diamond flaming and with gold.
Thither came Uriel, gliding through the even
On a sunbeam, swift as a shooting star
In autumn thwarts the night, when vapors fired
Impress the air, and show the mariner
From what point of his compass to beware
Impetuous winds: he thus began in haste.
  Gabriel, to thee thy course by lot hath given
Charge and strict watch, that to this happy place
No evil thing approach or enter in:
This day at highth of noon came to my sphere
A spirit, zealous, as he seem'd, to know
More of the Almighty's works, and chiefly man
God's latest image: I descried his way
Bent all on speed, and mark'd his aery gait:
But in the mount that lies from Eden north,
Where he first lighted, soon discern'd his looks
Alien from heav'n, with passions foul obscured:
Mine eye pursued him still, but under shade
Lost sight of him; one of the banish'd crew,
I fear, hath ventured from the deep to raise
New troubles; him thy care must be to find.
  To whom the wingèd warrior thus return'd:
Uriel, no wonder if thy perfect sight,
Amid the sun's bright circle where thou sitt'st,
See far and wide: in at this gate none pass
The vigilance here placed, but such as come
Well known from heav'n; and since meridian hour
No creature thence. If spirit of other sort,

---

[1] The angel sent to Daniel (Dan. ix. 21), and to the Virgin Mary
and to Zacharias (see Luke i. 19 and 26).

So minded, have o'erleap'd these earthy bounds
On purpose, hard thou know'st it to exclude
Spiritual substance with corporeal bar.
But if within the circuit of these walks
In whatsoever shape he lurk, of whom
Thou tell'st, by morrow dawning I shall know.

 So promised he, and Uriel to his charge
Return'd on that bright beam, whose point now raised
Bore him slope downward to the sun, now fall'n
Beneath th' Azores; whether the prime orb,
Incredible how swift, had hither roll'd
Diurnal, or this less volubil earth,
By shorter flight to th' east, had left him there,
Arraying with reflected purple and gold
The clouds that on his western throne attend.
Now came still evening on, and twilight gray
Had in her sober livery all things clad;
Silence accompanied; for beast and bird,
They to their grassy couch, these to their nests,
Were slunk, all but the wakeful nightingale;
She all night long her amorous descant sung;
Silence was pleased: now glow'd the firmament
With living sapphires; Hesperus that led
The starry host rode brightest, till the moon,
Rising in clouded majesty, at length
Apparent queen unveil'd her peerless light,
And o'er the dark her silver mantle threw.

 When Adam thus to Eve: Fair consort, the hour
Of night and all things now retired to rest
Mind us of like repose, since God hath set
Labor and rest, as day and night, to men
Successive, and the timely dew of sleep
Now falling with soft slumbrous weight inclines
Our eyelids: other creatures all day long
Rove idle, unemploy'd, and less need rest:
Man hath his daily work of body or mind
Appointed, which declares his dignity,
And the regard of heaven on all his ways;
While other animals unactive range,
And of their doings God takes no account
To-morrow ere fresh morning streak the east
With first approach of light we must be risen,

And at our pleasant labor, to reform
Yon flowery arbors, yonder alleys green,
Our walk at noon, with branches overgrown
That mock our scant manuring, and require
More hands than ours to lop their wanton growth:
Those blossoms also and those dropping gums,
That lie bestrown unsightly and unsmooth,
Ask riddance, if we mean to tread with ease:
Meanwhile, as nature wills, night bids us rest.

    To whom thus Eve with perfect beauty adorn'd.
My author and disposer, what thou bidd'st
Unargued I obey, so GOD ordains;
GOD is thy law, thou mine; to know no more
Is woman's happiest knowledge and her praise.
With thee conversing I forget all time,
All seasons and their change, all please alike:
Sweet is the breath of morn, her rising sweet,
With charm of earliest birds; pleasant the sun,
When first on this delightful land he spreads
His orient beams, on herb, tree, fruit, and flower,
Glist'ning with dew; fragrant the fertile earth
After soft showers; and sweet the coming on
Of grateful ev'ning mild; then silent night
With this her solemn bird, and this fair moon,
And these the gems of heav'n, her starry train:
But neither breath of morn when she ascends
With charm of earliest birds, nor rising sun
On this delightful land, nor herb, fruit, flower,
Glist'ring with dew, nor fragrance after showers,
Nor grateful evening mild, nor silent night
With this her solemn bird, nor walk by moon,
Or glittering starlight, without thee is sweet.
But wherefore all night long shine these? for whom
This glorious sight, when sleep hath shut all eyes?

    To whom our general ancestor replied.
Daughter of GOD and man, accomplish'd Eve,
Those have their course to finish, round the earth,
By morrow ev'ning, and from land to land
In order, though to nations yet unborn,
Minist'ring light prepared, they set and rise;
Lest total darkness should by night regain
Her old possession, and extinguish life

In nature and all things, which these soft fires
Not only enlighten, but with kindly heat
Of various influence foment and warm,
Temper or nourish, or in part shed down
Their stellar virtue on all kinds that grow
On earth, made hereby apter to receive
Perfection from the sun's more potent ray.
These then, though unbeheld in deep of night,
Shine not in vain; nor think, though men were none
That heav'n would want spectators, GOD want praise:
Millions of spiritual creatures walk the earth
Unseen, both when we wake, and when we sleep.
All these with ceaseless praise his works behold
Both day and night: how often from the steep
Of echoing hill or thicket have we heard
Celestial voices to the midnight air,
Sole, or responsive each to other's note,
Singing their great Creator? oft in bands
While they keep watch, or nightly rounding walk,
With heav'nly touch of instrumental sounds
In full harmonic number join'd, their songs
Divide the night, and lift our thoughts to heaven.

   Thus talking hand in hand alone they pass'd
On to their blissful bower; it was a place
Chosen by the sov'reign planter, when he framed
All things to man's delightful use: the roof
Of thickest covert was inwoven shade,
Laurel and myrtle, and what higher grew
Of firm and fragrant leaf; on either side
Acanthus and each odorous bushy shrub
Fenced up the verdant wall, each beauteous flower,
Iris all hues, roses, and jessamin
Rear'd high their flourish'd heads between, and wrought
Mosaic; under foot the violet,
Crocus, and hyacinth with rich inlay
Broider'd the ground, more color'd than with stone
Of costliest emblem: other creature here,
Beast, bird, insect, or worm, durst enter none;
Such was their awe of man. In shadier bower
More sacred and sequester'd, though but feign'd,
Pan or Sylvanus never slept; nor nymph,
Nor Faunus haunted. Here in close recess

With flowers, garlands, and sweet-smelling herbs,
Espousèd Eve deck'd first her nuptial bed,
And heav'nly choirs the Hymenæn sung,
What day the genial angel to our sire
Brought her in naked beauty more adorn'd,
More lovely than Pandora,[1] whom the Gods
Endow'd with all their gifts, and O too like
In sad event, when to the unwiser son
Of Japhet brought by Hermes she ensnared
Mankind with her fair looks, to be avenged
On him who had stole Jove's authentic fire.

Thus at their shady lodge arrived, both stood,
Both turn'd, and under open sky adored
The GOD that made both sky, air, earth, and heav'n
Which they beheld, the moon's resplendent globe,
And starry pole. Thou also mad'st the night,
Maker Omnipotent, and thou the day,
Which we in our appointed work employ'd
Have finish'd, happy in our mutual help
And mutual love, the crown of all our bliss
Ordain'd by thee, and this delicious place
For us too large, where thy abundance wants
Partakers, and uncropt falls to the ground.
But thou hast promised from us two a race
To fill the earth, who shall with us extol
Thy goodness infinite, both when we wake,
And when we seek, as now, thy gift of sleep.

This said unanimous, and other rites
Observing none, but adoration pure
Which GOD likes best, into their inmost bower
Handed they went; and, eased the putting off
These troublesome disguises which we wear,

[1] Pandora was a most beautiful woman on whom the gods bestowed all their gifts. Jupiter, enraged with Prometheus, the son of Japhet, for having stolen fire from heaven, sent Pandora, with a box of supposed treasures, to him, to punish him; but he refused to receive her. Hermes (or Mercury) then led her to Prometheus's "unwiser" brother Epimetheus, who received her, and was persuaded by her to open the box she brought as her dowry. It contained all the ills which have since afflicted humanity, but *Hope* remained at the bottom. It is very probable that this fable originated in the true story of Eve's disobedience, and her enticing Adam to share her sin.

Straight side by side were laid; nor turn'd, I ween,
Adam from his fair spouse; nor Eve the rites
Mysterious of connubial love refused
Whatever hypocrites austerely talk
Of purity, and place, and innocence,
Defaming as impure what GOD declares
Pure, and commands to some, leaves free to all.
Our Maker bids increase, who bids abstain
But our destroyer, foe to GOD and man?
Hail wedded love, mysterious law, true source
Of human offspring, sole propriety
In paradise of all things common else.
By thee adulterous lust was driv'n from men
Among the bestial herds to range; by thee
Founded in reason, loyal, just, and pure,
Relations dear, and all the charities[1]
Of father, son, and brother, first were known.
Far be it, that I should write thee sin or blame,
Or think thee unbefitting holiest place,
Perpetual fountain of domestic sweets,
Whose bed is undefiled and chaste pronounced,
Present, or past, as saints and patriarchs used.
Here Love his golden shafts employs, here lights
His constant lamp, and waves his purple wings,
Reigns here and revels; not in the bought smile
Of harlots, loveless, joyless, unendear'd,
Casual fruition; nor in court amours,
Mix'd dance, or wanton mask, or midnight ball,
Or serenate, which the starved lover sings
To his proud fair, best quitted with disdain.
These, lull'd by nightingales, embracing slept,
And on their naked limbs the flowery roof
Shower'd roses, which the morn repair'd. Sleep on,
Blest pair, and O! yet happiest if ye seek
No happier state, and know to know no more.
    Now had night measured with her shadowy cone
Half way up hill this vast sublunar vault,
And from their ivory port the Cherubim
Forth issuing at th' accustom'd hour stood arm'd
To their night watches in warlike parade,
When Gabriel to his next in power thus spake.

    [1] Affections.

Uzziel,[1] half these draw off, and coast the south
With strictest watch; these other wheel the north;
Our circuit meets full west. As flame they part,
Half wheeling to the shield, half to the spear.
From these two strong and subtle spirits he call'd
That near him stood, and gave them thus in charge.
　Ithuriel and Zephon,[2] with wing'd speed
Search through this garden, leave unsearch'd no nook;
But chiefly where those two fair creatures lodge,
Now laid perhaps asleep secure of harm.
This evening from the sun's decline arrived,
Who tells of some infernal spirit seen
Hitherward bent, who could have thought? escaped
The bars of hell, on errand bad no doubt:
Such where ye find, seize fast, and hither bring.
　So saying, on he led his radiant files,
Dazzling the moon; these to the bower direct
In search of whom they sought: him there they found,
Squat like a toad, close at the ear of Eve;
Assaying by his devilish art to reach
The organs of her fancy, and with them forge
Illusions as he list, phantasms, and dreams;
Or if, inspiring venom, he might taint
Th' animal spirits that from pure blood arise
Like gentle breaths from rivers pure, thence raise
At least distemper'd, discontented thoughts,
Vain hopes, vain aims, inordinate desires
Blown up with high conceits ingend'ring pride,
Him thus intent Ithuriel with his spear
Touch'd lightly; for no falsehood can endure
Touch of celestial temper, but returns
Of force to its own likeness: up he starts
Discover'd and surprized. As when a spark
Lights on a heap of nitrous powder, laid
Fit for the tun, some magazine to store
Against a rumor'd war, the smutty grain
With sudden blaze diffused inflames the air:
So started up in his own shape the fiend.
Back stepp'd those two fair angels, half amazed

　[1] This angel's name signifies the strength of God.
　[2] The name of Ithuriel signifies the discovery of God; of Zephon
a secret, or searcher of secrets.—*From* Hume.

So sudden to behold the grisly king;
Yet thus, unmoved with fear, accost him soon.
 Which of those rebel spirits adjudged to hell
Com'st thou, escaped thy prison? and transformed,
Why sat'st thou like an enemy in wait,
Here watching at the head of these that sleep?
 Know ye not then, said Satan fill'd with scorn,
Know ye not me? ye knew me once no mate
For you, there sitting where ye durst not soar;
Not to know me argues yourselves unknown,
The lowest of your throng; or if ye know,
Why ask ye, and superfluous begin
Your message, like to end as much in vain?
 To whom thus Zephon, answering scorn with scorn.
Think not, revolted spirit, thy shape the same
Or undiminish'd brightness, to be known
As when thou stood'st in heav'n upright and pure;
That glory then, when thou no more wast good,
Departed from thee, and thou resemblest now
Thy sin and place of doom obscure and foul.
But come, for thou, be sure, shalt give account
To him who sent us, whose charge is to keep
This place inviolable, and these from harm.
 So spake the Cherub, and his grave rebuke,
Severe in youthful beauty, added grace
Invincible: abash'd the devil stood,
And felt how awful goodness is, and saw
Virtue in her shape how lovely, saw, and pined
His loss; but chiefly to find here observed
His lustre visibly impair'd; yet seem'd
Undaunted. If I must contend, said he,
Best with the best, the sender not the sent,
Or all at once; more glory will be won,
Or less be lost. Thy fear, said Zephon bold,
Will save us trial what the least can do
Single against thee wicked, and thence weak.
 The fiend replied not, overcome with rage;
But like a proud steed rein'd went haughty on,
Champing his iron curb: to strive or fly
He held it vain; awe from above had quell'd
His heart, not else dismay'd. Now drew they nigh
The western point, where those half-rounding guards

Just met, and closing stood in squadron join'd,
Awaiting next command. To whom their chief
Gabriel from the front thus call'd aloud.

O friends, I hear the tread of nimble feet
Hasting this way, and now by glimpse discern
Ithuriel and Zephon through the shade,
And with them comes a third of regal port,
But faded splendor wan; who by his gait
And fierce demeanor seems the prince of hell,
Nor likely to part hence without contest:
Stand firm, for in his look defiance lours.

He scarce had ended, when those two approach'd,
And brief related whom they brought, where found,
How busied, in what form and posture couch'd,
To whom with stern regard thus Gabriel spake.

Why hast thou, Satan, broke the bounds prescribed
To thy transgression, and disturb'd the charge
Of others, who approve not to transgress
By thy example, but have power and right
To question thy bold entrance on this place,
Employ'd, it seems, to violate sleep, and those
Whose dwelling God hath planted here in bliss?

To whom thus Satan with contemptuous brow.
Gabriel, thou hadst in heav'n th' esteem of wise,
And such I held thee: but this question ask'd
Puts me in doubt. Lives there who loves his pain?
Who would not, finding way, break loose from hell,
Though hither doom'd? thou wouldst thyself, no doubt,
And boldly venture to whatever place
Farthest from pain, where thou migh'st hope to change
Torment with ease, and soonest recompense
Dole with delight, which in this place I sought:
To thee no reason, who know'st only good,
But evil hast not tried: and wilt object
His will who bound us? Let Him surer bar
His iron gates, if He intends our stay
In that dark durance: thus much what was ask'd.
The rest is true; they found me where they say;
But that implies not violence or harm.

Thus he in scorn. The warlike angel moved,
Disdainfully, half smiling, thus replied.
O loss of one in heav'n to judge of wise,

Since Satan fell, whom folly overthrew,
And now returns him from his prison scaped,
Gravely in doubt whether to hold them wise
Or not, who ask what boldness brought him hither
Unlicensed from his bounds in hell prescribed:
So wise he judges it to fly from pain
However, and to scape his punishment.
So judge thou still, presumptuous, till the wrath,
Which thou incurr'st by flying, meet thy flight
Sevenfold, and scourge that wisdom back to hell,
Which taught thee yet no better, that no pain
Can equal anger infinite provoked.
But wherefore thou alone? wherefore with thee
Came not all hell broke loose? is pain to them
Less pain, less to be fled, or thou than they
Less hardy to endure? courageous chief,
The first in flight from pain, hadst thou alleged
To thy deserted host this cause of flight,
Thou surely hadst not come sole fugitive.
　　To which the fiend thus answer'd, frowning stern.
Not that I less endure, or shrink from pain
Insulting angel, well thou know'st I stood
Thy fiercest, when in battle to thy aid
The blasting vollied thunder made all speed,
And seconded thy else not dreaded spear.
But still thy words at random, as before,
Argue thy inexperience what behoves
From hard assays and ill successes past
A faithful leader, not to hazard all
Through ways of danger by himself untried.
I therefore, I alone first undertook
To wing the desolate abyss, and spy
This new created world, whereof in hell
Fame is not silent, here in hope to find
Better abode, and my afflicted Powers
To settle here on earth, or in mid air;
Though for possession put to try once more
What thou and thy gay legions dare against;
Whose easier business were to serve their Lord
High up in heav'n, with songs to hymn his throne,
And practised distances to cringe, not fight.
　　To whom the warrior angel soon replied.

To say and straight unsay, pretending first
Wise to fly pain, professing next the spy,
Argues no leader, but a liar traced,
Satan, and couldst thou faithful add? O name,
O sacred name of faithfulness profaned!
Faithful to whom? to thy rebellious crew?
Army of fiends, fit body to fit head:
Was this your discipline and faith engaged,
Your military obedience, to dissolve
Allegiance to th' acknowledged Power supreme?
And thou sly hypocrite, who now wouldst seem
Patron of liberty, who more than thou
Once fawn'd, and cring'd, and servilely adored
Heav'n's awful Monarch? wherefore but in hope
To dispossess him, and thyself to reign?
But mark what I arreed thee now; Avaunt;
Fly thither whence thou fledst: if from this hour
Within these hallow'd limits thou appear,
Back to th' infernal pit I drag thee chain'd,
And seal thee so,[1] as henceforth not to scorn
The facile gates of hell too slightly barr'd.

So threaten'd he: but Satan to no threats
Gave heed, but waxing more in rage replied.

Then, when I am thy captive talk of chains,
Proud limitary Cherub; but ere then
Far heavier load thyself expect to feel
From my prevailing arm; though heaven's King
Ride on thy wings,[2] and thou with thy compeers,
Used to the yoke, draw'st his triumphant wheels
In progress through the road of heav'n star-paved.

While thus he spake, th' angelic squadron bright
Turn' fiery red, sharp'ning in moonèd horns
Their phalanx, and began to hem him round
With ported spears, as thick as when a field
Of Ceres, ripe for harvest, waving bends
Her bearded grove of ears, which way the wind
Sways them; the careful ploughman doubting stands,
Lest on the threshing floor his hopeful sheaves
Prove chaff. On the other side Satan alarm'd,
Collecting all his might, dilated stood,

[1] Rev. xx. 3.
[2] Ezek. i. x. and xi. 22.

Like Teneriffe or Atlas unremoved:
His stature reach'd the sky, and on his crest
Sat horror plumed; nor wanted in his grasp
What seem'd both spear and shield. Now dreadful deeds
Might have ensued, nor only Paradise
In this commotion, but the starry cope
Of heav'n perhaps, or all the elements
At least had gone to wrack, disturb'd and torn
With violence of this conflict, had not soon
Th' Eternal to prevent such horrid fray
Hung forth in heav'n his golden scales,[1] yet seen
Betwixt Astrea and the Scorpion sign,
Wherein all things created first he weigh'd,
The pendulous round earth with balanced air
In counterpoise; now ponders all events,
Battles, and realms: in these he put two weights,
The sequel each of parting and of fight;
The latter quick up flew and kick'd the beam:
Which Gabriel spying thus bespake the fiend.

Satan, I know thy strength, and thou know'st mine:
Neither our own but given; what folly then
To boast what arms can do, since thine no more
Than heav'n permits, nor mine, though doubled now
To trample thee as mire? for proof look up
And read thy lot in yon celestial sign,
Where thou art weigh'd,[2] and shown how light, how
     weak,
If thou resist. The fiend look'd up, and knew
His mounted scale aloft: nor more; but fled
Murmuring, and with him fled the shades of night.

[1] The constellation Libra. This image of the Deity weighing the
fates of the combatants is found both in Homer—XXII, "Iliad"—
and in Virgil, who represents Jupiter as weighing the fates of
Turnus and Æneas.—ADDISON. "In Homer and Virgil the com-
batants are weighed one against another, but here Satan only is
weighed; in one scale the consequence of his retreating, in the
other of his fighting. And there is this further improvement, that,
as in Homer and Virgil the fates are weighed to satisfy Jupiter
himself, it is here done to satisfy only the contending parties—
for Satan to read his own destiny!—NEWTON.
[2] Dan. v. 27.

BOOK V

The Argument

Morning approached, Eve relates to Adam her troublesome dream; he likes it not, yet comforts her: they come forth to their day-labors: their morning hymn at the door of their bower. God, to render man inexcusable, sends Raphael to admonish him of his obedience, of his free estate, of his enemy near at hand, who he is, and why his enemy, and whatever else may avail Adam to know. Raphael comes down to paradise; his appearance described, his coming discerned by Adam afar off, sitting at the door of his bower; he goes out to meet him, brings him to his lodge, entertains him with the choicest fruits of paradise got together by Eve; their discourse at table; Raphael performs his message, minds Adam of his state and of his enemy; relates at Adam's request, who that enemy is, and how he came to be so, beginning from his first revolt in heaven, and the occasion thereof; how he drew his legions after him to the parts of the north, and there incited them to rebel with him; persuading all but only Abdiel a seraph, who in argument dissuades and opposes him, then forsakes him.

Now morn, her rosy steps in th' eastern clime
Advancing, sow'd the earth with orient pearl,
When Adam waked, so custom'd for his sleep
Was aery light, from pure digestion bred,
And temperate vapors bland, which the only sound
Of leaves and fuming rills, Aurora's fan
Lightly dispersed, and the shrill matin song
Of birds on every bough: so much the more
His wonder was to find unwaken'd Eve
With tresses discomposed, and glowing cheek,
As through unquiet rest: he on his side
Leaning half-raised, with looks of cordial love
Hung over her enamor'd, and beheld
Beauty, which, whether waking or asleep,
Shot forth peculiar graces: then with voice
Mild, as when Zephyrus on Flora breathes,

Her hand soft touching, whisper'd thus: Awake,
My fairest, my espoused, my latest found,
Heav'n's last best gift, my ever new delight,
Awake, the morning shines, and the fresh field
Calls us, we lose the prime, to mark how spring
Our tended plants, how blows the citron grove,
What drops the myrrh, and what the balmy reed,
How nature paints her colors, how the bee
Sits on the bloom extracting liquid sweet.
　　Such whisp'ring waked her, but with startled eye
On Adam, whom embracing, thus she spake.
　　O sole in whom my thoughts find all repose,
My glory, my perfection, glad I see
Thy face and morn returned; for I this night,
Such night till this I never pass'd, have dream'd,
If dream'd, not, as I oft am wont, of thee,
Works of day pass'd, or morrow's next design,
But of offence and trouble, which my mind
Knew never till this irksome night: methought
Close at mine ear one call'd me forth to walk
With gentle voice; I thought it thine: it said,
Why sleep'st thou Eve? now is the pleasant time,
The cool, the silent, save where silence yields
To the night-warbling bird, that now awake
Tunes sweetest his love-labor'd song; now reigns
Full orb'd the moon, and with more pleasing light
Shadowy sets off the face of things; in vain,
If none regard: heav'n wakes with all his eyes,
Whom to behold but thee, nature's desire,
In whose sight all things joy, with ravishment
Attracted by thy beauty still to gaze.
I rose as at thy call, but found thee not;
To find thee I directed then my walk;
And on, methought, alone I pass'd through ways
That brought me on a sudden to the tree
Of interdicted knowledge: fair it seem'd,
Much fairer to my fancy than by day:
And as I wond'ring look'd, beside it stood
One shaped and wing'd like one of those from heav'n
By us oft seen; his dewy locks distill'd
Ambrosia; on that tree he also gazed;
And O fair plant, said he, with fruit surcharged,

Deigns none to ease thy load and taste thy sweet,
Nor GOD, nor man; is knowledge so despised?
Or envy, or what reserve forbids to taste?
Forbid who will, none shall from me withhold
Longer thy offer'd good; why else set here?
This said he paused not, but with vent'rous arm
He pluck'd, he tasted; me damp horror chill'd
At such bold words vouch'd with a deed so bold.
But he thus overjoy'd: O fruit divine,
Sweet of thyself, but much more sweet thus cropp'd,
Forbidden here, it seems, as only fit
For Gods, yet able to make Gods of men:
And why not Gods of men since good, the more
Communicated, more abundant grows,
The author not impair'd, but honor'd more
Here, happy creature, fair angelic Eve,
Partake thou also; happy though thou art,
Happier thou may'st be, worthier canst not be:
Taste this, and be henceforth among the Gods
Thyself a Goddess, not to earth confined,
But sometimes in the air, as we, sometimes
Ascend to heav'n, by merit thine, and see
What life the Gods live there, and such live thou.
So saying, he drew nigh, and to me held,
Even to my mouth, of that same fruit held part
Which he had pluck'd; the pleasant savory smell
So quicken'd appetite, that I, methought,
Could not but taste. Forthwith up to the clouds
With him I flew, and underneath beheld
The earth outstretch'd immense, a prospect wide
And various: wond'ring at my flight and change
To this high exaltation, suddenly
My guide was gone, and I methought, sunk down,
And fell asleep: but O how glad I waked
To find this but a dream! Thus Eve her night
Related, and thus Adam answer'd sad.
　　Best image of myself and dearer half,
The trouble of thy thoughts this night in sleep
Affects me equally; nor can I like
This uncouth dream, of evil sprung I fear:
Yet evil whence? in thee can harbor none,
Created pure. But know that in the soul

Are many lesser faculties that serve
Reason as chief: among these Fancy next
Her office holds; of all external things,
Which the five watchful senses represent
She forms imaginations, aery shapes,
Which Reason joining, or disjoining, frames
All what we affirm, or what deny, and call
Our knowledge or opinion; then retires
Into her private cell when nature rests.
Oft in her absence mimic Fancy wakes
To imitate her; but, misjoining shapes,
Wild work produces oft, and most in dreams,
Ill matching words and deeds long past or late.
Some such resemblances methinks I find
Of our last evening's talk in this thy dream,
But with addition strange; yet be not sad:
Evil into the mind of GOD or man
May come and go, so unapproved, and leave
No spot or blame behind; which gives me hope
That what in sleep thou didst abhor to dream,
Waking thou never wilt consent to do.
Be not dishearten'd then, nor cloud those looks
That wont to be more cheerful and serene
Than when fair morning first smiles on the world;
And let us to our fresh employments rise,
Among the groves, the fountains, and the flow'rs,
That open now their choicest bosom'd smells,
Reserved from night, and kept for thee in store.
So cheer'd he his fair spouse, and she was cheer'd;
But silently a gentle tear let fall
From either eye, and wiped them with her hair:
Two other precious drops that ready stood,
Each in their crystal sluice, he ere they fell
Kiss'd as the gracious signs of sweet remorse,
And pious awe that fear'd to have offended.
So all was clear'd, and to the field they haste.
But first, from under shady arborous roof
Soon as they forth were come to open sight
Of dayspring and the sun, who, scarce uprisen
With wheels yet hov'ring o'er the ocean brim
Shot parallel to the earth his dewy ray,
Discovering in wide landscape all the east

Of Paradise and Eden's happy plains,
Lowly they bow'd adoring, and began
Their orisons, each morning duly paid
In various style; for neither various style
Nor holy rapture wanted they to praise
Their Maker, in fit strains pronounced or sung
Unmeditated, such prompt eloquence
Flow'd from their lips, in prose or numerous verse,
More tuneable than needed lute or harp
To add more sweetness: and they thus began.

    These are thy glorious works, Parent of good,
Almighty, thine this universal frame,
Thus wondrous fair; thyself how wondrous then!
Unspeakable, who sitt'st above these heavens,
To us invisible, or dimly seen
In these thy lowest works; yet these declare
Thy goodness beyond thought, and power divine.
Speak ye who best can tell, ye sons of light,
Angels, for ye behold him, and with songs
And choral symphonies, day without night,
Circle his throne rejoicing, ye in heaven,
On earth join all ye creatures to extol
Him first, him last, him midst, and without end.
Fairest of stars, last in the train of night,
If better thou belong not to the dawn,
Sure pledge of day, that crown'st the smiling morn
With thy bright circlet, praise him in thy sphere
While day arises, that sweet hour of prime.
Thou sun, of this great world both eye and soul,
Acknowledge him thy greater, sound his praise
In thy eternal course, both when thou climb'st,
And when high noon hast gain'd, and when thou fall'st.
Moon, that now meet'st the orient sun, now fly'st,
With the fixed stars, fixed in their orb that flies,
And ye five other wand'ring fires that move
In mystic dance not without song,[1] resound
His praise, who out of darkness call'd up light.
Air, and ye elements the eldest birth
Of nature's womb, that in quaternion run
Perpetual circle, multiform, and mix
And nourish all things, let your ceaseless change

   [1] Alluding to the Pythagorean idea of the music of the spheres.

Vary to our great Maker still new praise.
Ye mists and exhalations that now rise
From hill or steaming lake, dusky or grey,
Till the sun paint your fleecy skirts with gold,
In honor to the world's great author rise,
Whether to deck with clouds the uncolor'd sky
Or wet the thirsty earth with falling showers,
Rising or falling still advance his praise.
His praise, ye winds that from four quarters blow,
Breathe soft or loud; and wave your tops, ye pines,
With every plant, in sign of worship wave.
Fountains and ye that warble, as ye flow,
Melodious murmurs, warbling tune his praise:
Join voices, all ye living souls, ye birds,
That singing up to heaven gate ascend,
Bear on your wings and in your notes his praise;
Ye that in waters glide, and ye that walk
The earth, and stately tread, or lowly creep;[1]
Witness if I be silent, morn or even,
To hill, or valley, fountain, or fresh shade,
Made vocal by my song, and taught his praise.
Hail universal Lord, be bounteous still
To give us only good; and if the night
Have gather'd aught of evil, or conceal'd,
Disperse it, as now light dispels the dark.
    So pray'd they innocent, and to their thoughts
Firm peace recover'd soon and wonted calm,
On to their morning's rural work they haste,
Among sweet dews and flowers, where any row
Of fruit-trees over woody reach'd too far
Their pamper'd [2] boughs, and needed hands to check
Fruitless embraces: or they led the vine
To wed her elm; she spoused about him twines
Her marriageable arms, and with her brings
Her dower, th' adopted clusters, to adorn
His barren leaves. Them thus employ'd beheld
With pity heav'n's high King, and to Him called
Raphael, the sociable spirit, that deign'd
To travel with Tobias, and secured
His marriage with the seventimes-wedded maid.

    [1] See Psalm cxlviii.
    [2] Unrestrained.

Raphael, said he, thou hear'st what stir on earth
Satan, from hell scap'd through the darksome gulf,
Hath raised in paradise, and how disturb'd
This night the human pair, how he designs
In them at once to ruin all mankind:
Go therefore, half this day as friend with friend
Converse with Adam, in what bower or shade
Thou find'st him from the heat of noon retired,
To respite his day-labor with repast,
Or with repose; and such discourse bring on,
As may advise him of his happy state,
Happiness in his power left free to will,
Left to his own free will, his will though free,
Yet mutable; whence warn him to beware
He swerve not too secure; tell him withal
His danger, and from whom; what enemy
Late fall'n himself from heaven, is plotting now
The fall of others from like state of bliss;
By violence? no; for that shall be withstood,
But by deceit and lies; this let him know,
Lest wilfully transgressing he pretend
Surprisal, unadmonish'd, unforewarn'd.

So spake th' eternal Father, and fulfill'd
All justice: nor delay'd the wingèd saint
After his charge received; but from among
Thousand celestial ardors, where he stood
Veil'd with his gorgeous wings, up springing light
Flew through the midst of heav'n; th' angelic choirs,
On each hand parting, to his speed gave way
Through all the empyreal road; till at the gate
Of heav'n arrived, the gate itself open'd wide
On golden hinges turning, as by work
Divine the sov'reign Architect had framed.
From hence, no cloud, or, to obstruct his sight,
Star interposed, however small he sees,
Not unconform to other shining globes,
Earth and the garden of GOD, with cedars crown'd
Above all hills: as when by night the glass
Of Galileo, less assured, observes
Imagined lands and regions in the moon:
Or pilot from amidst the Cyclades[1]

[1] Islands of the Archipelago.

Delos, or Samos, first appearing kens
A cloudy spot. Down thither prone in flight
He speeds, and through the vast ethereal sky
Sails between worlds and worlds, with steady wing
Now on the polar winds, then with quick fan
Winnows the buxom air; till within soar
Of tow'ring eagles, to all the fowls he seems
A phœnix, gazed by all, as that sole bird,
When to inshrine his reliques in the sun's
Bright temple, to Egyptian Thebes he flies.[1]
At once on th' eastern cliff of paradise
He lights, and to his proper shape returns
A seraph wing'd: six wings he wore, to shade
His lineaments divine; the pair that clad
Each shoulder broad came mantling o'er his breast
With regal ornament; the middle pair
Girt like a starry zone his waist, and round
Skirted his loins and thighs with downy gold
And colors dipp'd in heav'n; the third his feet
Shadow'd from either heel with feather'd mail
Sky-tinctured grain. Like Maia's son[2] he stood,
And shook his plumes, that heav'nly fragrance fill'd
The circuit wide. Straight knew him all the bands
Of angels under watch; and to his state,
And to his message high, in honor rise;
For on some message high they guess'd him bound.
Their glittering tents he pass'd and now is come
Into the blissful field, through groves of myrrh,
And flow'ring odors, cassia, nard, and balm;
A wilderness of sweets; for nature here
Wanton'd as in her prime, and play'd at will
Her virgin fancies, pouring forth more sweet,
Wild above rule or art; enormous bliss.

---

[1] The phœnix was a fabled bird, of which one only was said to exist at a time. It was exquisitely beautiful; and lived many hundred years. At the end of its life it made a pile of aromatic woods, which it kindled, and, fanning the flames with its wings, perished in the blaze. From its ashes sprang another phœnix. The phœnix made his funeral pyre in the sun's temple at Thebes.

[2] "The feathered Mercury."—SHAKESPEARE. Mercury had wings on his feet as well as his shoulders.

Him through the spicy forest onward come
Adam discern'd, as in the door he sat
Of his cool bower, while now the mounted sun
Shot down direct his fervid rays, to warm
Earth's inmost womb, more warmth than Adam needs;
And Eve within, due at her hour prepared
For dinner savory fruits, of taste to please
True appetite, and not disrelish thirst
Of nectarous draughts between, from milky stream,
Berry, or grape, to whom thus Adam call'd.

    Haste hither, Eve, and worth thy sight behold
Eastward among those trees, what glorious shape
Comes this way moving, seems another morn
Risen on mid-noon; some great behest from heav'n
To us perhaps he brings, and will vouchsafe
This day to be our guest. But go with speed,
And what thy stores contain bring forth, and pour
Abundance, fit to honor and receive
Our heavenly stranger; well we may afford
Our givers their own gifts, and large bestow
From large bestow'd, where nature multiplies
Her fertile growth, and by disburd'ning grows
More fruitful; which instructs us not to spare.

    To whom thus Eve. Adam, earth's hallow'd mould,
Of GOD inspired, small store will serve, where store
All seasons ripe for use hangs on the stalk;
Save what by frugal storing firmness gains
To nourish, and superfluous moist consumes.
But I will haste, and from each bough and brake,
Each plant and juiciest gourd, will pluck such choice
To entertain our angel guest, as he
Beholding shall confess, that here on earth
GOD hath dispensed his bounties as in heav'n.

    So saying, with dispatchful looks in haste
She turns, on hospitable thoughts intent
What choice to choose for delicacy best,
What order, so contrived as not to mix
Tastes, not well join'd, inelegant, but bring
Taste after taste upheld with kindliest change;
Bestirs her then, and from each tender stalk
Whatever earth, all-bearing mother, yields

In India east or west, or middle shore
In Pontus, or the Punic coast,[1] or where
Alcinous reign'd,[2] fruit of all kinds, in coat,
Rough, or smooth rind, or bearded husk, or shell,
She gathers, tribute large, and on the board
Heaps with unsparing hand: for drink the grape
She crushes, inoffensive must,[3] and meaths[4]
From many a berry, and from sweet kernels press'd
She tempers dulcet creams, nor these to hold
Wants her fit vessels pure; then strews the ground
With rose and odors from the shrub unfumed.
Meanwhile our primitive great sire, to meet
His god-like guest, walks forth, without more train
Accompanied than with his own complete
Perfections; in himself was all his state,
More solemn than the tedious pomp that waits
On princes, when their rich retinue long
Of horses led and grooms besmear'd with gold
Dazzles the crowd, and sets them all agape.
Nearer his presence Adam though not awed,
Yet with submiss approach and reverence meek,
As to a superior nature, bowing low,
Thus said. Native of heav'n, for other place
None can than heav'n such glorious shape contain,
Since by descending from the thrones above,
Those happy places thou hast deign'd a while
To want, and honor these, vouchsafe with us
Two only, who yet by sov'reign.gift possess
This spacious ground, in yonder shady bower
To rest, and what the garden choicest bears
To sit and taste, till this meridian heat
Be over, and the sun more cool decline.
   Whom thus the angelic Virtue answer'd mild.
Adam, I therefore came, nor art thou such
Created, or such place hast here to dwell,
As may not oft invite, though spirits of heav'n,
To visit thee: lead on then where thy bower
O'ershades: for these mid-hours, till ev'ning rise,

---

[1] Carthage.
[2] Phœacia, an island in the Ionian Sea.
[3] Grape juice, unfermented.
[4] Mead.

I have at will. So to the sylvan lodge
They came, that like Pomona's arbor smiled,
With flow'rets deck'd and fragrant smells: but Eve
Undeck'd, save with herself, more lovely fair
Than wood-nymph, or the fairest goddess feign'd
Of three that in Mount Ida naked strove,[1]
Stood to entertain her guest from heav'n; no veil
She needed, virtue-proof; no thought infirm
Alter'd her cheek. On whom the angel Hail
Bestow'd, the holy salutation used
Long after to blest Mary, second Eve.

Hail, mother of mankind, whose fruitful womb
Shall fill the world more numerous with thy sons,
Than with these various fruits the trees of GOD
Have heap'd this table. Raised of grassy turf
Their table was, and mossy seats had round,
And on her ample square from side to side
All autumn piled, though spring and autumn here
Danced hand in hand. A while discourse they hold,
No fear lest dinner cool, when thus began
Our author. Heav'nly stranger, please to taste
These bounties, which our Nourisher, from whom
All perfect good unmeasured out descends,
To us for food and for delight hath caused
The earth to yield; unsavory food, perhaps,
To spiritual natures: only this I know,
That one celestial Father gives to all.

To whom the angel. Therefore what He gives,
Whose praise be ever sung, to man in part
Spiritual, may of purest spirits be found
No ingrateful food: and food alike those pure
Intelligential substances require,
As doth your rational; and both contain
Within them every lower faculty
Of sense, whereby they hear, see, smell, touch, taste,
Tasting concoct, digest, assimilate,
And corporeal to incorporeal turn.
For know, whatever was created needs
To be sustain'd and fed; of elements
The grosser feeds the purer; earth the sea;

[1] Alluding to the judgment of Paris, when Juno, Minerva, and Venus contended for the apple inscribed, "To the fairest."

Earth and the sea feed air; the air those fires
Ethereal; and as lowest first the moon;
Whence in her visage round those spots, unpurged
Vapors not yet into her substance turn'd.
Nor doth the moon no nourishment exhale
From her moist continent to higher orbs.
The sun, that light imparts to all, receives
From all his alimental recompence
In humid exhalations, and at even
Sups with the ocean. Though in heav'n the trees[1]
Of life ambrosial fruitage bear, and vines
Yield nectar; tho' from off the boughs each morn
We brush mellifluous dews, and find the ground
Cover'd with pearly grain;[2] yet GOD hath here
Varied his bounty so with new delights,
As may compare with heaven; and to taste
Think not I shall be nice. So down they sat,
And to their viands fell; nor seemingly
The angel, nor in mist, the common gloss
Of theologians, but with keen dispatch
Of real hunger, and concoctive heat
To transubstantiate: what redounds, transpires
Through spirits with ease; nor wonder; if by fire
Of sooty coal the empyric alchymist
Can turn, or holds it possible to turn,
Metals of drossest ore to perfect gold
As from the mine. Meanwhile at table Eve
Minister'd naked, and their flowing cups
With pleasant liquors crown'd. O innocence
Deserving paradise! if ever, then,
Then had the sons of GOD excuse to have been
Enamor'd at that sight; but in those hearts
Love unlibidinous reign'd, nor jealousy,
Was understood, the injured lover's hell.

   Thus when with meats and drinks they had sufficed,
Not burden'd nature, sudden mind arose
In Adam, not to let th' occasion pass,
Given him by this great conference, to know
Of things above his world, and of their being
Who dwell in heav'n, whose excellence he saw

[1] Psalm lxxviii. 25; cv. 40.
[2] "The bread of Heaven," *i.e.* manna. Rev. xxii. 2. Matt. xxvi. 29.

Transcend his own so far; whose radiant forms,
Divine effulgence, whose high power so far
Exceeded human; and his wary speech
Thus to th' empyreal minister he framed.
   Inhabitant with GOD, now know I well
Thy favor, in this honor done to man,
Under whose lowly roof thou hast vouchsafed
To enter, and these earthly fruits to taste,
Food not of angels, yet accepted so,
As that more willingly thou could'st not seem
At heav'n's high feast to have fed: yet what compare?
   To whom the wingèd Hierarch replied.
O Adam, one Almighty is, from whom
All things proceed, and up to him return,
If not depraved from good, created all
Such to perfection, one first matter all,
Indued with various forms, various degrees
Of substance, and, in things that live, of life:
But more refined, more spirituous, and pure,
As nearer to him placed, or nearer tending,
Each in their several active spheres assign'd,
Till body up to spirit work, in bounds
Proportion'd to each kind. So from the root
Springs lighter the green stalk; from thence the leaves
More aery, last the bright consummate flow'r
Spirits odorous breathes; flowers and their fruit,
Man's nourishment, by gradual scale sublimed,
To vital spirits aspire, to animal,
To intellectual, give both life and sense,
Fancy and understanding, whence the soul
Reason receives, and reason is her being,
Discursive or intuitive; discourse
Is oftest yours, the latter most is ours,
Differing but in degree, of kind the same.
Wonder not then, what GOD for you saw good
If I refuse not, but convert, as you,
To proper substance: time may come, when men
With angels may participate, and find
No inconvenient diet, nor too light fare:
And from these corporal nutriments perhaps
Your bodies may at last turn all to spirit,
Improved by tract of time, and wing'd ascend

Ethereal, as we, or may at choice
Here or in heav'nly paradises dwell;
If ye be found obedient, and retain
Unalterably firm His love entire,
Whose progeny you are. Meanwhile enjoy
Your fill what happiness this happy state
Can comprehend, incapable of more.

　　To whom the patriarch of mankind replied.
O favorable spirit, propitious guest,
Well hast thou taught the way that might direct
Our knowledge, and the scale of nature set
From centre to circumference, whereon
In contemplation of created things
By steps we may ascend to God. But say,
What meant that caution join'd, If ye be found
Obedient? Can we want obedience then
To him, or possibly his love desert,
Who form'd us from the dust, and placed us here
Full to the utmost measure of what bliss
Human desires can seek or apprehend?

　　To whom the angel. Son of heav'n and earth
Attend: that thou art happy, owe to God;
That thou continu'st such, owe to thyself,
That is, to thy obedience; therein stand.
This was that caution given thee; be advised.
God made thee perfect, not immutable:
And good He made thee, but to persevere
He left it in thy power; ordain'd thy will
By nature free, not over-ruled by fate
Inextricable or strict necessity:
Our voluntary service he requires,
Not our necessitated, such with him
Finds no acceptance, nor can find; for how
Can hearts, not free, be tried whether they serve
Willing or no, who will but what they must
By destiny, and can no other choose?
Myself and all th' angelic host, that stand
In sight of God enthroned, our happy state
Hold, as you yours, while our obedience holds;
On other surety none; freely we serve,
Because we freely love, as in our will
To love or not; in this we stand or fall.

And some are fall'n, to disobedience fall'n,
And so from heaven to deepest hell: O fall
From what high state of bliss into what woe!

   To whom our great progenitor. Thy words
Attentive, and with more delighted ear,
Divine instructor, I have heard, than when
Cherubic songs by night from neighboring hills
Aereal music send: nor knew I not
To be both will and deed created free;
Yet that we never shall forget to love
Our Maker, and obey Him whose command
Single is yet so just, my constant thoughts
Assured me, and still assure: though what thou tell'st
Hath past in heav'n, some doubt within me move,
But more desire to hear, if thou consent,
The full relation, which must needs be strange,
Worthy of sacred silence to be heard;
And we have yet large day, for scarce the sun
Hath finish'd half his journey, and scarce begins
His other half in the great zone of heav'n.

   Thus Adam made request, and Raphael,
After short pause, assenting thus began.

   High matter thou enjoin'st me, O prime of men,
Sad task and hard; for how shall I relate
To human sense th' invisible exploits
Of warring spirits? how without remorse
The ruin of so many, glorious once
And perfect while they stood? how last unfold
The secrets of another world, perhaps
Not lawful to reveal? yet for thy good,
This is dispensed, and what surmounts the reach
Of human sense, I shall delineate so,
By lik'ning spiritual to corporal forms,
As may express them best: though what if earth
Be but the shadow of heav'n; and things therein
Each to other like, more than on earth is thought?

   As yet this world was not, and Chaos wild
Reign'd where these heav'ns now roll, where earth now
    rests
Upon her centre poised, when on a day,
For time, though in eternity, applied
To motion, measures all things durable

By present, past, and future; on such day
As heav'n's great year[1] brings forth, th' empyreal host[2]
Of angels, by imperial summons call'd,
Innumerable before th' Almighty's throne
Forthwith from all the ends of heav'n appear'd:
Under their hierarchs in orders bright
Ten thousand thousand ensigns high advanced,
Standards and gonfalons 'twixt van and rear
Stream in the air, and for distinction serve
Of hierarchies, of orders, and degrees:
Or in their glittering tissues bear imblazed
Holy memorials, acts of zeal and love
Recorded eminent. Thus when in orbs
Of circuit inexpressible they stood
Orb within orb, the Father infinite,
By whom in bliss imbosom'd sat the Son,
Amidst as from a flaming mount, whose top
Brightness had made invisible, thus spake.

Hear all ye Angels, progeny of light.
Thrones, Dominations, Princedoms, Virtues, Powers,
Hear my decree,[3] which unrevoked shall stand.
This day I have begot whom I declare
My only Son, and on this holy hill
Him have anointed, whom ye now behold
At my right hand; your head I him appoint
And by my Self have sworn to him shall bow
All knees in heav'n, and shall confess him Lord.
Under his great vice-gerent reign abide
United, as one individual soul,
For ever happy: him who disobeys
Me disobeys, breaks union, and, that day
Cast out from God and blessed vision, falls
Into utter darkness, deep ingulf'd, his place
Ordain'd without redemption, without end.

So spake th' Omnipotent, and with his words
All seemed well pleased; all seem'd, but were not all.
That day, as other solemn days, they spent

---

[1] Plato's great year was probably in Milton's mind. It was a revolution of all the spheres. "Everything returns to where it set out when their motion first began."—RICHARDSON.

[2] Job i. 6. Dan. vii. 10.

[3] See Psalm ii. Heb. i. 5.

In song and dance about the sacred hill,
Mystical dance, which yonder starry sphere
Of planets and of fix'd in all her wheels
Resembles nearest, mazes intricate,
Eccentric, intervolved, yet regular,
Then most, when most irregular they seem;
And in their motions harmony divine
So smooths her charming tones, that GOD's own ear
Listens delighted. Ev'ning now approach'd,
For we have also our ev'ning and our morn,
We ours for change delectable, not need,
Forthwith from dance to sweet repast they turn
Desirous, all in circles as they stood,
Tables are set, and on a sudden piled
With angels' food, and rubied nectar flows,
In pearl, in diamond, and massy gold;
Fruit of delicious vines, the growth of heav'n.
On flow'rs reposed and with fresh flowerets crown'd,
They eat, they drink, and in communion sweet
Quaff immortality and joy, secure
Of surfeit where full measure only bounds
Excess, before th' all-bounteous·King, who shower'd
With copious hand, rejoicing in their joy.
Now when ambrosial night with clouds exhaled
From that high mount of GOD, whence light and shade
Spring both, the face of brightest heav'n had changed
To grateful twilight, for night comes not there
In darker veil, and roseate dews disposed
All but the unsleeping eyes of GOD to rest,[1]
Wide over all the plain, and wider far
Than all this globous earth in plain outspread,
Such are the courts of GOD, th' angelic throng
Dispersed in bands and files, their camp extend
By living streams among the trees of life,[2]
Pavilions numberless and sudden rear'd,
Celestial tabernacles, where they slept
Fann'd with cool winds, save those who in their course
Melodious hymns about the sov'reign throne
Alternate all night long. But not so waked

[1] Psalm cxxi. 4: "He that keepeth Israel shall neither slumber nor sleep."
[2] Rev. xxii.

Satan, so call him now, his former name
Is heard no more in heav'n; he of the first
If not the first arch-angel, great in power,
In favor and pre-eminence, yet fraught
With envy against the Son of God, that day
Honor'd by his great Father, and proclaim'd
Messiah King anointed, could not bear
Thro' pride that sight, and thought himself impair'd.
Deep malice thence conceiving and disdain,
Soon as midnight brought on the dusky hour,
Friendliest to sleep and silence, he resolved
With all his legions to dislodge, and leave
Unworshipp'd, unobey'd, the throne supreme,
Contemptuous, and his next subordinate
Awak'ning, thus to him in secret spake.

   Sleep'st thou, companion dear, what sleep can close
Thy eyelids? and remember'st what decree
Of yesterday so late hath past the lips
Of heav'n's Almighty? Thou to me thy thoughts
Wast wont, I mine to thee was wont to impart:
Both waking we were one; how then can now
Thy sleep dissent? new laws thou see'st imposed;
New laws from Him who reigns new minds may raise
In us who serve, new counsels, to debate
What doubtful may ensue; more in this place
To utter is not safe. Assemble thou
Of all those myriads which we lead, the chief:
Tell them, that by command, ere yet dim night
Her shadowy cloud withdraws, I am to haste,
And all who under me their banners wave,
Homeward with flying march, where we possess
The quarters of the north,[1] there to prepare

---

[1] "How art thou fallen, O Lucifer, son of the morning. . . . For thou hast said in thine heart, I will ascend into heaven, I will exalt my throne above the stars of God; I will sit also upon the mount of the congregation *in the sides of the north*."—Isaiah xiv. part of 12 and 13 vs. In Shakespeare, 1st Part of *Henry VI.*, Act V. Sc. 3, Joan of Arc, addressing the fiends, calls them,—

'substitutes

      "Unto the lordly *monarch of the north*."

i.e., the devil. This was probably in accordance with popular superstition, which actually gave an ill name to the *north* side of even a churchyard.

Fit entertainment to receive our King
The great Messiah, and his new commands;
Who speedily through all the hierarchies
Intends to pass triumphant, and give laws.

   So spake the false arch-angel, and infused
Bad influence into th' unwary breast
Of his associate; he together calls,
Or several one by one, the regent Powers,
Under him regent, tells, as he was taught,
That the Most High commanding, now ere night,
Now ere dim night had disincumber'd heav'n,
The great hierarchial standard was to move;
Tells the suggested cause, and casts between
Ambiguous words and jealousies, to sound
Or taint integrity; but all obey'd
The wonted signal, and superior voice
Of their great potentate; for great indeed
His name, and high was his degree in heav'n;
His count'nance, as the morning star that guides
The starry flock, allured them, and with lies
Drew after him the third part of heav'n's host.[1]

   Meanwhile th' eternal Eye, whose sight discerns
Abstrusest thoughts, from forth His holy mount,
And from within the golden lamps[2] that burn
Nightly before Him, saw without their light
Rebellion rising, saw in whom, how spread
Among the sons of morn,[3] what multitudes
Where banded to oppose His high decree;
And smiling to His only Son thus said.

   Son, thou in whom my glory I behold
In full resplendence, heir of all my might,
Nearly it now concerns us to be sure
Of our omnipotence, and with what arms
We mean to hold what anciently we claim
Of deity or empire; such a foe
Is rising, who intends to erect his throne
Equal to ours, throughout the spacious north;
Nor so content, hath in his thought to try
In battle what our power is, or our right.

[1] Rev. xii. 3, 4.
[2] Rev. iv. 5.
[3] Isaiah xiv. 12.

Let us advise, and to this hazard draw
With speed what force is left, and all employ
In our defence, lest unawares we lose
This our high place, our sanctuary, our hill.
   To whom the Son with calm aspect and clear
Light'ning divine, ineffable, serene,
Made answer. Mighty Father, Thou Thy foes
Justly hast in derision, and secure
Laugh'st at their vain designs and tumults vain,[1]
Matter to me of glory, whom their hate
Illustrates, when they see all regal power
Giv'n me to quell their pride, and in event
Know whether I be dextrous to subdue
Thy rebels, or be found the worst in heav'n.
   So spake the Son: but Satan with his powers
Far was advanced on wingèd speed, an host
Innumerable as the stars of night,
Or stars of morning, dewdrops, which the sun
Impearls on every leaf and every flower.
Regions they pass'd, the mighty regencies
Of Seraphim, and Potentates, and Thrones
In their triple degrees, regions to which
All thy dominion, Adam, is no more
Than what this garden is to all the earth,
And all the sea, from one entire globose
Stretch'd into longitude: which having pass'd,
At length into the limits of the north
They came, and Satan to his royal seat
High on a hill, far blazing, as a mount
Raised on a mount, with pyramids and tow'rs
From diamond quarries hewn, and rocks of gold,
The palace of great Lucifer; so call
That structure in the dialect of men
Interpreted, which not long after he,
Affecting all equality with GOD,
In imitation of that mount[2] whereon
Messiah was declared in sight of heav'n,
The mountain of the congregation call'd;
For thither he assembled all his train,
Pretending so commanded to consult

[1] Psalm ii. 4.
[2] Psalm ii. 6.

About the great reception of their king,
Thither to come, and with calumnious art
Of counterfeited truth thus held their ears.

Thrones, dominations, princedoms, virtues, powers,
If these magnific titles yet remain
Not merely titular, since by decree
Another now hath to himself ingross'd
All power, and us eclipsed under the name
Of king anointed, for whom all this haste
Of midnight march and hurried meeting here,
This only to consult how we may best
With what may be devised of honors new
Receive him, coming to receive from us
Knee-tribute yet unpaid, prostration vile,
Too much to one, but double how endured,
To one and to his image now proclaim'd?
But what if better counsels might erect
Our minds, and teach us to cast off this yoke?
Will ye submit your necks, and choose to bend
The supple knee? ye will not, if I trust
To know ye right, or if ye know yourselves
Natives and sons of heav'n, possest before
By none, and if not equal all, yet free,
Equally free; for orders and degrees
Jar not with liberty, but well consist.
Who can in reason then or right assume
Monarchy over such as live by right
His equals, if in power and splendor less,
In freedom equal? or can introduce
Law and edict on us, who without law
Err not? much less for this to be our Lord,
And look for adoration, to th' abuse
Of those imperial titles, which assert
Our being ordain'd to govern, not to serve?

Thus far his bold discourse without control
Had audience, when among the seraphim
Abdiel, than whom none with more zeal adored
The Diety, and divine commands obey'd,
Stood up, and in a flame of zeal severe
The current of his fury thus opposed.

O argument blasphemous, false and proud,
Words which no ear ever to hear in heav'n

Expected, least of all from thee, ingrate,
In place thyself so high above thy peers.
Canst thou with impious obloquy condemn
The just decree of GOD, pronounced and sworn,
That to His only Son, by right endued
With regal sceptre, every soul in heav'n
Shall bend the knee,[1] and in that honor due
Confess him rightful king? unjust thou say'st,
Flatly unjust, to bind with laws the free,
And equal over equals to let reign,
One over all with unsucceeded power.
Shalt thou give law to GOD?[2] shalt thou dispute
With him the points of liberty, who made
Thee what thou art, and form'd the pow'rs of heav'n
Such as he pleased, and circumscribed their being?
Yet by experience taught we know how good,
And of our good, and of our dignity
How provident He is; how far from thought
To make us less, bent rather to exalt
Our happy state under one head more near
United. But to grant it thee unjust,
That equal over equals monarch reign:
Thyself though great and glorious dost thou count,
Or all angelic nature join'd in one,
Equal to him begotten Son, by whom
As by His word the mighty Father made
All things, ev'n thee, and all the spirits of heav'n
By him created in their bright degrees,[3]
Crown'd them with glory, and to their glory named
Thrones, dominations, princedoms, virtues, powers,
Essential powers; nor by his reign obscured,
But more illustrious made, since he the head
One of our number thus reduced becomes;
His laws our laws, all honor to him done
Returns our own. Cease then this impious rage,
And tempt not these; but hasten to appease
Th' incensèd Father, and th' incensèd Son,[4]
While pardon may be found in time besought.

[1] Philip. ii. 9, 10, 11.
[2] Rom. ix. 20.
[3] Colos. i. 15, 16, 17.
[4] Psalm ii.

So spake the fervent angel; but his zeal
None seconded, as out of season judged
Or singular and rash; whereat rejoiced
The Apostate, and more haughty thus replied.

That we were form'd then say'st thou? and the work
Of secondary hands by task transferr'd
From Father to his Son? strange point and new!
Doctrine which we would know whence learn'd: who
    saw
When this creation was? remember'st thou
Thy making, while the Maker gave thee being?
We know no time when we were not as now;
Know none before us, self-begot, self-raised
By our own quick'ning power, when fatal course
Had circled his full orb, the birth mature
Of this native heav'n, ethereal sons.
Our puissance is our own, our own right hand
Shall teach us highest deeds, by proof to try
Who is our equal: then thou shalt behold
Whether by supplication we intend
Address, and to begird th' Almighty throne
Beseeching or besieging. This report,
These tidings carry to th' anointed king;
And fly, ere evil intercept thy flight.

He said, and, as the sound of waters deep,
Hoarse murmur echo'd to his words applause
Through the infinite host; nor less for that
The flaming seraph fearless, though alone
Encompass'd round with foes, thus answer'd bold.

O alienate from GOD, O spirit accurst,
Forsaken of all good, I see thy fall
Determined, and thy hapless crew involved
In this perfidious fraud, contagion spread
Both of thy crime and punishment. Henceforth
No more be troubled how to quit the yoke
Of GOD's MESSIAH; those indulgent laws
Will not be now vouchsafed, other decrees
Against thee are gone forth without recall:
That golden sceptre which thou didst reject
Is now an iron rod, to bruise and break
Thy disobedience. Well thou didst advise;
Yet not for thy advice or threats I fly

These wicked tents devoted, lest the wrath
Impendent raging into sudden flame
Distinguish not; for soon expect to feel
His thunder on thy head, devouring fire.
Then who created thee lamenting learn,
When who can uncreate thee thou shalt know.
  So spake the seraph Abdiel faithful found,
Among the faithless faithful only he:
Among innumerable false unmoved,
Unshaken, unseduced, unterrified;
His loyalty he kept, his love, his zeal,
Nor number, nor example with him wrought
To swerve from truth, or change his constant mind
Though single. From amidst them forth he pass'd,
Long way through hostile scorn, which he sustain'd
Superior, nor of violence fear'd aught;
And with retorted scorn his back he turn'd
On those proud tow'rs to swift destruction doom'd.

BOOK VI

The Argument

Raphael continues to relate how Michael and Gabriel were sent forth to battle against Satan and his angels. The first fight described: Satan and his powers retire under night: he calls a council, invents devilish engines, which in the second day's fight put Michael and his angels to some disorder; but they at length pulling up mountains overwhelm both the force and machines of Satan; yet the tumult not so ending, God on the third day sends Messiah his Son, for whom he had reserved the glory of that victory. He in the power of his Father coming to the place, and causing all his legions to stand still on either side, with his chariot and thunder driving into the midst of his enemies, pursues them unable to resist towards the wall of heaven; which opening, they leap down with horror and confusion into the place of punishment prepared for them in the deep. Messiah returns with triumph to his Father.

ALL night the dreadless angel unpursued
Through heav'n's wide champaign held his way, till morn,
Waked by the circling hours, with rosy hand
Unbarr'd the gates of light. There is a cave
Within the mount of GOD, fast by his throne,
Where light and darkness in perpetual round
Lodge and dislodge by turns, which makes through heav'n
Grateful vicissitude, like day and night:
Light issues forth, and at the other door
Obsequious darkness enters, till her hour
To veil the heav'n, though darkness there might well
Seem twilight here; and now went forth the morn
Such as in highest heav'n, array'd in gold
Empyreal, from before her vanish'd night,
Shot through with orient beams: when all the plain
Cover'd with thick embattled squadrons bright,
Chariots, and flaming arms, and fiery steeds,
Reflecting blaze on blaze, first met his view.
War he perceived, war in procinct, and found

Already known what he for news had thought
To have reported: gladly then he mix'd
Among those friendly powers, who him received
With joy and acclamations loud, that one,
That of so many myriads fall'n yet one
Return'd not lost. On to the sacred hill
They led him high applauded, and present
Before the seat supreme; from whence a voice
From midst a golden cloud thus mild was heard.

    Servant of GOD, well done, well hast thou fought
The better fight, who single hast maintain'd
Against revolted multitudes the cause
Of truth, in word mightier than they in arms;
And for the testimony of truth hast borne
Universal reproach, far worse to bear
Than violence: for this was all thy care,
To stand approved in sight of GOD, though worlds
Judged thee perverse. The easier conquest now
Remains thee, aided by this host of friends,
Back on thy foes more glorious to return
Than scorn'd thou didst depart, and to subdue
By force, who reason for their law refuse,
Right reason for their law, and for their king
Messiah, who by right of merit reigns.
Go, Michael of celestial armies prince,
And thou, in military prowess next,
Gabriel, lead forth to battle these my sons
Invincible, lead forth my armèd Saints
By thousands and by millions ranged for fight;
Equal in number to that godless crew
Rebellious; them with fire and hostile arms
Fearless assault, and to the brow of heav'n
Pursuing drive them out from GOD and bliss,
Into their place of punishment, the gulf
Of Tartarus, which ready opens wide
His fiery chaos to receive their fall.

    So spake the sovereign voice, and clouds began
To darken all the hill, and smoke to roll
In dusky wreaths reluctant flames the sign
Of wrath awaked: nor with less dread the loud
Ethereal trumpet from on high gan blow:
At which command the powers militant

That stood for heav'n, in mighty quadrate join'd
Of union irresistible, moved on
In silence their bright legions, to the sound
Of instrumental harmony, that breathed
Heroic ardor to advent'rous deeds,
Under their godlike leaders, in the cause
Of God and his Messiah. On they move
Indissolubly firm: nor obvious hill,
Nor straight'ning vale, nor wood, nor stream, divides
Their perfect ranks; for high above the ground
Their march was, and the passive air upbore
Their nimble tread; as when the total kind
Of birds in orderly array on wing
Came summon'd over Eden to receive
Their names of thee: so over many a tract
Of heav'n they march'd, and many a province wide
Tenfold the length of this terrene. At last
Far in the horizon to the north appear'd
From skirt to skirt a fiery region, stretch'd
In battailous aspect, and nearer view
Bristled with upright beams innumerable
Of rigid spears, and helmets throng'd, and shields
Various, with boastful argument portray'd,[1]
The banded powers of Satan hasting on
With furious expedition; for they ween'd
That self-same day, by fight or by surprize,
To win the mount of God, and on his throne
To set the envier of his state, the proud
Aspirer; but their thoughts proved fond and vain
In the mid way. Though strange to us it seem'd
At first, that angel should with angel war,
And in fierce hosting[2] meet, who wont to meet
So oft in festivals of joy and love
Unanimous, as sons of one great Sire,
Hymning th' eternal Father; but the shout
Of battle now began,[3] and rushing sound
Of onset ended soon each milder thought.

[1] Here is an allusion to the designs and mottoes on shields.
[2] Mustering of *hosts* or armies.
[3] "There was war in heaven, Michael and his angels fought against the dragon, and the dragon fought and his angels and prevailed not," &c. See Rev. xii. 7, 8, 9.

High in the midst exalted as a God
Th' apostate in his sun-bright chariot sat,
Idol [1] of Majesty divine, enclosed
With flaming Cherubim and golden shields:
Then lighted from his gorgeous throne, for now
'Twixt host and host but narrow space was left,
A dreadful interval, and front to front
Presented stood in terrible array
Of hideous length: before the cloudy van,
On the rough edge of battle ere it join'd,
Satan, with vast and haughty strides advanced,
Came tow'ring, arm'd in adamant and gold:
Abdiel that sight endured not, where he stood
Among the mightiest, bent on highest deeds,
And thus his own undaunted heart explores.

O heav'n! that such resemblance of the Highest
Should yet remain, where faith and reälty [2]
Remain not; wherefore should not strength and might
There fail where virtue fails, or weakest prove
Where boldest, though to sight uncor querable?
His puissance, trusting in th' Almighty's aid.
I mean to try, whose reason I have tried
Unsound and false; nor is it aught but just,
That he, who in debate of truth hath won,
Should win in arms, in both disputes alike
Victor: though brutish that contest and foul,
When reason hath to deal with force, yet so
Most reason is that reason overcome.

So pondering, and, from his armèd peers
Forth stepping opposite, half way he met
His daring foe, at this prevention more
Incensed, and thus securely him defied.

Proud, art thou met? thy hope was to have reach'd
The highth of thy aspiring unopposed,
The throne of God unguarded, and his side
Abandon'd at the terror of thy power
Or potent tongue: fool, not to think how vain
Against th' Omnipotent to rise in arms;
Who out of smallest things could without end
Have raised incessant armies to defeat

[1] For Counterfeit—false deity.
[2] Reality.

Thy folly; or, with solitary hand
Reaching beyond all limit, at one blow
Unaided could have finish'd thee, and whelm'd
Thy legions under darkness: but thou seest
All are not of thy train; there be, who faith
Prefer and piety to GOD; though then
To thee not visible, when I alone
Seem'd in thy world erroneous to dissent
From all: my sect thou seest; now learn too late
How few sometimes may know, when thousands err.

    Whom the grand foe, with scornful eye askance,
Thus answer'd. Ill for thee, but in wish'd hour
Of my revenge, first sought for thou return'st
From flight, seditious angel, to receive
Thy merited reward, the first assay
Of this right hand provoked, since first that tongue
Inspired with contradiction durst oppose
A third part of the Gods, in synod met
Their deities to assert, who while they feel
Vigor divine within them, can allow
Omnipotence to none. But well thou com'st
Before thy fellows, ambitious to win
From me some plume, that thy success may show
Destruction to the rest: this pause between,
Unanswer'd lest thou boast, to let thee know,
At first I thought that liberty and heav'n
To heav'nly souls had been all one; but now
I see that most through sloth had rather serve,
Minist'ring spirits, train'd up in feast and song;
Such hast thou arm'd, the minstrelsy of heav'n,
Servility with freedom to contend,
As both their deeds compared this day shall prove.

    To whom in brief thus Abdiel stern replied.
Apostate, still thou err'st, nor end wilt find
Of erring, from the path of truth remote:
Unjustly thou deprav'st it with the name
Of servitude to serve whom GOD ordains,
Or Nature; GOD and Nature bid the same,
When he who rules is worthiest, and excels
Them whom he governs. This is servitude,
To serve th' unwise, or him who hath rebell'd
Against his worthier, as thine now serve thee,

Thyself not free, but to thyself enthrall'd;
Yet lewdly dar'st our minist'ring upbraid.
Reign thou in hell thy kingdom, let me serve
In heav'n GOD ever bless'd, and His divine
Behests obey, worthiest to be obey'd;
Yet chains in hell, not realms expect: meanwhile
From me return'd, as erst thou saidst, from flight,
This greeting on thy impious crest receive.
  So saying, a noble stroke he lifted high,
Which hung not, but so swift with tempest fell
On the proud crest of Satan, that no sight,
Nor motion of swift thought, less could his shield
Such ruin intercept: ten paces huge
He back recoil'd; the tenth on bended knee
His massy spear upstay'd; as if on earth
Winds under ground or waters, forcing way
Side-long had push'd a mountain from his seat,
Half sunk with all his pines. Amazement seized
The rebel thrones, but greater rage to see
Thus foil'd their mightiest; ours joy fill'd, and shout,
Presage of victory, and fierce desire
Of battle: whereat Michael bid sound
The arch-angel trumpet; through the vast of heav'n
It sounded, and the faithful armies rung
Hosanna to the Highest: nor stood at gaze
The adverse legions, nor less hideous join'd
The horrid shock. Now storming fury rose,
And clamor, such as heard in heaven till now
Was never; arms on armour clashing bray'd
Horrible discord, and the madding wheels
Of brazen chariots raged; dire was the noise
Of conflict; over head the dismal hiss
Of fiery darts in flaming volleys flew,
And flying vaulted either host with fire.
So under fiery cope together rush'd
Both battles main, with ruinous assault
And inextinguishable rage; all heav'n
Resounded, and had earth been then, all earth
Had to her centre shook. What wonder? when
Millions of fierce encount'ring angels fought
On either side, the least of whom could wield
These elements, and arm him with the force

Of all their regions: how much more of power
Army against army numberless to raise
Dreadful combustion warring, and disturb,
Though not destroy, their happy native seat;
Had not the eternal King omnipotent
From his strong hold of heav'n high overruled
And limited their might; though number'd such,
As each divided legion might have seem'd
A numerous host; in strength each armèd hand
A legion; led in fight, yet leader seem'd
Each warrior single as in chief, expert
When to advance, or stand, or turn the sway
Of battle, open when, and when to close
The ridges of grim war; no thought of flight,
None of retreat, no unbecoming deed
That argued fear; each on himself relied,
As only in his arm the moment lay
Of victory: deeds of eternal fame
Were done, but infinite; for wide was spread
That war and various; sometimes on firm ground
A standing fight: then soaring on main wing
Tormented all the air; all air seem'd then
Conflicting fire. Long time in even scale
The battle hung; till Satan, who that day
Prodigious power had shown, and met in arms
No equal, ranging through the dire attack
Of fighting Seraphim confused, at length
Saw where the sword of Michael smote, and fell'd
Squadrons at once; with huge two-handed sway
Brandish'd aloft the horrid edge came down
Wide wasting: such destruction to withstand
He hasted, and opposed the rocky orb
Of tenfold adamant, his ample shield,
A vast circumference. At his approach
The great arch-angel from his warlike toil
Surceased; and glad, as hoping here to end
Intestine war in heav'n, th' arch-foe subdued
Or captive dragg'd in chains, with hostile frown
And visage all inflamed, first thus began.

Author of evil, unknown till thy revolt,
Unnamed in heav'n; now plenteous, as thou seest
These acts of hateful strife, hateful to all,

Though heaviest by just measure on thyself
And thy adherents: how hast thou disturb'd
Heav'n's blessed peace, and into nature brought
Misery, uncreated till the crime
Of thy rebellion! how hast thou instill'd
Thy malice into thousands, once upright
And faithful, now proved false! But think not here
To trouble holy rest; heav'n casts thee out
From all her confines: heav'n the seat of bliss
Brooks not the works of violence and war.
Hence then, and evil go with thee along,
Thy offspring, to the place of evil, hell;
Thou and thy wicked crew: there mingle broils,
Ere this avenging sword begin thy doom,
Or some more sudden vengeance wing'd from GOD
Precipitate thee with augmented pain.
   So spake the prince of angels; to whom thus
The adversary. Nor think thou with wind
Of aery threats to awe whom yet with deeds
Thou canst not. Hast thou turn'd the least of these
To flight, or if to fall, but that they rise
Unvanquish'd, easier to transact with me
That thou shouldst hope, imperious and with threats
To chase me hence? err not that so shall end
The strife which thou call'st evil, but we style
The strife of glory: which we mean to win,
Or turn this heav'n itself into the hell
Thou fablest; here however to dwell free,
If not to reign: meanwhile thy utmost force,
And join Him named Almighty to thy aid,
I fly not, but have sought thee far and nigh.
   They ended parle, and both address'd for fight
Unspeakable; for who, though with the tongue
Of angels, can relate, or to what things
Liken on earth conspicuous, that may lift
Human imagination to such highth
Of Godlike power? for likest gods they seem'd,
Stood they or moved, in stature, motion, arms,
Fit to decide the empire of great heav'n.
Now waved their fiery swords, and in the air
Made horrid circles; two broad suns their shields
Blazed opposite, while expectation stood

In horror; from each hand with speed retired,
Where erst was thickest fight, th' angelic throng,
And left large field, unsafe within the wind
Of such commotion, such as, to set forth
Great things by small, if, nature's concord broke,
Among the constellations war were sprung,
Two planets, rushing from aspect malign
Of fiercest opposition, in mid sky
Should combat, and their jarring spheres confound.
Together both, with next to Almighty arm,
Uplifted imminent, one stroke they aim'd
That might determine, and not need repeat,
As not of power, at once; nor odds appear'd
In might or swift prevention; but the sword
Of Michael from the armory of GOD
Was giv'n him temper'd so, that neither keen
Nor solid might resist that edge: it met
The sword of Satan with steep force to smite
Descending, and in half cut sheer; nor stay'd,
But with swift wheel reverse, deep entering, shared
All his right side; then Satan first knew pain,
And writhed him to and fro convolved; so sore
The griding sword with discontinuous wound
Pass'd thro' him, but th' ethereal substance closed,
Not long divisible, and from the gash
A stream of nectarous humour issuing flow'd
Sanguine, such as celestial spirits may bleed,[1]
And all his armour stain'd ere while so bright.
Forthwith on all sides to his aid was run
By angels many and strong, who interposed
Defence, while others bore him on their shields
Back to his chariot; where it stood retired
From off the files of war: there they him laid
Gnashing for anguish, and despite, and shame,
To find himself not matchless, and his pride
Humbled by such rebuke, so far beneath
His confidence to equal God in power.
Yet soon he heal'd; for spirits that live throughout
Vital in every part, not as frail man

---

[1] Homer calls the blood of the gods *ichor*, and describes it as
differing from human blood, as Milton does that of Satan the
Archangel.

In entrails, heart or head, liver or reins,
Cannot but by annihilating die;
Nor in their liquid texture mortal wound
Receive, no more than can the fluid air:
All heart they live, all head, all eye, all ear,
All intellect, all sense, and as they please
They limb themselves, and color, shape, or size
Assume, as likes them best, condense or rare.

Meanwhile in other parts like deeds deserved
Memorial, where the might of Gabriel fought,
And with fierce ensigns pierced the deep array
Of Moloch furious king, who him defied,
And at his chariot wheels to drag him bound
Threaten'd, nor from the Holy One of heav'n
Refrain'd his tongue blasphemous; but anon,
Down cloven to the waist, with shatter'd arms
And uncouth pain fled bellowing. On each wing
Uriel and Raphael, his vaunting foe
Though huge and in a rock of diamond arm'd,
Vanquish'd, Adrameleck[1] and Asmadai,[2]
Two potent thrones, that to be less than Gods
Disdain'd, but meaner thoughts learn'd in their flight,
Mangled with ghastly wounds thro' plate and mail
Nor stood unmindful Abdiel to annoy
The atheist crew, but with redoubled blow
Ariel, and Arioc, and the violence
Of Ramiel scorch'd and blasted, overthrew.
I might relate of thousands, and their names
Eternize here on earth; but those elect
Angels, contented with their fame in heav'n,
Seek not the praise of men: the other sort,
In might though wondrous and in acts of war,
Nor of renown less eager, yet by doom
Cancell'd from heav'n and sacred memory,
Nameless in dark oblivion let them dwell.
For strength from truth divided and from just,
Illaudable, naught merits but dispraise
And ignominy; yet to glory aspires
Vain glorious, and through infamy seeks fame:
Therefore eternal silence be their doom.

[1] One of the idols of Sepharvaim. 2 Kings xvii. 31.
[2] The same as Asmodeus, the persecutor of Sara in Tobit.

And now, their mightiest quell'd, the battle swerved,
With many an inroad gored; deformed rout
Enter'd and foul disorder: all the ground
With shiver'd armor strown, and on a heap
Chariot and charioteer lay overturn'd,
And fiery foaming steeds; what stood, recoil'd
O'erwearied, through the faint Satanic host
Defensive scarce, or with pale fear surprized,
Then first with fear surprized and sense of pain
Fled ignominious, to such evil brought
By sin of disobedience till that hour
Not liable to fear, or flight, or pain.
Far otherwise th' inviolable saints
In cubic phalanx firm advanced entire,
Invulnerable, impenetrably arm'd:
Such high advantages their innocence
Gave them above their foes, not to have sinn'd,
Not to have disobey'd; in fight they stood
Unwearied, unobnoxious to be pain'd
By wound, tho' from their place by violence moved.

Now night her course began, and, over heav'n
Inducing darkness, grateful truce imposed,
And silence on the odious din of war:
Under her cloudy covert both retired,
Victor and vanquish'd. On the foughten field
Michael and his angels prevalent
Encamping placed in guard their watches round,
Cherubic waving fires: on th' other part
Satan with his rebellious disappear'd,
Far in the dark dislodged, and void of rest
His potentates to council call'd by night;
And in the midst thus undismay'd began.

O now in danger tried, now known in arms
Not to be overpower'd, companions dear,
Found worthy not of liberty alone,
Too mean pretence, but what we more affect,
Honor, dominion, glory, and, renown;
Who have sustain'd one day in doubtful fight,
(And if one day why not eternal days?)
What heaven's Lord had powerfullest to send
Against us from about His throne, and judged
Sufficient to subdue us to His will

But proves not so: then fallible, it seems,
Of future we may deem Him, though till now
Omniscient thought. True is, less firmly arm'd,
Some disadvantage we endured and pain,
Till now not known, but known, as soon contemn'd;
Since now we find this our empyreal form
Incapable of mortal injury,
Imperishable, and though pierced with wound
Soon closing, and by native vigor heal'd.
Of evil then so small as easy think
The remedy; perhaps more valid arms,
Weapons more violent, when next we meet,
May serve to better us, and worse our foes:
Or equal what between us made the odds,
In nature none: if other hidden cause
Left them superior, while we can preserve
Unhurt our minds and understanding sound,
Due search and consultation will disclose.

He sat; and in th' assembly next upstood
Nisroch,[1] of principalities the prime;
As one he stood escaped from cruel fight,
Sore toil'd, his riven arms to havock hewn;
And cloudy in aspect thus answering spake.

Deliverer from new lords, leader to free
Enjoyment of our right as Gods; yet hard
For Gods, and too unequal work we find
Against unequal arms to fight in pain,
Against unpain'd, impassive; from which evil
Ruin must needs ensue, for what avails
Valor or strength, though matchless, quell'd with pain,
Which all subdues, and makes remiss the hand
Of mightiest? sense of pleasure we may well
Spare out of life perhaps, and not repine,
But live content, which is the calmest life:
But pain is perfect misery, the worst
Of evils, and excessive overturns
All patience. He who therefore can invent
With what more forcible we may offend
Our yet unwounded enemies, or arm
Ourselves with like defence, to me deserves

---

[1] Nisroch was worshipped by the Assyrians. It was in his temple that Sennacherib was slain by his two sons. See 2 Kings xix. 37.

No less than for deliverance what we owe.
   Whereto with look composed Satan replied.
Not uninvented that, which thou aright
Believ'st so main to our success, I bring:
Which of us who beholds the bright surface
Of this ethereous mould whereon we stand,
This continent of spacious heav'n, adorn'd
With plant, fruit, flow'r ambrosial, gems, and gold,
Whose eye so superficially surveys
These things, as not to mind from whence they grow
Deep under ground, materials dark and crude,
Of spirituous and fiery spume, till touch'd
With heaven's ray, and temper'd they shoot forth
So beauteous, op'ning to the ambient light?
These in their dark nativity the deep
Shall yield us pregnant with infernal flame,
Which into hollow engines long and round
Thick-ramm'd, at th' other bore with touch of fire
Dilated and infuriate, shall send forth
From far with thund'ring noise among our foes
Such implements of mischief, as shall dash
To pieces, and o'erwhelm whatever stands
Adverse, that they shall fear we have disarm'd
The Thunderer of his only dreaded bolt.
Nor long shall be our labor; yet ere dawn,
Effect shall end our wish. Meanwhile revive;
Abandon fear; to strength and counsel join'd
Think nothing hard, much less to be despair'd.
   He ended, and his words their drooping cheer
Enlighten'd, and their languish'd hope revived.
Th' invention all admired, and each, how he
To be th' inventor miss'd, so easy it seem'd
Once found, which yet unfound most would have
      thought
Impossible: yet haply of thy race
In future days, if malice should abound,
Some one intent on mischief, or inspired
With dev'lish machination, might devise
Like instrument, to plague the sons of men
For sin, on war and mutual slaughter bent.
Forthwith from council to the work they flew,
None arguing stood; innumerable hands

Were ready; in a moment up they turn'd
Wide the celestial soil, and saw beneath
Th' originals of nature in their crude
Conception: sulphurous and nitrous foam
They found, they mingled, and with subtle art
Concocted and adusted they reduced
To blackest grain, and into store convey'd.
Part hidden veins digg'd up, nor hath this earth
Entrails unlike, of mineral and stone,
Whereof to found their engines and their balls
Of missive ruin; part incentive reed
Provide, pernicious with one touch to fire.
So all ere day-spring, under conscious night
Secret, they finish'd, and in order set,
With silent circumspection unespied.

Now when fair morn orient in heav'n appear'd,
Up rose the victor angels, and to arms
The matin trumpet sung: in arms they stood
Of golden panoply, refulgent host,
Soon banded; others from the dawning hills
Look'd round, and scouts each coast light-armèd scour,
Each quarter, to descry the distant foe,
Where lodged, or whither fled, or if for fight,
In motion or in halt: him soon they met
Under spread ensigns moving nigh, in slow
But firm battalion: back with speediest sail
Zophiel, of cherubim the swiftest wing,
Came flying, and in mid air aloud thus cried.

Arm warriors, arm for fight, the foe at hand,
Whom fled we thought, will save us long pursuit
This day. Fear not his flight, so thick a cloud
He comes, and settled in his face I see
Sad resolution and secure: let each
His adamantine coat gird well, and each
Fit well his helm, gripe fast his orbèd shield,
Borne ev'n or high; for this day will pour down,
If I conjecture aught, no drizzling show'r,
But rattling storm of arrows barb'd with fire.

So warn'd he them, aware themselves, and soon
In order, quit of all impediment;
Instant without disturb they took alarm,
And onward move embattell'd; when behold

Not distant far with heavy pace the foe
Approaching gross and huge; in hollow cube
Training his devilish enginry, impaled
On every side with shadowing squadrons deep,
To hide the fraud. At interview both stood
Awhile; but suddenly at head appear'd
Satan; and thus was heard commanding loud.

    Vanguard, to right and left the front unfold;
That all may see, who hate us, how we seek
Peace and composure, and with open breast
Stand ready to receive them, if they like
Our overture, and turn not back perverse;
But that I doubt; however witness heaven,
Heav'n witness thou anon, while we discharge
Freely our part: ye who appointed stand
Do as you have in charge, and briefly touch
What we propound, and loud that all may hear.

    So scoffing in ambiguous words, he scarce
Had ended; when to right and left the front
Divided, and to either flank retired:
Which to our eyes discover'd, new and strange,
A triple mounted row of pillars, laid
On wheels, for like to pillars most they seem'd,
Or hollow'd bodies made of oak or fir
With branches lopp'd, in wood or mountain fell'd,
Brass, iron, stony mould, had not their mouths
With hideous orifice gaped on us wide,
Portending hollow truce; at each behind
A seraph stood, and in his hand a reed
Stood waving tipp'd with fire; while we suspense
Collected stood within our thoughts amused;
Not long, for sudden all at once their reeds
Put forth, and to a narrow vent applied
With nicest touch. Immediate in a flame,
But soon obscured with smoke all heav'n appear'd,
From those deep-throated engines belch'd, whose roar
Embowell'd with outrageous noise the air,
And all her entrails tore, disgorging foul
Their devilish glut, chain'd thunderbolts and hail
Of iron globes, which on the victor host
Levell'd with such impetuous fury smote,
That whom they hit, none on their feet might stand,

Though standing else as rocks; but down they fell
By thousands, angel on archangel roll'd,
The sooner for their arms; unarm'd they might
Have easily as spirits evaded swift
By quick contraction or remove: but now
Foul dissipation follow'd and forced rout:
Nor served it to relax their serried files.
What should they do? if on they rush'd, repulse
Repeated, and indecent overthrow
Doubled, would render them yet more despised,
And to their foes a laughter: for in view
Stood rank'd of seraphim another row,
In posture to displode their second tire
Of thunder; back defeated to return
They worse abhorr'd. Satan beheld their plight,
And to his mates thus in derision call'd.

O friends, why come not on these victors proud?
Ere while they fierce were coming, and when we,
To entertain them fair with open front
And breast (what could we more?) propounded terms
Of composition, straight they changed their minds,
Flew off, and into strange vagaries fell,
As they would dance: yet for a dance they seem'd
Somewhat extravagant and wild, perhaps
For joy of offer'd peace: but I suppose,
If our proposals once again were heard,
We should compel them to a quick result.

To whom thus Belial in like gamesome mood.
Leader, the terms we sent were terms of weight,
Of hard contents, and full of force urged home,
Such as we might perceive amused them all,
And stumbled many; who receives them right,
Had need from head to foot well understand;
Not understood, this gift they have besides,
They show us when our foes walk not upright.

So they among themselves in pleasant vein
Stood scoffing, heighten'd in their thoughts beyond
All doubt of victory; eternal might
To match with their inventions they presumed
So easy, and of His thunder made a scorn,
And all His host derided, while they stood
Awhile in trouble; but they stood not long;

Rage prompted them at length, and found them arms
Against such hellish mischief fit to oppose.
Forthwith, behold the excellence, the power
Which GOD hath in his mighty angels placed!
Their arms away they threw, and to the hills,
For earth hath this variety from heav'n
Of pleasure situate in hill and dale,
Light as the lightning glimpse they ran, they flew,
From their foundations loos'ning to and fro
They pluck'd the seated hills with all their load,
Rocks, waters, woods, and by the shaggy tops
Up lifting bore them in their hands. Amaze,
Be sure, and terror seized the rebel host,
When coming towards them so dread they saw
The bottom of the mountains upward turn'd;
Till on those cursed engines triple-row
They saw them whelm'd, and all their confidence
Under the weight of mountains buried deep,
Themselves invaded next, and on their heads
Main promontories flung, which in the air
Came shadowing, and opprest whole legions arm'd;
Their armor help'd their harm, crush'd in and bruised
Into their substance pent, which wrought them pain
Implacable, and many a dolorous groan,
Long struggling underneath, ere they could wind
Out of such prison, though spirits of purest light,
Purest at first, now gross by sinning grown.
The rest in imitation to like arms
Betook them, and the neighboring hills uptore;
So hills amid the air encounter'd hills,
Hurl'd to and fro with jaculation dire,
That under ground they fought in dismal shade;
Infernal noise; war seem'd a civil game
To this uproar; horrid confusion heap'd
Upon confusion rose: and now all heav'n
Had gone to wrack, with ruin overspread,
Had not th' Almighty Father, where he sits
Shrined in his sanctuary of heav'n secure,
Consulting on the sum of things, foreseen
This tumult, and permitted all, advised:
That his great purpose he might so fulfil,
To honor his anointed Son avenged

Upon his enemies, and to declare
All power on him transferr'd: whence to his Son
Th' assessor of his throne he thus began.
    Effulgence of my glory, Son beloved,
Son in whose face invisible is beheld
Visibly, what by Deity I am,
And in whose hand what by decree I do,
Second Omnipotence, two days are past,
Two days, as we compute the days of heav'n,
Since Michael and his powers went forth to tame
These disobedient; sore hath been their fight,
As likeliest was, when two such foes met arm'd;
For to themselves I left them, and thou know'st,
Equal in their creation they were form'd,
Save what sin hath impair'd, which yet hath wrought
Insensibly, for I suspend their doom;
Whence in perpetual fight they needs must last
Endless, and no solution will be found.
War wearied hath perform'd what war can do,
And to disorder'd rage let loose the reins,
With mountains as with weapons arm'd, which makes
Wild work in heav'n and dangerous to the main.
Two days are therefore past, the third is thine;
For thee I have ordain'd it, and thus far
Have suffer'd, that the glory may be thine
Of ending this great war, since none but thou
Can end it. Into thee such virtue and grace
Immense I have transfused, that all may know
In heav'n and hell thy power above compare,
And this perverse commotion govern'd thus,
To manifest thee worthiest to be heir
Of all things, to be heir and to be king
By sacred unction,[1] thy deserved right.
Go then, thou Mightiest, in thy Father's might,
Ascend my chariot, guide the rapid wheels
That shake heav'n's basis, bring forth all my war,
My bow and thunder, my almighty arms
Gird on, and sword upon thy puissant thigh;[2]
Pursue these sons of darkness, drive them out
From all heav'n's bounds into the utter deep:

[1] Psalm xlv. 7.
[2] Psalm xlv. 3, 4.

There let them learn, as likes them, to despise
GOD and Messiah his anointed king.

He said, and on his Son with rays direct
Shone full, He all his Father full exprest
Ineffably into His face received,
And thus the filial Godhead answering spake.

O Father, O Supreme of heav'nly thrones,
First, Highest, Holiest, Best, thou always seek'st
To glorify thy Son,[1] I always thee,
As is most just; this I my glory account,
My exaltation, and my whole delight,
That thou in me well pleased declar'st thy will
Fulfill'd, which to fulfill is all my bliss.
Sceptre and power, thy giving, I assume,
And gladlier shall resign, when in the end
Thou shalt be all in all,[2] and I in thee
For ever, and in me all whom thou lov'st:[3]
But whom thou hat'st, I hate, and can put on
Thy terrors, as I put thy mildness on,
Image of thee in all things; and shall soon,
Arm'd with thy might, rid heav'n of these rebell'd,
To their prepared ill mansion driven down
To chains of darkness,[4] and th' undying worm;[5]
That from thy just obedience could revolt,
Whom to obey is happiness entire.
Then shall thy saints unmix'd, and from th' impure
Far separate, circling thy holy mount
Unfainèd hallelujahs to thee sing,
Hymns of high praise, and I among them chief.

So said, he, o'er his sceptre bowing, rose
From the right hand of glory where he sat,
And the third sacred morn began to shine,
Dawning through heav'n: forth rush'd with whirlwind
    sound
The chariot of paternal Deity,
Flashing thick flames, wheel within wheel undrawn,
Itself instinct with spirit, but convoy'd

[1] John xvii. 4, 5.
[2] 1 Cor. xv. 28.
[3] John xvii. 21, 23.
[4] 2 Peter ii. 4.
[5] Mark ix. 44.

By four cherubic shapes; four faces each
Had wondrous, as with stars their bodies all
And wings were set with eyes, with eyes the wheels
Of beryl,[1] and careering fires between:[2]
Over their heads a crystal firmament,
Whereon a sapphire throne, inlaid with pure
Amber, and colors of the show'ry arch.
He, in celestial panoply all arm'd
Of radiant Urim[3] work divinely wrought,
Ascended; at his right hand Victory
Sate eagle-winged, beside him hung his bow
And quiver with three-bolted thunder stored,
And from about him fierce effusion roll'd
Of smoke,[4] and bickering flame, and sparkles dire.
Attended with ten thousand thousand saints[5]
He onward came, far off his coming shone,
And twenty thousand,[6] I their number heard,
Chariots of GOD, half on each hand were seen.
He on the wings of Cherub rode sublime.[7]
On the crystalline sky, in sapphire throned.
Illustrious far and wide, but by his own
First seen, them unexpected joy surprised,
When the great ensign of Messiah blazed,
Aloft by angels borne, his sign in heav'n:[8]
Under whose conduct Michael soon reduced
His army, circumfused on either wing,
Under their Head [9] embodied all in one.
Before him power divine his way prepared:
At his command the uprooted hills retired
Each to his place, they heard his voice and went
Obsequious: Heav'n his wonted face renew'd,
And with fresh flow'rets hill and valley smiled.
    This saw his hapless foes, but stood obdured,

---

[1] A beryl is a precious stone of sea-green color.—NEWTON.
[2] See Ezek. i.
[3] Exod. xxviii. 2.
[4] Psalm xviii. 8; 1. 3.
[5] Jude 14.
[6] Psalm lxviii. 17.
[7] Psalm xviii. 10.
[8] Matt. xxiv. 30.
[9] Rom. xii. 5.

And to rebellious fight rallied their powers
Insensate hope conceiving from despair:
In heav'nly spirits could such perverseness dwell?
But to convince the proud what signs avail,
Or wonders move the obdurate to relent?
They harden'd more by what might most reclaim;
Grieving to see His glory, at the sight
Took envy, and, aspiring to His highth,
Stood reimbattled fierce, by force or fraud
Weening to prosper, and at length prevail
Against God and Messiah, or to fall
In universal ruin last; and now
To final battle drew, disdaining flight,
Or faint retreat; when the great Son of God
To all his hosts on either hand thus spake.

    Stand still in bright array, ye saints, here stand,
Ye angels arm'd, this day from battle rest;
Faithful hath been your warfare, and of God
Accepted, fearless in His righteous cause,
And as ye have received, so have ye done
Invincibly: but of this cursed crew
The punishment to other hand belongs;
Vengeance is His,[1] or whose He sole appoints:
Number to this day's work is not ordain'd,
Nor multitude, stand only and behold
God's indignation on these godless pour'd
By Me; not you, but me they have despised,
Yet envied: against me is all their rage,
Because the Father, to whom in heav'n supreme
Kingdom, and power, and glory appertains,
Hath honor'd me according to his will.
Therefore to me their doom he hath assign'd;
That they may have their wish, to try with me
In battle which the stronger proves, they all,
Or I alone against them; since by strength
They measure all, of other excellence
Not emulous, nor care who then excels;
Nor other strife with them do I vouchsafe.

    So spake the Son, and into terror changed
His count'nance, too severe to be beheld
And full of wrath bent on his enemies.

[1]Deut. xxxii. 35. Rom. xii. 19.

At once the Four[1] spread out their starry wings
With dreadful shake contiguous, and the orbs
Of his fierce chariot roll'd, as with the sound
Of torrent floods, or of a numerous host
He on His impious foes right onward drove,
Gloomy as night; under His burning wheels
The steadfast empyrean shook throughout,
All but the throne itself of GOD. Full soon
Among them He arrived, in His right hand
Grasping ten thousand thunders, which He sent
Before Him, such as in their souls infix'd
Plagues; they astonish'd all resistance lost,
All courage; down their idle weapons dropp'd;
O'er shields, and helms, and helmèd heads He rode
Of thrones and mighty seraphim prostrate,
That wish'd the mountains now might be again.[2]
Thrown on them as a shelter from his ire.
Nor less on either side tempestuous fell
His arrows, from the fourfold visaged Four,
Distinct with eyes, and from the living wheels
Distinct alike with multitude of eyes;
One spirit in them ruled, and every eye
Glared light'ning, and shot forth pernicious fire
Among th' accurst, that wither'd all their strength,
And of their wonted vigor left them drain'd,
Exhausted, spiritless, afflicted, fall'n.
Yet half his strength He put not forth, but check'd
His thunder in mid volley, for He meant
Not to destroy, but root them out of heav'n.
The overthrown He raised, and as a herd
Of goats or timorous flock together throng'd
Drove them before Him thunder-struck, pursued
With terrors and with furies to the bounds
And crystal wall of heav'n, which op'ning wide
Roll'd inward, and a spacious gap disclosed
Into the wasteful deep; the monstrous sight
Struck them with horror backward; but far worse
Urged them behind; headlong themselves they threw
Down from the verge of heav'n, eternal wrath
Burn'd after them to the bottomless pit.

[1] The four Cherubim. Ezek. i.
[2] Rev. vi. 16.

Hell heard th' unsufferable noise, hell saw
Heav'n ruining from heav'n, and would have fled
Affrighted; but strict fate had cast too deep
Her dark foundations, and too fast had bound.
Nine days they fell; confounded Chaos roar'd,
And felt tenfold confusion in their fall
Through his wild anarchy; so huge a rout
Incumber'd him with ruin: hell at last
Yawning received them whole, and on them closed;
Hell their fit habitation, fraught with fire
Unquenchable, the house of woe and pain.
Disburden'd heav'n rejoiced, and soon repair'd
Her mural breach, returning whence it roll'd.

Sole victor from th' expulsion of his foes
Messiah His triumphal chariot turn'd:
To meet Him all His saints, who silent stood
Eye-witnesses of His almighty acts,
With jubilee advanced; and as they went,
Shaded with branching palm, each order bright
Sung triumph, and Him sung victorious King,
Son, Heir, and Lord, to Him dominion given,
Worthiest to reign: He celebrated rode
Triumphant through mid heav'n, into the courts
And temple of His mighty Father throned
On high; who into glory Him received,[1]
Where now He sits at the right hand of bliss.

Thus measuring things in heav'n by things on earth,
At thy request, and that thou may'st beware
By what is past, to thee I have reveal'd
What might have else to human race been hid:
The discord which befell, and war in heav'n
Among th' angelic powers, and the deep fall
Of those too high aspiring, who rebell'd
With Satan, he who envies now thy state,
Who now is plotting how he may seduce
Thee also from obedience, that with him
Bereaved of happiness thou may'st partake
His punishment, eternal misery,
Which would be all his solace and revenge,
As a despite done against the Most High,
Thee once to gain companion of his woe.

[1] 1 Tim. iii. 16. Heb. i. 3.

But listen not to his temptations, warn
Thy weaker, let it profit thee to have heard
By terrible example the reward
Of disobedience; firm they might have stood,
Yet fell: remember, and fear to transgress.

BOOK VII

The Argument

Raphael, at the request of Adam, relates how, and where-fore, this world was first created; that God, after the expelling of Satan and his angels out of heaven, declared his pleasure to create another world, and other creatures to dwell therein; sends his Son with glory and attendance of angels to perform the work of creation in six days; the angels celebrate with hymns the performance thereof, and his re-ascension into heaven.

DESCEND from heav'n, Urania,[1] by that name
If rightly thou art call'd, whose voice divine
Following, above th' Olympian hill I soar,
Above the flight of Pegasean wing.[2]
The meaning, not the name, I call: for thou
Nor of the Muses nine,[3] nor on the top
Of old Olympus dwell'st, but heav'nly born,
Before the hills appear'd, or fountain flow'd,
Thou with eternal Wisdom didst converse,
Wisdom thy sister, and with her didst play
In presence of th' almighty Father, pleased
With thy celestial song. Up led by thee
Into the heav'n of heav'ns I have presumed,
An earthly guest, and drawn empyreal air
Thy temp'ring; with like safety guided down
Return me to my native element:
Least from this flying steed unrein'd, as once
Bellerophon,[4] though from a lower clime,

[1] The word "Urania" signifies heavenly. Here the Poet means *Heavenly Muse.*
[2] The winged horse, Pegasus, said to belong to the Muses, was emblematical of flights of imagination.
[3] Urania, amongst the Muses, was the patroness of Astronomy.
[4] Bellerophon, the son of Glaucus, was a beautiful youth, who was falsely accused by Sthenobœa, Queen of Argos, to her husband. Prœtus, King of Argos, sent him, in consequence, into Lycia with letters commanding that he should be exposed to destruction. He escaped from many perilous enterprises forced on him;

Dismounted, on the Aleian field I fall
Erroneous, there to wander and forlorn.
Half yet remains unsung, but narrower bound,
Within the visible diurnal sphere;
Standing on earth, not rapt above the pole,
More safe I sing with mortal voice, unchanged
To hoarse or mute, though fall'n on evil days,
On evil days though fall'n and evil tongues;
In darkness, and with dangers compast round,
And solitude; yet not alone, while thou
Visit'st my slumbers nightly, or when morn
Purples the east. Still govern thou my song,
Urania, and fit audience find, though few.
But drive far off the barbarous dissonance
Of Bacchus and his revellers, the race
Of that wild rout that tore the Thracian bard
In Rhodope, where woods and rocks had ears
To rapture, till the savage clamor drown'd
Both harp and voice; nor could the Muse defend
Her son.[1] So fail not thou, who thee implores:
For thou art heav'nly, she an empty dream.
Say, Goddess, what ensued when Raphael,
The affable arch-angel, had forewarn'd
Adam by dire example to beware
Apostasy, by what befell in heav'n
To those apostates, lest the like befall
In Paradise to Adam or his race,
Charged not to touch the interdicted tree,
If they transgress, and slight that sole command,
So easily obey'd, amid the choice
Of all tastes else to please their appetite
Though wand'ring. He with his consorted Eve
The story heard attentive, and was fill'd
With admiration and deep muse, to hear

---

but when he attempted to mount to heaven on the winged horse,
Pegasus (incited to the trial by vain-glory), he was thrown off,
and wandered on the Aleian plains for the remainder of his life.
The Aleian plains were in Cilicia.

[1] Orpheus was torn to pieces by the Bacchanalian women of
Rhodope, a mountain of Thrace; nor could his mother, the Muse
Calliope, save him. Newton thinks that Milton here alludes to the
dissolute Court of Charles II.

Of things so high and strange, things to their thought
So unimaginable as hate in heav'n,
And war so near the peace of GOD in bliss
With such confusion: but the evil soon
Driven back redounded as a flood on those
From whom it sprung, impossible to mix
With blessedness. Whence Adam soon repeal'd
The doubts that in his heart arose: and now
Led on, yet sinless, with desire to know
What nearer might concern him, how this world
Of heav'n and earth conspicuous first began,
When, and whereof created, for what cause,
What within Eden, or without was done
Before his memory, as one whose drouth
Yet scarce allay'd still eyes the current stream,
Whose liquid murmur heard new thirst excites,
Proceeded thus to ask his heav'nly guest.

  Great things, and full of wonder in our ears,
Far differing from this world, thou hast reveal'd,
Divine interpreter, by favor sent
Down from the empyrean to forewarn
Us timely of what might else have been our loss,
Unknown, which human knowledge could not reach:
For which to the infinitely Good we owe
Immortal thanks, and His admonishment
Receive with solemn purpose to observe
Immutably His sovereign will, the end
Of what we are. But since thou hast vouchsafed
Gently for our instruction to impart
Things above earthly thought, which yet concern'd
Our knowing, as to highest wisdom seem'd,
Deign to descend now lower, and relate
What may no less perhaps avail us known;
How first began this heav'n which we behold
Distant so high, with moving fires adorn'd
Innumerable, and this which yields or fills
All space, the ambient air wide interfused
Embracing round this florid earth; what cause
Moved the Creator in his holy rest
Through all eternity so late to build
In Chaos; and the work begun, how soon
Absolved; if unforbid thou may'st unfold

What we, not to explore, the secrets, ask
Of His eternal empire, but the more
To magnify His works, the more we know.
And the great light of day yet wants to run
Much of his race though steep; suspense in heav'n
Held by thy voice, thy potent voice, he hears,
And longer will delay to hear thee tell
His generation, and the rising birth
Of nature from the unapparent deep:
Or if the star of ev'ning and the moon
Haste to thy audience, night with her will bring
Silence, and sleep list'ning to thee will watch;
Or we can bid his absence, till thy song
End, and dismiss thee ere the morning shine.

    Thus Adam his illustrious guest besought;
And thus the Godlike Angel answer'd mild.

    This also thy request with caution ask'd
Obtain: though to recount almighty works
What words or tongue of seraph can suffice,
Or heart of man suffice to comprehend?
Yet what thou canst attain, which best may serve
To glorify the Maker, and infer
Thee also happier, shall not be withheld
Thy hearing, such commission from above
I have received, to answer thy desire
Of knowledge within bounds; beyond abstain
To ask, nor let thine own inventions hope
Things not reveal'd, which th' invisible King,[1]
Only omniscient, hath suppress in night,
To none communicable in earth or heav'n:
Enough is left besides to search and know.
But knowledge is as food, and needs no less
Her temperance over appetite, to know
In measure what the mind may well contain,
Oppresses else with surfeit, and soon turns
Wisdom to folly, as nourishment to wind.

    Know then, that after Lucifer from heav'n,
So call him, brighter once amidst the host
Of angels, than that star the stars among,
Fell with his flaming legions through the deep

[1] 1 Tim. i. 17.

Into his place, and the great Son return'd
Victorious with his saints, th' omnipotent
Eternal Father from his throne beheld
Their multitude, and to his Son thus spake.

    At least our envious foe hath fail'd, who thought
All like himself rebellious, by whose aid
This inaccessible high strength, the seat
Of deity supreme, us dispossest,
He trusted to have seized, and into fraud
Drew many, whom their place knows here no more:
Yet far the greater part have kept, I see,
Their station, heav'n yet populous retains
Number sufficient to possess her realms
Though wide, and this high temple to frequent
With ministries due and solemn rites.
But lest his heart exalt him in the harm
Already done, to have dispeopled heav'n,
My damage fondly deem'd, I can repair
That detriment, if such it be to lose
Self-lost, and in a moment will create
Another world, out of one man a race
Of men innumerable, there to dwell,
Not here, till by degrees of merit raised,
They open to themselves at length the way
Up hither, under long obedience tried;
And earth be changed to heav'n, and heav'n to earth,
One kingdom, joy and union without end.
Meanwhile inhabit lax,[1] ye powers of heav'n,
And thou my Word, begotten Son, by thee,
This I perform, speak thou, and be it done.
My overshadowing spirit and might with thee
I send along; ride forth, and bid the deep
Within appointed bounds be heav'n and earth;
Boundless the deep, because I AM who fill
Infinitude, nor vacuous the space;
Though I uncircumscribed myself retire,
And put not forth my goodness, which is free
To act, or not, necessity and chance
Approach not me, and what I will is fate.

  [1] The meaning seems to be, "Occupy the space left by the fall of
the angels."

So spake th' Almighty, and to what he spake
His Word, the Filial Godhead, gave effect.
Immediate are the acts of GOD, more swift
Than time or motion, but to human ears
Cannot without process of speech be told,
So told as earthly notion can receive.
Great triumph and rejoicing was in heav'n,
When such was heard declared the Almighty's will;
Glory they sung to the Most High, good will
To future men, and in their dwellings peace;
Glory to Him, whose just avenging ire
Had driven out th' ungodly from His sight
And th' habitations of the just; to Him,
Glory and praise, whose wisdom had ordain'd
Good out of evil to create, instead
Of spirits malign a better race to bring
Into their vacant room, and thence diffuse
His good to worlds and ages infinite.
  So sang the Hierarchies. Meanwhile the Son
On his great expedition now appear'd,
Girt with omnipotence, with radiance crown'd
Of Majesty divine, sapience and love
Immense, and all his Father in him shone.
About his chariot numberless were pour'd
Cherub and Seraph, Potentates and Thrones,
And Virtues, wingèd Spirits, and Chariots wing'd,
From the armory of GOD, where stand of old
Myriads, between two brazen mountains lodged
Against a solemn day, harness'd at hand,
Celestial equipage; and now came forth
Spontaneous, for within them spirit lived,
Attendant on their Lord: heav'n open'd wide
Her ever-during gates, harmonious sound
On golden hinges moving, to let forth
The King of glory, in his powerful Word
And Spirit coming to create new worlds.
On heav'nly ground they stood, and from the shore
They view'd the vast immeasurable abyss
Outrageous as a sea, dark, wasteful, wild,
Up from the bottom turn'd by furious winds
And surging waves, as mountains, to assault

Heav'n's highth, and with the centre mix the pole.
   Silence, ye troubled waves, and, thou deep, peace,
Said then th' omnific Word, your discord end.
   Nor stay'd; but, on the wings of Cherubim
Uplifted, in Paternal Glory rode
Far into Chaos and the world unborn;
For Chaos heard his voice. Him all his train
Followed in bright procession to behold
Creation, and the wonders of his might.
Then stay'd the fervid wheels, and in his hand
He took the golden compasses, prepared
In GOD's eternal store, to circumscribe
This universe, and all created things.
One foot he centered, and the other turn'd
Round through the vast profundity obscure,
And said, Thus far extend, thus far thy bounds,
This be thy just circumference, O world.
Thus GOD the heav'n created, thus the earth,
Matter unform'd and void. Darkness profound
Cover'd th' Abyss; but on the watery calm
His brooding wings the Spirit of GOD outspread,[1]
And vital virtue infused and vital warmth
Throughout the fluid mass, but downward purged
The black, tartareous, cold infernal dregs,
Adverse to life: then founded, then conglobed
Like things to like; the rest to several place
Disparted, and between spun out the air,
And earth self-balanced on her centre hung.
   Let there be light, said GOD, and forthwith light
Ethereal, first of things, quintessence pure,
Sprung from the deep, and from her native east
To journey through the aery gloom began,
Sphered in a radiant cloud, for yet the sun
Was not; she in a cloudy tabernacle
Sojourn'd the while. GOD saw the light was good;
And light from darkness by the hemisphere
Divided: light the day, and darkness night,
He named. Thus was the first day ev'n and morn:
Nor past uncelebrated, nor unsung

[1] Gen. i. 1, 2.

By the celestial choirs, when orient light
Exhaling first from darkness they beheld,
Birth day of heav'n and earth; with joy and shout[1]
The hollow universal orb they fill'd,
And touch'd their golden harps, and hymning praised
God and his works, creator him they sung,
Both when first evening was, and when first morn.
    Again GOD said, Let there be firmament[2]
Amid the waters, and let it divide
The waters from the waters: and GOD made
The firmament, expanse of liquid, pure,
Transparent, elemental air, diffused
In circuit to the uttermost convex
Of this great round; partition firm and sure,
The waters underneath from those above
Dividing: for as earth, so he the world
Built on circumfluous waters calm, in wide
Crystalline ocean, and the loud misrule
Of Chaos far removed, lest fierce extremes
Contiguous might distemper the whole frame:
And heav'n He named the firmament: so ev'n
And morning chorus sung the second day.
    The earth was form'd, but, in the womb as yet
Of waters embryon immature involved,
Appear'd not: over all the face of earth
Main ocean flow'd, not idle, but with warm
Prolific humor soft'ning all her globe
Fermented the great mother to conceive,
Satiate with genial moisture, when GOD said,
Be gather'd now, ye waters under heav'n,
Into one place, and let dry land appear.
Immediately the mountains huge appear
Emergent, and their broad bare backs upheave
Into the clouds, their tops ascend the sky.
So high as heaved the tumid hills, so low
Down sunk a hollow bottom broad and deep,
Capacious bed of waters: thither they
Hasted with glad precipitance, uproll'd

[1] Job xxxviii. 4, 7.
[2] Firmament signifies expansion.—NEWTON.

As drops on dust conglobing from the dry:
Part rise in crystal wall, or ridge direct,
For haste; such flight the great command imprest
On the swift floods: as armies at the call
Of trumpet, for of armies thou hast heard,
Troop to their standard, so the watery throng,
Wave rolling after wave, where way they found;
If steep, with torrent rapture, if through plain,
Soft-ebbing: nor withstood them rock or hill,
But they, or under ground, or circuit wide
With serpent error wandering, found their way,
And on the washy oose deep channels wore,
Easy, ere GOD had bid the ground be dry,
All but within those banks, where rivers now
Stream, and prepetual draw their humid train.
The dry land, earth; and the great receptacle
Of congregated waters He call'd seas;
And saw that it was good, and said, Let the earth
Put forth the verdant grass, herb yielding seed,
And fruit-tree yielding fruit after her kind;
Whose seed is in herself upon the earth.
He scarce had said, when the bare earth, till then
Desert and bare, unsightly, unadorned,
Brought forth the tender grass, whose verdure clad
Her universal face with pleasant green;
Then herbs of every leaf, that sudden flow'd
Opening their various colors, and made gay
Her bosom smelling sweet: and these scarce blown,
Forth flourish'd thick the clustering vine, forth crept
The swelling gourd, up stood the corny reed
Embattled in her field; and the humble shrub,
And bush with frizzled hair implicit: last
Rose, as in dance, the stately trees, and spread
Their branches hung with copious fruit, or gemm'd
Their blossoms: with high woods the hills were crown'd,
With tufts the valleys and each fountain side:
With borders long the rivers: that earth now
Seem'd like to heav'n, a seat where Gods might dwell,
Or wander with delight, and love to haunt
Her sacred shades: though GOD had yet not rain'd
Upon the earth, and man to till the ground

None was; but from the earth a dewy mist
Went up and water'd all the ground, and each
Plant of the field, which, ere it was in the earth,
GOD made, and every herb, before it grew
On the green stem: GOD saw that it was good:
So ev'n and morn recorded the third day.

    Again th' Almighty spake: Let there be lights
High in th' expanse of heaven to divide
The day from night; and let them be for signs,
For seasons, and for days, and circling years;
And let them be for lights, as I ordain
Their office in the firmament of heav'n
To give light on the earth; and it was so.
And GOD made two great lights, great for their use
To man, the greater to have rule by day,
The less by night, altern: and made the stars,
And set them in the firmament of heav'n,
To illuminate the earth, and rule the day
In their vicissitude, and rule the night,
And light from darkness to divide. GOD saw,
Surveying His great work, that it was good:
For of celestial bodies first the sun,
A mighty sphere, He framed, unlightsome first,
Though of ethereal mould: then form'd the moon
Globose, and every magnitude of stars,
And sow'd with stars the heav'n thick as a field.
Of light by far the greater part he took,
Transplanted from her cloudy shrine, and placed
In the sun's orb, made porous to receive
And drink the liquid light, firm to retain
Her gather'd beams, great palace now of light.
Hither, as to their fountain, other stars
Repairing, in their golden urns draw light,
And hence the morning planet gilds her horns:
By tincture or reflection they augment
Their small peculiar, though from human sight
So far remote, with diminution seen.
First in his east the glorious lamp was seen,
Regent of day, and all the horizon round
Invested with bright rays, jocund to run
His longitude through heav'n's high road: the gray
Dawn and the Pleiades before him danced,

Shedding sweet influence.[1] Less bright the moon,
But opposite in levell'd west was set
His mirror, with full face borrowing her light
From him, for other light she needed none
In that respect; and still that distance keeps
Till night, then in the east her turn she shines,
Revolved on heav'n's great axle, and her reign
With thousand lesser lights dividual holds,
With thousand thousand stars that then appear'd
Spangling the hemisphere: then first adorn'd
With their bright luminaries, that set and rose,
Glad ev'ning and glad morn crown'd the fourth day.

    And GOD said, Let the waters generate[2]
Reptile with spawn abundant, living soul:
And let fowl fly above the earth, with wings
Display'd on the open firmament of heav'n.
And GOD created the great whales, and each
Soul living, each that crept, which plenteously
The waters generated by their kinds,
And every bird of wing after his kind;
And saw that it was good, and bless'd them, saying,
Be fruitful, multiply, and in the seas,
And lakes, and running streams, the waters fill;
And let the fowl be multiplied on the earth.
Forthwith the sounds and seas, each creek and bay,
With fry innumerable swarm, and shoals
Of fish, that with their fins and shining scales
Glide under the green wave, in sculls[3] that oft
Bank the mid sea: part single, or with mate,
Graze the seaweed their pasture, and through groves

---

[1] The Pleiades are seven stars in the neck of the constellation Taurus, which, rising about the time of the vernal equinox, are called by the Latins "Vergiliæ." Milton, therefore, in saying that the Pleiades danced before the sun at his creation, implies that creation began with the spring.—*From* NEWTON. It has been a recent idea of astronomers, that the Pleiades, or seven suns—for fixed stars *are* suns—are the centre of the universe round which the heavens revolve; but this is not yet clearly ascertained. Job speaks of "the sweet influences of the Pleiades."—See Job xxxviii. 31.

[2] Gen. i. 20, 22.

[3] *Schools.* We say a "school of whales" for a shoal now. Scull comes from the Saxon *sceole*, an assembly.

Of coral stray, or sporting with quick glance
Show to the sun their waved coats dropt with gold;
Or in their pearly shells at ease attend
Moist nutriment, or under rocks their food
In jointed armour watch: on smooth the seal
And bended dolphins play; part huge of bulk,
Wallowing unwieldy, enormous in their gait,
Tempest the ocean: there Leviathian,
Hugest of living creatures, on the deep
Stretch'd like a promontory sleeps, or swims
And seems a moving land, and at his gills
Draws in, and at his trunk spouts out a sea.
Meanwhile the tepid caves, and fens, and shores,
Their brood as numerous hatch from the egg, that soon
Bursting with kindly rupture forth disclosed
Their callow young; but feather'd soon and fledge,
They summ'd their pens,[1] and soaring the air sublime
With clang despised the ground, under a cloud
In prospect: there the eagle and the stork
On cliffs and cedar tops their eyries build:[2]
Part loosely wing the region, part more wise
In common ranged in figure[3] wedge their way,
Intelligent of seasons,[4] and set forth
Their aery caravan, high over seas
Flying, and over lands, with mutual wing
Easing their flight; so steers the prudent crane
Her annual voyage, borne on winds; the air
Floats, as they pass, fann'd with unnumber'd plumes,
From branch to branch the smaller birds with song
Solaced the woods, and spread their painted wings
Till even; nor then the solemn nightingale
Ceased warbling, but all night tuned her soft lays.
Others on silver lakes and rivers bath'd
Their downy breast; the swan, with archèd neck
Between her white wings mantling proudly, rows
Her state with oary feet: yet oft they quit

---

[1] Pens are feathers. Here the meaning is, "They used their pinions as full fledged birds."

[2] Jeremiah xxxix. 27, 28.

[3] Migratory birds fly in shape of a wedge, one bird leading alternately.

[4] Jeremiah viii. 7.

The dank, and rising on stiff pennons tower
The mid aërial sky. Others on ground
Walk'd firm; the crested cock, whose clarion sounds
The silent hours, and the other, whose gay train
Adorns him, color'd with the florid hue
Of rainbows and starry eyes. The waters thus
With fish replenish'd, and the air with fowl,
Ev'ning and morn solemnized the fifth day.

    The sixth, and of creation last, arose
With ev'ning harps and matin; when God said,
Let the earth bring forth soul living in her kind,
Cattle and creeping things, and beast of the earth
Each in their kind. The earth obey'd, and straight
Op'ning her fertile womb teem'd at a birth
Innumerous living creatures, perfect forms,
Limb'd and full grown. Out of the ground up rose
As from his lair the wild beast where he wonns[1]
In forest wild, in thicket, brake, or den;
Among the trees in pairs they rose, they walk'd;
The cattle in the fields and meadows green:
Those rare and solitary, these in flocks
Pasturing at once, and in broad herds upsprung.
The grassy clods now calved; now half appear'd
The tawny lion, pawing to get free
His hinder parts, then springs as broke from bonds,
And rampant shakes his brinded mane; the ounce,
The libbard,[2] and the tiger, as the mole
Rising, the crumbled earth above them threw
In hillocks; the swift stag from under ground
Bore up his branching head; scarce from his mould
Behemoth, biggest born of earth, upheaved
His vastness: fleeced the flocks and bleating rose,
As plants: ambiguous between sea and land
The river horse and scaly crocodile.
At once came forth whatever creeps the ground,
Insect or worm; those waved their limber fans
For wings, and smallest lineaments exact
In all the liveries deck'd of summer's pride
With spots of gold and purple, azure and green:

---

[1] *Wone* is Saxon for to dwell, to inhabit.—*See* CHAUCER, *Sompnoure's Tale*, line 7745.

[2] Leopard.

These as a line their long dimension drew,
Streaking the ground with sinuous trace; not all
Minims[1] of nature; some of serpent kind,
Wondrous in length and corpulence, involved
Their snaky folds and added wings. First crept
The parsimonious emmet, provident
Of future, in small room large heart inclosed,
Pattern of just equality perhaps
Hereafter, join'd in her popular tribes
Of commonalty: swarming next appear'd
The female bee, that feeds her husband drone
Deliciously, and builds her waxen cells
With honey stored: the rest are numberless,
And thou their natures know'st, and gav'st them names,
Needless to thee repeated; nor unknown
The serpent, subtlest beast of all the field,
Of huge extent sometimes, with brazen eyes
And hairy mane terrific, though to thee
Not noxious, but obedient at thy call.

Now heav'n in all her glory shone, and roll'd
Her motions, as the great First Mover's hand
First wheel'd their course; earth in her rich attire
Consummate lovely smiled; air, water, earth,
By fowl, fish, beast, was flown, was swum, was walk'd
Frequent; and of the sixth day yet remain'd;
There wanted yet the master work, the end
Of all yet done; a creature, who not prone
And brute as other creatures, but indued
With sanctity of reason, might erect
His stature, and upright with front serene
Govern the rest, self-knowing; and from thence
Magnanimous to correspond with heav'n;
But grateful to acknowledge whence his good
Descends, thither with heart and voice, and eyes
Directed in devotion, to adore
And worship God supreme, who made him chief
Of all His works: therefore the omnipotent
Eternal Father,—for where is not He
Present?—thus to his Son audibly spake.

Let us make now man in our image, man[2]

---

[1] Something exceedingly small, a dwarf.
[2] Gen. i, 26–28.

In our similitude, and let them rule
Over the fish and fowl of sea and air,
Beast of the field and over all the earth,
And every creeping thing that creeps the ground.
This said, He form'd thee, Adam, thee, O man,
Dust of the ground, and in thy nostrils breathed
The breath of life: in his own image he
Created thee, in the image of GOD
Express, and thou becam'st a living soul.
Male he created thee, but thy consort
Female for race; then bless'd mankind, and said,
Be fruitful, multiply, and fill the earth,
Subdue it, and throughout dominion hold
Over fish of the sea, and fowl of the air,
And every living thing that moves on the earth.
Wherever thus created, for no place
Is yet distinct by name, thence, as thou know'st,
He brought thee into this delicious grove,
This garden, planted with the trees of GOD,
Delectable both to behold and taste;
And freely all their pleasant fruit for food
Gave thee, all sorts are here that all th' earth yields,
Variety without end; but of the tree,
Which tasted works knowedge of good and evil,
Thou may'st not: in the day thou eat'st thou diest;
Death is the penalty imposed; beware,
And govern well thy appetite; lest sin
Surprise thee, and her black attendant death.
   Here finish'd He, and all that He had made
View'd, and behold all was entirely good;
So ev'n and morn accomplish'd the sixth day:
Yet not, till the Creator from His work
Desisting, though unwearied, up return'd,
Up to the heav'n of heav'ns His high abode,
Thence to behold this new-created world,
Th' addition of His empire, how it show'd
In prospect from His throne, how good, how fair,
Answering His great idea. Up He rode,
Follow'd with acclamation and the sound
Symphonious of ten thousand harps, that tuned
Angelic harmonies: the earth, the air
Resounded, thou remember'st, for thou heard'st;

The heav'ns and all the constellations rung,
The planets in their station list'ning stood,
While the bright pomp ascended jubilant.
Open, ye everlasting gates, they sung,[1]
Open, ye heavens, your living doors; let in
The great Creator, from His work return'd
Magnificent, His six days' work, a world:
Open, and henceforth oft; for GOD will deign
To visit oft the dwellings of just men
Delighted, and with frequent intercourse
Thither will send his wingèd messengers
On errands of supernal grace. So sung
The glorious train ascending: He through heav'n,
That open'd wide her blazing portals, led
To GOD's eternal house direct the way,
A broad and ample road, whose dust is gold,
And pavement stars, as stars to thee appear
Seen in the galaxy, that milky way
Which nightly as a circling zone thou seest
Powder'd with stars. And now on earth the seventh
Ev'ning arose in Eden, for the sun
Was set, and twilight from the east came on,
Forerunning night; when at the holy mount
Of heaven's high seated top, th' imperial throne
Of Godhead, fix'd forever firm and sure,
The Filial Power arrived, and sat Him down
With His great Father; for He also went
Invisible, yet stay'd, such privilege
Hath Omnipresence, and the work ordain'd,
Author and end of all things, and from work
Now resting, bless'd and hallow'd the seventh day,
As resting on that day from all His work,
But not in silence holy kept; the harp
Had work, and rested not; the solemn pipe
And dulcimer, all organs of sweet stop,
All sounds on fret by string or golden wire,
Temper'd soft tunings, intermix'd with voice
Choral or unison: of incense, clouds

---

[1] Psalm xxiv. 7. This Psalm was sung by the Levites when the ark of God was carried up into the sanctuary on Mount Sion, and is understood as a prophecy of our Lord's ascension.—*From* NEWTON, and Mant's "Bible."

Fuming from golden censers, hid the mount.
Creation and the six days' acts they sung;
Great are thy works, Jehovah, infinite
Thy power; what thought can measure thee, or tongue
Relate thee? greater now in thy return
Than from the giant angels; thee that day
Thy thunders magnified; but to create
Is greater than created to destroy.
Who can impair thee, mighty King, or bound
Thy empire? easily the proud attempt
Of Spirits apostate and their counsels vain
Thou hast repell'd, while impiously they thought
Thee to diminish, and from thee withdraw
The number of thy worshippers. Who seeks
To lessen thee, against his purpose serves
To manifest the more thy might: his evil
Thou usest, and from thence creat'st more good.
Witness this new-made world, another heav'n
From heaven gate not far, founded in view
On the clear hyaline, the glassy sea;
Of amplitude almost immense, with stars
Numerous, and every star perhaps a world
Of destined habitation; but thou know'st
Their seasons: among these the seat of men,
Earth, with her nether ocean circumfused,
Their pleasant dwelling place. Thrice happy men,
And sons of men, whom GOD hath thus advanced,
Created in His image, there to dwell
And worship Him; and in reward to rule
Over His works, on earth, in sea, or air,
And multiply a race of worshippers
Holy and just: thrice happy, if they know
Their happiness, and persevere upright.
   So sung they, and the empyrean rung
With Hallelujahs: thus was Sabbath kept.
And thy request think now fulfill'd, that ask'd
How first this world and face of things began,
And what before thy memory was done
From the beginning, that posterity
Inform'd by thee might know. If else thou seek'st
Aught, not surpassing human measure say.

BOOK VIII

The Argument

Adam inquires concerning celestial motions, is doubtfully answer'd, and exhorted to search rather things more worthy of knowledge. Adam assents; and still desirous to detain Raphael, relates to him what he remember'd since his own creation; his placing in Paradise; his talk with God concerning solitude and fit society; his first meeting and nuptials with Eve; his discourse with the angel thereupon: who, after admonitions repeated, departs.

THE angel ended, and in Adam's ear
So charming left his voice, that he awhile
Thought him still speaking, still stood fix'd to hear:
Then, as new waked, thus gratefully replied.
  What thanks sufficient, or what recompence
Equal, have I to render thee, divine
Historian? who thus largely hast allay'd
The thirst I had of knowledge, and vouchsafed
This friendly condescension to relate
Things else by me unsearchable, now heard
With wonder, but delight, and, as is due,
With glory attributed to the high
Creator: something yet of doubt remains
Which only thy solution can resolve.
When I behold this goodly frame, this world,
Of heav'n and earth consisting, and compute
Their magnitudes, this earth a spot, a grain,
An atom, with the firmament compared
And all her number'd stars, that seem to roll
Spaces incomprehensible, for such
Their distance argues, and their swift return
Diurnal, merely to officiate light
Round this opacous earth, this punctual [1] spot.
One day and night, in all their vast survey
Useless besides; reasoning I oft admire,
How nature wise and frugal could commit

[1] Small as a point in punctuation.

Such disproportions, with superfluous hand
So many nobler bodies to create,
Greater so manifold, to this one use,
For aught appears, and on their orbs impose
Such restless revolution day by day
Repeated, while the sedentary earth,
That better might with far less compass move,
Served by more noble than herself, attains
Her end without least motion, and receives,
As tribute, such a sumless journey brought
Of incorporeal speed, her warmth and light;
Speed, to describe whose swiftness number fails.[1]

So spake our sire, and by his count'nance seem'd
Entering on studious thoughts abstruse; which Eve
Perceiving where she sat retired in sight,
With lowliness majestic from her seat,
And grace that won who saw to wish her stay,
Rose, and went forth among her fruits and flow'rs,
To visit how they prosper'd, bud and bloom,
Her nursery; they at her coming sprung
And touch'd by her fair tendance gladlier grew.
Yet went she not, as not with such discourse
Delighted, or not capable her ear
Of what was high: such pleasure she reserved,
Adam relating, she sole auditress;
Her husband the relater she preferr'd
Before the angel, and of him to ask
Chose rather; he, she knew, would intermix
Grateful digressions, and solve high dispute
With conjugal caresses; from his lip
Not words alone pleased her. O when meet now
Such pairs, in love and mutual honor join'd?
With Goddess-like demeanor forth she went;
Not unattended, for on her as queen
A pomp of winning graces waited still,
And from about her shot darts of desire
Into all eyes to wish her still in sight.
And Raphael now to Adam's doubt proposed
Benevolent and facile thus replied.

To ask or search I blame thee not, for heav'n

[1] One is here reminded of the fact that Milton had held communion with Galileo, whose "Eppure si muove" is historical.

Is as the book of GOD before thee set,
Wherein to read his wondrous works, and learn
His seasons, hours, or days, or months, or years.
This to attain, whether heav'n move or earth,
Imports not, if thou reckon right;[1] the rest
From man or angel the great architect
Did wisely to conceal, and not divulge
His secrets to be scann'd by them who ought
Rather admire; or if they list to try
Conjecture, He his fabric of the heav'ns
Hath left to their disputes, perhaps to move
His laughter at their quaint opinions wide
Hereafter, when they come to model heav'n
And calculate the stars, how they will wield
The mighty frame, how build, unbuild, contrive,
To save appearances; how gird the sphere
With centric and eccentric scribbled o'er,
Cycle and epicycle,[2] orb in orb.
Already by thy reasoning this I guess,
Who art to lead thy offspring, and supposest,
That bodies bright and greater should not serve
The less not bright, nor heav'n such journeys run,
Earth sitting still, when she alone receives
The benefit. Consider first, that great
Or bright infers not excellence: the earth
Though, in comparison of heav'n, so small,
Nor glistering, may of solid good contain
More plenty than the sun, that barren shines,
Whose virtue on itself works no effect,
But in the fruitful earth: there first received
His beams, unactive else, their vigor find.
Yet not to earth are those bright luminaries
Officious, but to thee earth's habitant.

[1] The subject was then matter of discussion, and, in the Roman Church, of persecution. The Ptolemaic system made the earth the centre of the system, and the sun and stars move round it; the Copernican made the sun the centre, and the earth move, as Galileo asserted.

[2] These terms were used by Ptolemaic astronomers to explain their system. *Centric* means a sphere whose centre is the same as that of the earth; *eccentric*, a sphere whose centre is quite different to that of the earth. *Cycle* is a circle; *epicycle*, a circle *on* another circle.

And for the heav'n's wide circuit, let it speak
The Maker's high magnificence, who built
So spacious, and His line stretch'd out so far;
That man may know he dwells not in his own;
An edifice too large for him to fill,
Lodged in a small partition, and the rest
Ordain'd for uses to his Lord best known.
The swiftness of those circles attribute,
Though numberless, to his omnipotence,
That to corporeal substances could add
Speed almost spiritual: me thou think'st not slow,
Who since the morning hour set out from heav'n
Where GOD resides, and ere midday arrived
In Eden, distance inexpressible
By numbers that have name. But this I urge,
Admitting motion in the heav'ns, to show
Invalid that which thee to doubt it moved;
Not that I so affirm, though so it seem
To thee who hast thy dwelling here on earth.
GOD, to remove his ways from human sense,
Placed heav'n from earth so far, that earthly sight,
If it presume, might err in things too high,
And no advantage gain. What if the sun
Be centre to the world, and other stars,
By his attractive virtue and their own
Incited, dance about him various rounds?
Their wand'ring course now high, now low, then hid,
Progressive, retrograde, or standing still,
In six thou seest;[1] and what if sev'nth to these
The planet earth, so steadfast though she seem,
Insensibly three different motions[2] move?
Which else to several spheres thou must ascribe,
Moved contrary with thwart obliquities,
Or save the sun his labor, and that swift
Nocturnal and diurnal rhomb supposed,
Invisible else above all stars, the wheel

---

[1] The moon and the five planets visible to Adam.
[2] Three motions were attributed by the Copernicans to the earth.
The *diurnal*, round her own axis, causing day and night; the *annual*, round the sun; and the *motion of libration*, as it is called,
whereby the earth so proceeds in her orbit, as that her axis is
constantly parallel to the axis of the world.—NEWTON.

Of day and night; which needs not thy belief,
If earth industrious of herself fetch day
Travelling east, and with her part averse
From the sun's beam meet night, her other part
Still luminous by his ray. What if that light,
Sent from her through the wide transpicuous air,
To the terrestrial moon be as a star
Enlight'ning her by day, as she by night
This earth? reciprocal, if land be there,
Fields and inhabitants: her spots thou seest
As clouds, and clouds may rain, and rain produce
Fruits in her soften'd soil, for some to eat
Allotted there; and other suns perhaps
With their attendant moons thou wilt descry,
Communicating male and female light,
Which two great sexes animate the world,
Stored in each orb perhaps with some that live.
For such vast room in nature unpossess'd
By living soul, desert and desolate,
Only to shine, yet scarce to cóntribute
Each orb a glimpse of light, convey'd so far
Down to this habitable, which returns
Light back to them, is obvious to dispute.
But whether thus these things, or whether not,
Whether the sun predominant in heav'n
Rise on the earth, or earth rise on the sun,
He from the east his flaming road begin,
Or she from west her silent course advance
With inoffensive pace, that spinning sleeps
On her soft axle, while she paces ev'n,
And bears thee soft with the smooth air along,
Solicit not thy thoughts with matters hid,
Leave them to God above, Him serve and fear:
Of other creatures, as Him pleases best,
Wherever placed, let Him dispose: joy thou
In what He gives to thee, this paradise
And thy fair Eve; heav'n is for thee too high
To know what passes there; be lowly wise:
Think only what concerns thee and thy being;
Dream not of other worlds, what creatures there
Live, in what state, condition, or degree,
Contented that thus far hath been reveal'd

Not of earth only, but of highest heav'n.
 To whom thus Adam, clear'd of doubt, replied.
How fully hast thou satisfied me, pure
Intelligence of heav'n, angel serene,
And freed from intricacies, taught to live
The easiest way, nor with perplexing thoughts
To interrupt the sweet of life, from which
GOD hath bid dwell far off all anxious cares,
And not molest us, unless we ourselves
Seek them with wand'ring thoughts, and notions vain.
But apt the mind or fancy is to rove
Uncheck'd, and of her roving is no end;
Till warn'd, or by experience taught, she learn,
That not to know at large of things remote
From use, obscure and subtle, but to know
That which before us lies in daily life,
Is the prime wisdom; what is more, is fume,
Or emptiness, or fond impertinence,
And renders us in things that most concern
Unpractised, unprepared, and still to seek.
Therefore from this high pitch let us descend
A lower flight, and speak of things at hand
Useful, whence haply mention may arise
Of something not unseasonable to ask
By sufferance, and thy wonted favor deign'd.
Thee I have heard relating what was done
Ere my remembrance: now hear me relate
My story, which perhaps thou hast not heard;
And day is not yet spent; till then thou seest
How subtly to detain thee I devise,
Inviting thee to hear while I relate,
Fond, were it not in hope of thy reply.
For while I sit with thee, I seem in heav'n,
And sweeter thy discourse is to my ear
Than fruits of palm-tree pleasantest to thirst
And hunger both, from labor, at the hour
Of sweet repast: they satiate, and soon fill,
Though pleasant; but thy words, with grace divine
Imbued, bring to their sweetness no satiety.
 To whom thus Raphael answer'd heav'nly meek.
Nor are thy lips ungraceful, sire of men,
Nor tongue ineloquent; for GOD on thee

Abundantly His gifts hath also pour'd
Inward and outward both, His image fair:
Speaking or mute all comeliness and grace
Attends thee, and each word, each motion forms.
Nor less think we in heav'n of thee on earth,
Than of our fellow-servant, and inquire
Gladly into the ways of GOD with man:
For GOD we see hath honor'd thee, and set
On man his equal love. Say therefore on;
For I that day was absent, as befell,
Bound on a voyage uncouth and obscure,
Far on excursion toward the gates of hell,
Squared in full legion, such command we had,
To see that none thence issued forth a spy,
Or enemy, while GOD was in his work,
Lest He, incensed at such eruption bold,
Destruction with creation might have mix'd.
Not that they durst without His leave attempt,
But us He sends upon his high behests
For state, as Sov'reign King, and to enure
Our prompt obedience. Fast we found, fast shut
The dismal gates, and barricadoed strong;
But long ere our approaching heard within
Noise, other than the sound of dance or song,
Torment, and loud lament, and furious rage.
Glad we return'd up to the coasts of light
Ere sabbath ev'ning: so we had in charge.
But thy relation now; for I attend,
Pleased with thy words, no less than thou with mine.
    So spake the godlike Power, and thus our sire.
For man to tell how human life began
Is hard; for who himself beginning knew?
Desire with thee still longer to converse
Induced me. As new waked from soundest sleep
Soft on the flow'ry herb I found me laid,
In balmy sweat, which with his beams the sun
Soon dried, and on the reeking moisture fed.
Straight toward heav'n my wond'ring eyes I turn'd,
And gazed a while the ample sky, till raised
By quick instinctive motion up I sprung,
As thitherward endeavoring, and upright
Stood on my feet: about me round I saw

Hill, dale, and shady woods, and sunny plains,
And liquid lapse of murmuring streams; by these
Creatures that lived, and moved, and walk'd, or flew;
Birds on the branches warbling; all things smiled
With fragrance and with joy my heart o'erflow'd.
Myself I then perused, and limb by limb
Survey'd, and sometimes went, and sometimes ran
With supple joints, as lively vigor led:
But who I was, or where, or from what cause,
Knew not: to speak I tried, and forthwith spake;
My tongue obey'd, and readily could name
Whate'er I saw. Thou sun, said I, fair light,
And thou enlighten'd earth, so fresh and gay,
Ye hills and dales, ye rivers, woods, and plains,
And ye that live and move, fair creatures, tell,
Tell, if ye saw, how came I thus, how here?
Not of myself, by some great Maker then,
In goodness and in power pre-eminent:
Tell me, how may I know Him, how adore,
From whom I have that thus I move and live,
And feel that I am happier than I know.
While thus I call'd and stray'd I knew not whither,
From where I first drew air, and first beheld
This happy light, when answer none return'd,
On a green shady bank profuse of flow'rs
Pensive I sat me down; there gentle sleep
First found me, and with soft oppression seized
My drowsèd sense, untroubled, though I thought
I then was passing to my former state
Insensible, and forthwith to dissolve:
When suddenly stood at my head a dream,
Whose inward apparition gently moved
My fancy to believe I yet had being,
And lived: one came, methought, of shape divine,
And said, Thy mansion wants thee, Adam, rise,
First man, of men innumerable ordain'd
First father! call'd by thee, I come thy guide
To the garden of bliss, thy seat prepared.
So saying, by the hand He took me raised
And over fields and waters, as in air
Smooth sliding without step, last led me up
A woody mountain; whose high top was plain,

A circuit wide, enclosed, with goodliest trees
Planted, with walks, and bowers, that what I saw
Of earth before scarce pleasant seem'd. Each tree
Loaden with fairest fruit, that hung to the eye
Tempting, stirr'd in me sudden appetite
To pluck and eat: whereat I waked, and found
Before mine eyes all real, as the dream
Had lively shadow'd: here had new begun
My wand'ring, had not He, who was my guide
Up hither, from among the trees appear'd,
Presence divine. Rejoicing, but with awe,
In adoration at His feet I fell
Submiss: He rear'd me, and, Whom thou sought'st I am
Said mildly, author of all this thou seest
Above, or round about thee, or beneath.
This paradise I give thee, count it thine
To till and keep, and of the fruit to eat:
Of every tree that in the garden grows
Eat freely with glad heart; fear here no dearth:
But of the Tree whose operation brings
Knowledge of good and ill, which I have set
The pledge of thy obedience and thy faith
Amid the garden by the Tree of Life,
Remember what I warn thee, shun to taste,
And shun the bitter consequence: for know,
The day thou eat'st thereof, my sole command
Transgrest, inevitably thou shalt die;
From that day mortal, and this happy state
Shalt lose, expell'd from hence into a world
Of woe and sorrow. Sternly He pronounced
The rigid interdiction, which resounds
Yet dreadful in mine ear, though in my choice
Not to incur; but soon His clear aspect
Return'd and gracious purpose thus renew'd.
Not only these fair bounds, but all the earth
To thee and to thy race I give; as lords
Possess it, and all things that therein live,
Or live in sea, or air, beast, fish, and fowl.
In sign whereof each bird and beast behold
After their kinds; I bring them to receive
From thee their names, and pay thee fealty
With low subjection; understand the same

Of fish within their wat'ry residence,
Not hither summon'd since they cannot change
Their element to draw the thinner air.
As thus he spake, each bird and beast behold
Approaching two and two; these cow'ring low
With blandishment, each bird stoop'd on his wing.
I named them, as they pass'd and understood
Their nature, with such knowledge God indued
My sudden apprehension: but in these
I found not what methought I wanted still;
And to the heav'nly vision thus presumed.

O by what name, for thou above all these,
Above mankind, or aught than mankind higher,
Surpassest far my naming, how may I
Adore thee, Author of this universe,
And all this good to man, for whose well being
So amply, and with hands so liberal,
Thou hast provided all things? but with me
I see not who partakes. In solitude
What happiness, who can enjoy alone,
Or all enjoying, what contentment find?
Thus I presumptuous; and the vision bright,
As with a smile more brighten'd, thus replied.

What call'st thou solitude? Is not the earth
With various living creatures and the air
Replenish'd, and all these at thy command
To come and play before thee? Know'st thou not
Their language and their ways? They also know,
And reason not contemptibly; with these
Find pastime, and bear rule; thy realm is large.

So spake the universal Lord, and seem'd
So ordering. I, with leave of speech implored,
And humble deprecation, thus replied.
Let not my words offend thee, heav'nly Power,
My Maker, be propitious while I speak.
Hast thou not made me here thy substitute,
And these inferior far beneath me set?
Among unequals what society
Can sort, what harmony, or true delight?
Which must be mutual, in proportion due,
Given and received; but in disparity,
The one intense, the other still remiss,

Cannot well suit with either, but soon prove
Tedious alike: of fellowship I speak
Such as I seek, fit to participate
All rational delight, wherein the brute
Cannot be human consort: they rejoice
Each with their kind, lion with lioness;
So fitly them in pairs thou hast combined;
Much less can bird with beast, or fish with fowl,
So well converse, nor with the ox the ape;
Worse then can man with beast, and least of all.
　　Whereto the Almighty answer'd, not displeased.
A nice and subtle happiness I see
Thou to thyself proposest, in the choice
Of thy associates, Adam, and wilt taste
No pleasure, though in pleasure, solitary.
What think'st thou then of me, and this my state?
Seem I to thee sufficiently possest
Of happiness, or not? who am alone
From all eternity; for none I know
Second to me or like, equal much less.
How have I then with whom to hold converse,
Save with the creatures which I made, and those
To me inferior, infinite descents
Beneath what other creatures are to thee?
　　He ceased, I lowly answer'd. To attain
The highth and depth of thy eternal ways
All human thoughts come short, Supreme of things,
Thou in thyself art perfect, and in thee
Is no deficience found: not so is man,
But in degree, the cause of his desire
By conversation with his like to help,
Or solace his defects. No need that thou
Should'st propagate, already infinite,
And through all numbers absolute, though one.
But man by number is to manifest
His single imperfection, and beget
Like of his like, his image multiplied,
In unity defective, which requires
Collateral love, and dearest amity.
Thou in thy secrecy although alone,
Best with thyself accompanied, seek'st not
Social communication; yet so pleased

Canst raise thy creature to what highth thou wilt
Of union or communion, deified;
I by conversing cannot these erect
From prone, nor in their ways complacence find.
Thus I embolden'd spake, and freedom used
Permissive and acceptance found; which gain'd
This answer from the gracious Voice Divine.

Thus far to try thee, Adam, I was pleased,
And find thee knowing not of beasts alone,
Which thou hast rightly named, but of thyself,
Expressing well the spirit within thee free,
My image, not imparted to the brute;
Whose fellowship therefore unmeet for thee
Good reason was thou freely should'st dislike
And be so minded still: I, ere thou spak'st,
Knew it not good for man to be alone,
And no such company as then thou saw'st
Intended thee, for trial only brought,
To see how thou could'st judge of fit and meet.
What next I bring shall please thee, be assured,
Thy likeness, thy fit help, thy other self,
Thy wish exactly to thy heart's desire.

He ended, or I heard no more; for now
My earthly by His heav'nly overpower'd,
Which it had long stood under, strain'd to the highth
In that celestial colloquy sublime,
As with an object that excels the sense,
Dazzled, and spent, sunk down, and sought repair
Of sleep, which instantly fell on me, call'd
By nature as in aid, and closed mine eyes.[1]
Mine eyes He closed, but open left the cell
Of fancy my internal sight, by which
Abstract as in a trance methought I saw,
Though sleeping, where I lay, and saw the shape
Still glorious before whom awake I stood;
Who stooping open'd my left side, and took
From thence a rib, with cordial spirits warm,
And life-blood streaming fresh; wide was the wound,
But suddenly with flesh fill'd up and heal'd.
The rib he form'd and fashion'd with His hands;
Under His forming hands a creature grew

[1] Gen. ii. 21.

Manlike, but different sex, so lovely fair,
That what seem'd fair in all the world, seem'd now
Mean, or in her summ'd up, in her contain'd
And in her looks, which from that time infused
Sweetness into my heart, unfelt before,
And into all things from her air inspired
The spirit of love and amorous delight.
She disappear'd, and left me dark, I waked
To find her, or for ever to deplore
Her loss, and other pleasures all abjure.
When out of hope, behold her, not far off,
Such as I saw her in my dream, adorn'd
With what all earth or heaven could bestow
To make her amiable: on she came,
Led by her heav'nly Maker, though unseen,
And guided by his voice, nor uninform'd
Of nuptial sanctity and marriage rites:
Grace was in all her steps, heav'n in her eye,
In every gesture dignity and love.
I overjoy'd could not forbear aloud.
    This turn hath made amends; thou hast fulfill'd
Thy words, Creator bounteous and benign,
Giver of all things fair, but fairest this
Of all thy gifts, nor enviest. I now see
Bone of my bone, flesh of my flesh, myself
Before me; woman is her name, of man
Extracted; for this cause he shall forego
Father and mother, and to his wife adhere;
And they shall be one flesh, one heart, one soul.
    She heard me thus, and though divinely brought.
Yet innocence and virgin modesty,
Her virtue and the conscience of her worth,
That would be woo'd, and not unsought be won,
Not obvious, not obtrusive, but retired,
The more desirable, or to say all,
Nature herself, though pure of sinful thought,
Wrought in her so, that seeing me she turn'd;
I follow'd her, she what was honor knew.
And with obsequious majesty approved
My pleaded reason. To the nuptial bow'r
I led her blushing like the morn: all heav'n,
And happy constellations on that hour

Shed their selectest influence; the earth
Gave sign of gratulation, and each hill;
Joyous the birds; fresh gales and gentle airs
Whisper'd it to the woods, and from their wings
Flung rose, flung odors from the spicy shrub,
Disporting, till the amorous bird of night
Sung spousal, and bid haste the ev'ning star
On his hill top to light the bridal lamp.

    Thus I have told thee all my state, and brought
My story to the sum of earthly bliss,
Which I enjoy, and must confess to find
In all things else delight indeed, but such
As, used or not, works in the mind no change,
Nor vehement desire; these delicacies
I mean of taste, sight, smell, herbs, fruits, and flow'rs,
Walks, and the melody of birds: but here
Far otherwise, transported I behold,
Transported touch; here passion first I felt,
Commotion strange, in all enjoyments else
Superior and unmoved, here only weak
Against the charm of beauty's powerful glance.
Or nature fail'd in me, and left some part
Not proof enough such object to sustain,
Or from my side subducting took perhaps
More than enough; at least on her bestow'd
Too much of ornament, in outward show
Elaborate, of inward less exact.
For well I understand in the prime end
Of nature her th' inferior, in the mind
And inward faculties, which most excel,
In outward also her resembling less
His image who made both, and less expressing
The character of that dominion giv'n
O'er other creatures: yet when I approach
Her loveliness, so absolute she seems
And in herself complete, so well to know
Her own, that what she wills to do or say
Seems wisest, virtuousest, discreetest, best:
All higher knowledge in her presence falls
Degraded, wisdom in discourse with her
Loses discountenanced, and like folly shows:
Authority and reason on her wait,

As one intended first, not after made
Occasionally; and, to consummate all,
Greatness of mind and nobleness their seat
Build in her loveliest, and create an awe
About her, as a guard angelic placed.
 To whom the angel with contracted brow.
Accuse not nature, she hath done her part;
Do thou but thine, and be not diffident
Of wisdom; she deserts thee not, if thou
Dismiss not her, when most thou need'st her nigh,
By attributing overmuch to things
Less excellent, as thou thyself perceiv'st.
For what admir'st thou, what transports thee so?
An outside? fair no doubt, and worthy well
Thy cherishing, thy honoring, and thy love,
Not thy subjection: weigh with her thyself;
Then value: oft times nothing profits more
Than self-esteem, grounded on just and right
Well managed: of that skill the more thou know'st,
The more she will acknowledge thee her head,
And to realities yield all her shows;
Made so adorn for thy delight the more,
So awful, that with honor thou may'st love
Thy mate, who sees when thou art seen least wise
But if the sense of touch whereby mankind
Is propagated seem such dear delight
Beyond all other, think the same vouchsafed
To cattle and each beast; which would not be
To them made common and divulged, if aught
Therein enjoy'd were worthy to subdue
The soul of man, or passion in him move.
What higher in her society thou find'st
Attractive, human, rational, love still:
In loving thou dost well, in passion not,
Wherein true love consists not: love refines
The thoughts, and heart enlarges: hath his seat
In reason, and is judicious; is the scale
By which to heav'nly love thou may'st ascend,
Not sunk in carnal pleasure; for which cause
Among the beasts no mate for thee was found.
 To whom thus half abash'd Adam replied.

Neither her outside form'd so fair, nor aught
In procreation common to all kinds,
(Though higher of the genial bed by far
And with mysterious reverence I deem,)
So much delights me, as those graceful acts,
Those thousand decencies that daily flow
From all her words and actions, mix'd with love
And sweet compliance, which declare unfeign'd
Union of mind, or in us both one soul;
Harmony to behold in wedded pair,
More grateful than harmonious sound to the ear.
Yet these subject not; I to thee disclose
What inward thence I feel, not therefore foil'd,
Who meet with various objects, for the sense
Variously representing; yet still free
Approve the best, and follow what I approve.
To love thou blam'st me not, for love thou say'st
Leads up to heav'n, is both the way and guide;
Bear with me then, if lawful what I ask:
Love not the heav'nly spirts, and how their love
Express they? by looks only? or do they mix
Irradiance, virtual or immediate touch?

   To whom the angel with a smile that glow'd
Celestial rosy red, love's proper hue,
Answer'd. Let it suffice thee that thou know'st
Us happy, and without love no happiness.
Whatever pure thou in the body enjoy'st,
(And pure thou wert created,) we enjoy
In eminence, and obstacle find none
Of membrane, joint, or limb, exclusive bars:
Easier than air with air, if spirits embrace,
Total they mix, union of pure with pure
Desiring; nor restrain'd conveyance need
As flesh to mix with flesh, or soul with soul.
But I can now no more; the parting sun
Beyond the earth's green Cape and Verdant Isles,[1]
Hesperean[2] sets, my signal to depart.
Be strong, live happy, and love, but first of all

[1] Cape de Verde and the Cape de Verde Islands.
[2] In the West, where Hesperus, the evening star, appears.—*From* NEWTON.

Him whom to love is to obey,[1] and keep
His great command; take heed lest passion sway
Thy judgment to do aught, which else free will
Would not admit; thine and of all thy sons
The weal or woe in thee is placed; beware.
I in thy persevering shall rejoice,
And all the blest: stand fast; to stand or fáll
Free in thine own arbitrement it lies;
Perfect within, no outward aid require,
And all temptation to transgress repel.

  So saying, he arose; whom Adam thus
Follow'd with benediction. Since to part,
Go, heavenly guest, ethereal messenger,
Sent from whose sov'reign goodness I adore.
Gentle to me and affable hath been
Thy condescension, and shall be honor'd ever
With grateful memory: thou to mankind
Be good and friendly still, and oft return.

  So parted they, the angel up to heav'n
From the thick shade, and Adam to his bower.

[1] 1 John v. 3.

BOOK IX

The Argument

Satan having compassed the earth, with meditated guile returns as a mist by night into paradise, and enters into the serpent sleeping. Adam and Eve in the morning go forth to their labors, which Eve proposes to divide in several places, each laboring apart: Adam consents not, alleging the danger, lest that enemy, of whom they were forewarned, should attempt her found alone: Eve, loth to be thought not circumspect or firm enough, urges her going apart, the rather desirous to make trial of her strength: Adam at last yields: the serpent finds her alone; his subtle approach, first gazing, then speaking, with much flattery extolling Eve above all other creatures. Eve, wondering to hear the serpent speak, asks how he attained to human speech and such understanding not till now; the serpent answers, that by tasting of a certain tree in the garden he attained both to speech and reason, till then void of both: Eve requires him to bring her to that tree, and finds it to be the Tree of Knowledge forbidden; the serpent, now grown bolder, with many wiles and arguments induces her at length to eat: she, pleased with the taste, deliberates a while whether to impart thereof to Adam, or not; at last brings him of the fruit, relates what persuaded her to eat thereof: Adam at first amazed, but perceiving her lost, resolves, through vehemence of love, to perish with her, and extenuating the trespass eats also of the fruit: the effects thereof in them both: they seek to cover their nakedness: then fall to variance and accusation of one another.

No more of talk where GOD or Angel guest
With man, as with his friend, familiar used
To sit indulgent, and with him partake
Rural repast, permitting him the while
Venial discourse unblamed; I now must change
These notes to tragic; foul distrust, and breach
Disloyal on the part of man, revolt,
And disobedience: on the part of heav'n
Now alienated, distance and distaste,
Anger, and just rebuke, and judgment giv'n,

That brought into this world a world of woe;
Sin and her shadow Death, and misery
Death's harbinger; sad task, yet argument
Not less but more heroic than the wrath
Of stern Achilles on his foe[1] pursued
Thrice fugitive about Troy wall; or rage
Of Turnus for Lavinia disespoused,[2]
Or Neptune's ire or Juno's, that so long
Perplex'd the Greek[3] and Cytherea's son:[4]
If answerable style I can obtain
Of my celestial patroness, who deigns
Her nightly visitation unimplored,
And dictates to me slumb'ring, or inspires
Easy my unpremeditated verse:
Since first this subject for heroic song
Pleased me, long choosing and beginning late,[5]
Not sedulous by nature to indite
Wars, hitherto the only argument
Heroic deem'd, chief mast'ry to dissect
With long and tedious havock fabled knights
In battles feign'd; the better fortitude
Of patience and heroic martyrdom
Unsung; or to describe races and games,
Or tilting furniture, emblazon'd shields,
Impresses quaint,[6] caparisons and steeds;
Bases[7] and tinsel trappings, gorgeous knights
At joust and tournament; then marshall'd feast
Served up in hall with sewers, and seneshals;
The skill of artifice or office mean,
Not that which justly gives heroic name
To person or to poem. Me of these
Nor skill'd nor studious higher argument
Remains, sufficient of itself to raise
That name, unless an age too late, or cold

[1] Hector. See *Iliad*.
[2] See *Æneid*.
[3] Ulysses.
[4] Eneas.
[5] Milton is supposed to have begun his great poem in his forty-eighth year, and finished it in his fifty-seventh. It was published in 1667, when the Poet was in his sixtieth year.
[6] Devices on shields.
[7] The mantles worn by knights.

Climate, or years, damp my intended wing
Depress'd, and much they may, if all be mine,
Not hers who brings it nightly to my ear.

    The sun was sunk, and after him the star
Of Hesperus, whose office is to bring
Twilight upon the earth, short arbiter
'Twixt day and night, and now from end to end
Night's hemisphere had veil'd the horizon round:
When Satan who late fled before the threats
Of Gabriel out of Eden, now improved
In meditated fraud and malice, bent
On man's destruction, maugre what might hap
Of heavier on himself, fearless return'd.
By night he fled, and at midnight return'd
From compassing the earth, cautious of day,
Since Uriel regent of the sun descried
His entrance, and forewarn'd the Cherubim
That kept their watch; thence full of anguish driv'n,
The space of seven continued nights he rode
With darkness, thrice the equinoctial line
He circled, four times cross'd the car of night,
From pole to pole, traversing each colure;[1]
On the eighth return'd, and on the coast averse
From entrance or Cherubic watch by stealth
Found unsuspected way. There was a place,
Now not, though sin, not time, first wrought the change,
Where Tigris at the foot of paradise
Into a gulf shot under ground, till part
Rose up a fountain by the Tree of Life:
In with the river sunk, and with it rose
Satan involved in rising mist, then sought
Where to lie hid: sea he had search'd, and land
From Eden over Pontus,[2] and the pool
Mæotis, up beyond the river Ob;[3]
Downward as far Antartic; and in length
West from Orontes[4] to the ocean barr'd

---

[1] The colures are two great imaginary circles encompassing the globe from north to south. Satan moved thus to keep in the shades of night.—*From* NEWTON.

[2] The Euxine, or Black Sea.

[3] Oby, a river of Siberia, near the pole.

[4] A river of Syria.

At Darien:[1] thence to the land where flows
Ganges and Indus:[2] thus the orb he roam'd
With narrow search; and with inspection deep
Consider'd every creature, which of all
Most opportune might serve his wiles, and found
The serpent subtlest beast of all the field.[3]
Him after long debate, irresolute
Of thoughts revolved, his final sentence chose
Fit vessel, fittest imp of fraud, in whom
To enter, and his dark suggestions hide
From sharpest sight: for in the wily snake
Whatever sleights none would suspicious mark,
As from his wit and native subtlety
Proceeding, which in other beast observed
Doubt might beget of diabolic pow'r
Active within beyond the sense of brute.
Thus he resolved, but first from inward grief
His bursting passion into plaints thus pour'd.

O earth, how like to heav'n, if not preferr'd
More justly; seat worthier of gods, as built
With second thoughts, reforming what was old!
For what GOD after better worse would build?
Terrestrial heav'n, danced round by other heav'ns
That shine, yet bear their bright officious lamps,
Light above light, for thee alone, as seems,
In thee concentring all their precious beams
Of sacred influence. As GOD in heav'n
Is centre, yet extends to all, so thou
Centring receiv'st from all those orbs: in thee,
Not in themselves, all their known virtue appears
Productive in herb, plant, and nobler birth
Of creatures animate with gradual life
Of growth, sense, reason, all summ'd up in man.
With what delight could I have walk'd thee round,
If I could joy in aught, sweet interchange
Of hill and valley, rivers, woods, and plains,
Now land, now sea, and shores with forest crown'd,
Rocks, dens, and caves! but I in none of these
Find place or refuge; and the more I see

[1] The Isthmus of Panama.
[2] India.
[3] Gen. iii. 1.

Pleasures about me, so much more I feel
Torment within me, as from the hateful siege
Of contraries; all good to me becomes
Bane, and in heav'n much worse would be my state.
But neither here seek I, no nor in heav'n
To dwell, unless by mast'ring heav'n's Supreme;
Nor hope to be myself less miserable
By what I seek, but others to make such
As I, though thereby worse to me redound:
For only in destroying I find ease
To my relentless thoughts; and him destroy'd,
Or won to what may work his utter loss,
For whom all this was made, all this will soon
Follow, as him link'd in weal or woe;
In woe then; that destruction wide may range.
To me shall be the glory sole among
The infernal powers, in one day to have marr'd
What He, Almighty styled, six nights and days
Continued making, and who knows how long
Before had been contriving, though perhaps
Not longer than since I in one night freed
From servitude inglorious well nigh half
Th' angelic name, and thinner left the throng
Of His adorers. He to be avenged,
And to repair His numbers thus impair'd,
Whether such virtue spent of old now fail'd
More angels to create, if they at least
Are His created, or to spite us more,
Determined to advance into our room
A creature form'd of earth, and him endow,
Exalted from so base original,
With heav'nly spoils, our spoils: what he decreed
He effected; man he made, and for him built
Magnificent this world, and earth his seat,
Him lord pronounced, and, O indignity!
Subjected to his service angel wings,[1]
And flaming ministers, to watch and tend
Their earthly charge. Of these the vigilance
I dread, and to elude, thus wrapp'd in mist
Of midnight vapor, glide obscure, and pry
In every bush and brake, where hap may find

[1] Psalm civ. 4.

The serpent sleeping, in whose mazy folds
To hide me, and the dark intent I bring.
O foul descent! that I, who erst contended
With Gods to sit the highest, am now constrain'd
Into a beast, and mix'd with bestial slime,
This essence to incarnate and imbrute,
That to the highth of deity aspired;
But what will not ambition and revenge
Descend to? who aspires must down as low
As high he soar'd, obnoxious first or last
To basest things. Revenge, at first though sweet,
Bitter ere long, back on itself recoils:
Let it; I reck not, so it light well aim'd,
Since higher I fall short, on him who next
Provokes my envy, this new favorite
Of heav'n, this man of clay, son of despite,
Whom us the more to spite his Maker raised
From dust: spite then with spite is best repaid.

So saying, through each thicket dank or dry,
Like a black mist low creeping he held on
His midnight search, where soonest he might find
The serpent: him fast sleeping soon he found,
In labyrinth of many a round self-roll'd,
His head the midst, well stored with subtle wiles:
Not yet in horrid shade or dismal den,
Nor nocent yet, but on the grassy herb,
Fearless, unfear'd he slept. In at his mouth
The devil enter'd, and his brutal sense,
In heart or head, possessing soon inspired
With act intelligential; but his sleep
Disturb'd not, waiting close th' approach of morn.

Now, when as sacred light began to dawn
In Eden on the humid flow'rs, that breathed
Their morning incense, when all things that breathe
From th' earth's great altar send up silent praise
To the Creator and His nostrils fill
With grateful smell, forth came the human pair,
And join'd their vocal worship to the choir
Of creatures wanting voice; that done partake
The season, prime for sweetest scents and airs:
Then commune, how that day they best may ply
Their growing work; for much their work outgrew

The hands' dispatch of two, gard'ning so wide.
And Eve first to her husband thus began.

   Adam, well may we labor still to dress
This garden, still to tend plant, herb, and flow'r,
Our pleasant task enjoin'd; but till more hands
Aid us, the work under our labor grows,
Luxurious by restraint; what we by day
Lop overgrown, or prune, or prop, or bind,
One night or two with wanton growth derides,
Tending to wild. Thou therefore now advise,
Or hear what to my mind first thoughts present;
Let us divide our labors, thou where choice
Leads thee, or where most needs, whether to wind
The woodbine round this arbor, or direct
The clasping ivy where to climb, while I
In yonder spring[1] of roses intermix'd
With myrtle find what to redress till noon:
For while so near each other thus all day
Our task we choose, what wonder if so near
Looks intervene and smiles, or object new
Casual discourse draw on; which intermits
Our day's work, brought to little, though begun
Early, and the hour of supper comes unearn'd.

   To whom mild answer Adam thus return'd.
Sole Eve, associate sole, to me beyond
Compare above all living creatures dear,
Well hast thou motion'd, well thy thoughts employ'd,
How we might best fulfil the work which here
God hath assign'd us, nor of me shall pass
Unpraised; for nothing lovelier can be found
In woman, than to study household good,
And good works in her husband to promote.
Yet not so strictly hath our Lord imposed
Labor, as to debar us when we need
Refreshment, whether food, or talk between,
Food of the mind, or this sweet intercourse
Of looks and smiles; for smiles from reason flow,
To brute denied, and are of love the food,
Love not the lowest end of human life.
For not to irksome toil, but to delight,
He made us, and delight to reason join'd

   [1] A spring is a small coppice or thicket.

These paths and bowers doubt not but our joint hands
Will keep from wilderness with ease, as wide
As we need walk, till younger hands ere long
Assist us: but if much converse perhaps
Thee satiate, to short absence I could yield:
For solitude sometimes is best society,
And short retirement urges sweet return.
But other doubt possesses me, lest harm
Befall thee sever'd from me; for thou know'st
What hath been warn'd us, what malicious foe
Envying our happiness, and of his own
Despairing, seeks to work us woe and shame
By sly assault; and somewhere nigh at hand
Watches, no doubt, with greedy hope to find
His wish and best advantage, us asunder,
Hopeless to circumvent us join'd, where each
To other speedy aid might lend at need:[1]
Whether his first design be to withdraw
Our fealty from God, or to disturb
Conjugal love, than which perhaps no bliss
Enjoy'd by us excites his envy more;
Or this, or worse, leave not the faithful side
That gave thee being, still shades thee and protects.
The wife, where danger or dishonor lurks,
Safest and seemliest by her husband stays,
Who guards her, or with her the worst endures.

To whom the virgin majesty of Eve,
As one who loves, and some unkindness meets,
With sweet austere composure thus replied.

Offspring of heav'n and earth, and all earth's lord,
That such an enemy we have, who seeks
Our ruin, both by thee inform'd I learn,
And from the parting angel overheard,
As in a shady nook I stood behind,
Just then return'd at shut of evening flow'rs.
But that thou shouldst my firmness therefore doubt
To God or thee, because we have a foe
May tempt it, I expected not to hear.
His violence thou fear'st not, being such,
As we, not capable of death or pain,
Can either not receive, or can repel.

[1] Eccles. iv. 9, 10.

His fraud is then thy fear, which plain infers
Thy equal fear, that my firm faith and love
Can by his fraud be shaken or seduced:
Thoughts, which how found they harbor in thy breast,
Adam, misthought of her to thee so dear?
   To whom with healing words Adam replied.
Daughter of God and man, immortal Eve,
For such thou art, from sin and blame entire:
Not diffident of thee do I dissuade
Thy absence from my sight, but to avoid
Th' attempt itself, intended by our foe:
For he who tempts, though in vain, at least asperses
The tempted with dishonor foul, supposed
Not incorruptible of faith, not proof
Against temptation. Thou thyself with scorn
And anger wouldst resent the offer'd wrong,
Though ineffectual found: misdeem not then,
If such affront I labor to avert
From thee alone, which on us both at once
The enemy, though bold, will hardly dare,
Or daring, first on me th' assault shall light.
Nor thou his malice and false guile contemn;
Subtle he needs must be, who could seduce
Angels; nor think superfluous others' aid.
I from the influence of thy looks receive
Access in every virtue, in thy sight
More wise, more watchful, stronger, if need were
Of outward strength; while shame, thou looking on,
Shame to be overcome or over-reach'd,
Would utmost vigor raise, and raised unite.
Why shouldst not thou like sense within thee feel
When I am present, and thy trial choose
With me, best witness of thy virtue tried?
   So spake domestic Adam in his care
And matrimonial love; but Eve, who thought
Less attributed to her faith sincere,
Thus her reply with accent sweet renew'd.
   If this be our condition, thus to dwell
In narrow circuit straiten'd by a foe,
Subtle or violent, we not endued
Single with like defence, wherever met,
How are we happy, still in fear of harm?

But harm precedes not sin: only our foe
Tempting affronts us with his foul esteem
Of our integrity: his foul esteem
Sticks no dishonor on our front, but turns
Foul on himself; then wherefore shunn'd or fear'd
By us? who rather double honor gain
From his surmise proved false, find peace within,
Favor from heav'n, our witness, from th' event.
And what is faith, love, virtue, unassay'd
Alone, without exterior help sustain'd?
Let us not then suspect our happy state
Left so imperfect by the Maker wise,
As not secure to single or combined.
Frail is our happiness, if this be so,
And Eden were no Eden thus exposed.
　To whom thus Adam fervently replied.
O woman, best are all things as the will
Of God ordain'd them; His creating hand
Nothing imperfect or deficient left
Of all that He created, much less man,
Or aught that might his happy state secure,
Secure from outward force; within himself
The danger lies, yet lies within his power:
Against his will he can receive no harm.
But God left free the will, for what obeys
Reason is free, and reason He made right;
But bid her well beware, and still erect,
Lest by some fair appearing good surprized
She dictate false, and misinform the will
To do what God expressly hath forbid.
Not then mistrust, but tender love enjoins,
That I should mind thee oft, and mind thou me.
Firm we subsist, yet possible to swerve,
Since reason not impossibly may meet
Some specious object by the foe suborn'd,
And fall into deception unaware,
Not keeping strictest watch, as she was warn'd.
Seek not temptation then, which to avoid
Were better, and most likely, if from me
Thou sever not: trial will come unsought.
Wouldst thou approve thy constancy, approve

First thy obedience; th' other who can know?
Not seeing thee attempted, who attest?
But if thou think trial unsought may find
Us both securer than thus warn'd thou seem'st,
Go; for thy stay, not free, absents thee more;
Go in thy native innocence, rely
On what thou hast of virtue, summon all,
For GOD towards thee hath done His part, do thine.

    So spake the patriarch of mankind, but Eve
Persisted, yet submiss, though last, replied.

    With thy permission then, and thus forewarn'd,
Chiefly by what thy own last reasoning words
Touch'd only, that our trial, when least sought,
May find us both perhaps far less prepared,
The willinger I go, nor much expect
A foe so proud will first the weaker seek;
So bent, the more shall shame him his repulse.

    Thus saying, from her husband's hand her hand
Soft she withdrew; and like a wood-nymph light,
Oread or Dryad, or of Delia's[1] train,
Betook her to the groves, but Delia's self
In gait surpass'd and goddess-like deport,
Though not as she with bow and quiver arm'd,
But with such gard'ning tools as art, yet rude,
Guiltless of fire had form'd, or angels brought,
To Pales,[2] or Pomona,[3] thus adorn'd,
Likest she seem'd Pomona when she fled
Vertumnus,[4] or to Ceres in her prime,
Yet virgin of Proserpina from Jove.
Her long with ardent look his eye pursued
Delighted, but desiring more her stay:
Oft he to her his charge of quick return
Repeated, she to him as oft engaged
To be return'd by noon amid the bow'r,
And all things in best order to invite
Noontide repast, or afternoon's repose.

[1] A surname of Diana, because born in Delos.
[2] Goddess of sheepfolds.
[3] Goddess of fruits.
[4] The god of orchards, who assumed many shapes to win Pomona.

O much deceived, much failing, hapless Eve,
Of thy presumed return! event perverse!
Thou never from that hour in paradise
Found'st either sweet repast, or sound repose;
Such ambush hid among sweet flow'rs and shades
Waited with hellish rancor imminent
To intercept thy way, or send thee back
Despoil'd of innocence, of faith, of bliss.
For now, and since first break of dawn the fiend,
Mere serpent in appearance, forth was come,
And on his quest, where likeliest he might find
The only two of mankind, but in them
The whole included race, his purposed prey.
In bow'r and field he sought, where any tuft
Of grove or garden-plot more pleasant lay
Their tendance or plantation for delight,
By fountain or by shady rivulet
He sought them both, but wish'd his hap might find
Eve separate; he wish'd, but not with hope
Of what so seldom chanced, when to his wish,
Beyond his hope, Eve separate he spies,
Veil'd in a cloud of fragrance, where she stood,
Half spied, so thick the roses brushing round
About her glow'd, oft stooping to support
Each flow'r of slender stalk, whose head though gay
Carnation, purple, azure, or speck'd with gold,
Hung drooping unsustain'd; them she upstays
Gently with myrtle band, mindless the while
Herself, though fairest unsupported flow'r,
From her best prop so far, and storm so nigh.
Nearer he drew, and many a walk traversed
Of stateliest covert, cedar, pine, or palm,
Then voluble and bold, now hid, now seen
Among thick-woven arborets and flow'rs
Imborder'd on each bank, the hand of Eve:
Spot more delicious than those gardens feign'd
Or of revived Adonis,[1] or renown'd
Alcinous, host of old Laertes' son,[2]
Or that, not mystic, where the Sapient king

[1] At the request of Venus, he was restored to life.
[2] Ulysses. For description of the gardens of Alcinous see the "Odyssey."

Held dalliance with his fair Egyptian spouse.[1]
Much he the place admired, the person more.
As one who long in populous city pent
Where houses thick and sewers annoy the air,
Forth issuing on a summer's morn to breathe
Among the pleasant villages and farms
Adjoin'd, from each thing met conceives delight,
The smell of grain, or tedded grass,[2] or kine,
Or dairy, each rural sight, each rural sound;
If chance with nymph-like step fair virgin pass,
What pleasing seem'd, for her now pleases more,
She most, and in her look sums all delight:
Such pleasure took the serpent to behold
This flow'ry plat, the sweet recess of Eve
Thus early, thus alone: her heav'nly form
Angelic, but more soft and feminine,
Her graceful innocence, her every air
Of gesture or least action, over awed
His malice, and with rapine sweet bereaved
His fierceness of the fierce intent it brought
That space the evil one abstracted stood
From his own evil, and for the time remain'd
Stupidly good, of enmity disarm'd,
Of guile, of hate, of envy, of revenge;
But the hot hell that always in him burns,
Though in mid heav'n, soon ended his delight,
And tortures him now more, the more he sees
Of pleasure not for him ordain'd: then soon
Fierce hate he recollects, and all his thoughts
Of mischief, gratulating, thus excites.

Thoughts, whither have ye led me, with what sweet
Compulsion thus transported to forget
What hither brought us? hate, not love, nor hope
Of paradise for hell, hope here to taste
Of pleasure, but all pleasure to destroy,
Save what is in destroying: other joy
To me is lost. Then let me not let pass
Occasion which now smiles; behold alone
The woman opportune to all attempts,
Her husband, (for I view far round,) not nigh,

[1] Gardens of Solomon.
[2] Hay spread out.

Whose higher intellectual more I shun,
And strength, of courage haughty, and of limb
Heroic built, though of terrestrial mould;
Foe not informidable! exempt from wound,
I not: so much hath hell debased, and pain
Infeebled me, to what I was in heav'n.
She fair, divinely fair, fit love for gods,
Not terrible, though terror be in love,
And beauty, not approach'd by stronger hate,
Hate stronger under show of love well feign'd;
The way which to her ruin now I tend.

So spake the enemy of mankind, enclosed
In serpent, inmate bad, and toward Eve
Address'd his way, not with indented wave,
Prone on the ground, as since, but on his rear,
Circular base of rising folds, that tower'd
Fold above fold a surging maze, his head
Crested aloft, and carbuncle his eyes;
With burnish'd neck of verdant gold, erect
Amidst his circling spires, that on the grass
Floated redundant: pleasing was his shape,
And lovely, never since of serpent kind
Lovelier, not those that in Illyria changed
Hermione and Cadmus,[1] or the God [2]
In Epidaurus; nor to which transform'd
Ammonian[3] Jove or Capitoline[4] was seen.
He with Olympias, this with her who bore
Scipio the highth of Rome. With tract oblique
At first, as one who sought access, but fear'd
To interrupt, side-long he works his way.
As when a ship by skillful steersman wrought
Nigh river's mouth or foreland, where the wind
Veers oft, as oft so steers, and shifts her sail:
So varied he, and of his tortuous train

[1] Cadmus, who introduced letters into Greece, and Hermione his
wife. They were changed by serpents into serpents.

[2] Esculapius, the god of medicine. He is said to have taken the
form of a serpent when he appeared at Rome during a pestilence.
—*From* WARTON.

[3] Lybian.

[4] Roman. These lines relate to the fable of Jupiter being the
father of Alexander the Great, and of Scipio also. All these images
picture the magnificence of the serpent's form.

Curl'd many a wanton wreath in sight of Eve,
To lure her eye; she, busied, heard the sound
Of rustling leaves, but minded not as used
To such disport before her through the field,
From every beast, more duteous at her call,
Than at Circean call the herd disguised.
He bolder now uncall'd before her stood;
But as in gaze admiring: oft he bow'd
His turret crest, and sleek enamell'd neck,
Fawning, and lick'd the ground whereon she trod.
His gentle dumb expression turn'd at length
The eye of Eve to mark his play; he glad
Of her attention gain'd, with serpent tongue
Organic, or impulse of vocal air,
His fraudulent temptation thus began.

    Wonder not, sov'reign mistress, if perhaps
Thou canst, who art sole wonder, much less arm
Thy looks, the heav'n of mildness, with disdain,
Displeased that I approach thee thus, and gaze
Insatiate, I thus single, nor have fear'd
Thy awful brow, more awful thus retired.
Fairest resemblance of thy Maker fair,
Thee all things living gaze on, all things thine
By gift, and thy celestial beauty adore
With ravishment beheld, there best beheld
Where universally admired: but here
In this enclosure wild, these beasts among,
Beholders rude, and shallow to discern
Half what in thee is fair, one man except,
Who sees thee? and what is one? who shouldst be seen
A Goddess among Gods, adored and served
By angels numberless, thy daily train.

    So glozed the tempter, and his proem tuned;
Into the heart of Eve his words made way,
Though at the voice much marvelling: at length
Not unamazed she thus in answer spake.
What may this mean? Language of man pronounced
By tongue of brute, and human sense express'd?
The first at least of these I thought denied
To beasts, whom GOD on their creation-day
Created mute to all articulate sound;
The latter I demur, for in their looks

Much reason, and in their actions, oft appears.
Thee, serpent, subtlest beast of all the field
I knew, but not with human voice endued;
Redouble then this miracle, and say,
How cam'st thou speakable of mute, and how
To me so friendly grown above the rest
Of brutal kind, that daily are in sight?
Say, for such wonder claims attention due.
     To whom the guileful tempter thus replied.
Empress of this fair world, resplendent Eve,
Easy to me it is to tell thee all
What thou command'st, and right thou shouldst be
          obey'd.
I was at first as other beasts that graze
The trodden herb, of abject thoughts and low,
As was my food, nor aught but food discern'd
Or sex, and apprehended nothing high:
Till on a day roving the field, I chanced
A goodly tree far distant to behold
Loaden with fruit of fairest colors mixt,
Ruddy and gold: I nearer drew to gaze;
When from the boughs a savory odor blown,
Grateful to appetite, more pleased my sense
Than smell of sweetest fennel, or the teats
Of ewe or goat dropping with milk at ev'n,
Unsuck'd of lamb or kid, that tend their play.
To satisfy the sharp desire I had
Of tasting those fair apples, I resolved
Not to defer; hunger and thirst at once,
Powerful persuaders, quicken'd at the scent
Of that alluring fruit, urged me so keen.
About the mossy trunk I wound me soon,
For high from ground the branches would require
Thy utmost reach or Adam's: round the tree
All other beasts that saw with like desire,
Longing and envying, stood, but could not reach.
Amid the tree now got, where plenty hung
Tempting so nigh, to pluck and eat my fill
I spared not, for such pleasure till that hour
At feed or fountain never had I found.
Sated at length, ere long I might perceive
Strange alteration in me, to degree

Of reason in my inward powers and speech
Wanted not long, though to this shape retain'd.
Thenceforth to speculations high or deep
I turn'd my thoughts, and with capacious mind
Consider'd all things visible in heav'n,
Or earth, or middle, all things fair and good;
But all that fair and good in thy divine
Semblance and in thy beauty's heav'nly ray
United I beheld; no fair to thine
Equivalent or second, which compell'd
Me thus, though importune perhaps, to come
And gaze, and worship thee of right declared
Sov'reign of creatures, universal dame.

   So talk'd the spirited sly snake; and Eve
Yet more amazed unwary thus replied.

   Serpent, thy overpraising leaves in doubt
The virtue of that fruit, in thee first proved:
But say, where grows the tree? from hence how far?
For many are the trees of God that grow
In paradise, and various, yet unknown
To us, in such abundance lies our choice,
As leaves a greater store of fruit untouch'd,
Still hanging incorruptible, till men
Grow up to their provision, and more hands
Help to disburden nature of her birth.

   To whom the wily adder, blithe and glad.
Empress; the way is ready, and not long,
Beyond a row of myrtles on a flat,
Fast by a fountain, one small thicket past
Of blowing myrrh and balm: if thou accept
My conduct, I can bring thee hither soon.

   Lead then, said Eve. He leading swiftly roll'd
In tangles, and made intricate seem straight,
To mischief swift: hope elevates, and joy
Brightens his crest: as when a wand'ring fire
Compact of unctuous vapor, which the night
Condenses, and the cold environs round,
Kindled through agitation to a flame,
Which oft, they say, some evil spirit attends,
Hovering and blazing with delusive light,
Misleads th' amazed night-wanderer from his way
To bogs and mires, and oft through pond or pool,

There swallow'd up and lost, from succor far:
So glister'd the dire snake, and into fraud
Led Eve our credulous mother to the tree
Of prohibition, root of all our woe:
Which when she saw, thus to her guide she spake.

    Serpent, we might have spared our coming hither,
Fruitless to me, though fruit be here to excess,
The credit of whose virtue rest with thee;
Wond'rous indeed, if cause of such effects.
But of this tree we may not taste nor touch,
GOD so commanded; and left that command
Sole daughter of his voice; the rest, we live
Law to ourselves, our reason is our law.

    To whom the tempter guilefully replied.
Indeed! hath GOD then said that of the fruit
Of all these garden trees ye shall not eat,
Yet lords declared of all in earth or air?

    To whom thus Eve yet sinless. Of the fruit
Of each tree in the garden we may eat,
But of the fruit of this fair tree amidst
The garden, GOD hath said, ye shall not eat
Thereof, nor shall ye touch it, lest ye die.

    She scarce had said, though brief, when now more bold
The tempter, but with show of zeal and love
To man, and indignation at his wrong,
New part puts on, and as to passion moved,
Fluctuates disturb'd, yet comely, and in act
Raised, as of some great matter to begin.
As when of old some orator renown'd
In Athens or free Rome, where eloquence
Flourish'd, since mute, to some great cause address'd
Stood in himself collected, while each part,
Motion, each act won audience ere the tongue;
Sometimes in highth began, as no delay
Of preface brooking through his zeal of right:
So standing, moving, or to highth upgrown,
The tempter all impassion'd thus began.

    O sacred, wise, and wisdom-giving plant,
Mother of science, now I feel thy power
Within me clear, not only to discern
Things in their causes, but to trace the ways
Of highest agents, deem'd however wise.

Queen of this universe! do not believe
Those rigid threats of death; ye shall not die:[1]
How should ye? by the fruit? it gives you life
To knowledge: by the threatener? look on me,
Me who have touch'd and tasted, yet both live,
And life more perfect have attain'd than fate
Meant me, by vent'ring higher than my lot.
Shall that be shut to man, which to the beast
Is open? or will GOD incense His ire
For such a petty trespass, and not praise
Rather your dauntless virtue, whom the pain
Of death denounced, whatever thing death be,
Deterr'd not from achieving what might lead
To happier life, knowledge of good and evil?
Of good, how just? of evil, if what is evil
Be real, why not known, since easier shunn'd?
GOD therefore cannot hurt ye, and be just;
Not just, not GOD; not fear'd then, nor obey'd:
Your fear itself of death removes the fear.
Why then was this forbid? Why but to awe,
Why but to keep ye low and ignorant,
His worshippers; he knows that in the day
Ye eat thereof, your eyes that seem so clear,
Yet are but dim, shall perfectly be then
Open'd and clear'd, and ye shall be as Gods,
Knowing both good and evil, as they know.
That ye should be as Gods, since I as man,
Internal man, is but proportion meet,
I of brute, human, ye of human, Gods.
So shall ye die perhaps, by putting off
Human, to put on Gods: death to be wish'd,
Though threaten'd, which no worse than this can bring.
And what are Gods that man may not become
As they, participating godlike food?
The Gods are first, and that advantage use
On our belief, that all from them proceeds;
I question it, for this fair earth I see,
Warm'd by the sun, producing every kind,
Them nothing: if they all things who enclosed
Knowledge of good and evil in this tree,
That whoso eats thereof forthwith attains

[1] Gen. iii. 4.

Wisdom without their leave? and wherein lies
Th' offence, that man should thus attain to know?
What can your knowledge hurt him, or this tree
Impart against his will if all be his?
Or is it envy; and can envy dwell
In heav'nly breasts? These, these, and many more
Causes import your need of this fair fruit.
Goddess humane, reach then, and freely taste.

   He ended, and his words replete with guile
Into her heart too easy entrance won:
Fix'd on the fruit she gazed, which to behold
Might tempt alone, and in her ears the sound
Yet rung of his persuasive words, impregn'd
With reason, to her seeming, and with truth:
Meanwhile the hour of noon drew on, and waked
An eager appetite, raised by the smell
So savory of that fruit, which with desire,
Inclinable now grown to touch or taste,
Solicited her longing eye; yet first
Pausing a while, thus to herself she mused.

   Great are thy virtues, doubtless, best of fruits,
Though kept from man, and worthy to be admired,
Whose taste, too long forborne, at first assay
Gave elocution to the mute, and taught
The tongue not made for speech to speak thy praise:
Thy praise He also who forbids thy use
Conceals not from us, naming thee the Tree
Of Knowledge, knowledge both of good and evil;
Forbids us then to taste, but His forbidding
Commends thee more, while it infers the good
By thee communicated, and our want:
For good unknown sure is not had, or had
And yet unknown is as not had at all.
In plain then, what forbids He but to know?
Forbids us good, forbids us to be wise?
Such prohibitions bind not. But if death
Bind us with after-bands, what profits then
Our inward freedom? In the day we eat
Of this fair fruit, our doom is, we shall die.
How dies the serpent? he hath eaten and lives,
And knows, and speaks, and reasons, and discerns,

Irrational till then. For us alone
Was death invented? or to us denied
This intellectual food, for beasts reserved?
For beasts it seems: yet that one beast which first
Hath tasted envies not, but brings with joy
The good befall'n him, author unsuspect,
Friendly to man, far from deceit or guile.
What fear I then, rather what know to fear
Under this ignorance of good and evil,
Of GOD or death, of law or penalty?
Here grows the cure of all, this fruit divine,
Fair to the eye, inviting to the taste,
Of virtue to make wise: what hinders then
To reach, and feed at once both body and mind?
  So saying, her rash hand in evil hour
Forth reaching to the fruit, she pluck'd, she eat:
Earth felt the wound, and Nature from her seat
Sighing through all her works gave signs of woe,
That all was lost. Back to the thicket slunk
The guilty serpent, and well might, for Eve
Intent now only on her taste, naught else
Regarded, such delight till then, as seem'd,
In fruit she never tasted, whether true
Or fancied so, through expectation high
Of knowledge; nor was Godhead from her thought.
Greedily she ingorged without restraint,
And knew not eating death: satiate at length,
And highten'd as with wine, jocund and boon,
Thus to herself she pleasingly began.
  O sov'reign, virtuous, precious of all trees
In Paradise, of operation blest
To sapience, hitherto obscured, infamed,
And thy fair fruit let hang, as to no end
Created: but henceforth my early care,
Not without song, each morning, and due praise
Shall tend thee, and the fertile burden ease
Of thy full branches offer'd free to all;
Till dieted by thee I grow mature
In knowledge, as the Gods who all things know;
Though others envy what they cannot give;
For had the gift been theirs it had not here

Thus grown. Experience, next to thee I owe,
Best guide;[1] not following thee I had remain'd
In ignorance; thou open'st wisdom's way,
And giv'st access, though secret she retire,
And I perhaps am secret: heav'n is high,
High and remote to see from thence distinct
Each thing on earth; and other care perhaps
May have diverted from continual watch
Our great Forbidder, safe with all his spies
About him. But to Adam in what sort
Shall I appear? shall I to him make known
As yet my change, and give him to partake
Full happiness with me, or rather not,
But keep the odds of knowledge in my power
Without co-partner? so to add what wants
In female sex, the more to draw his love,
And render me more equal, and perhaps,
A thing not undesirable, sometime
Superior; for inferior who is free?
This may be well: but what if GOD have seen,
And death ensue? then I shall be no more,
And Adam wedded to another Eve
Shall live with her enjoying, I extinct.
A death to think. Confirm'd then I resolve,
Adam shall share with me in bliss or woe:
So dear I love him, that with him all deaths
I could endure; without him live no life.

So saying, from the tree her step she turn'd,
But first low reverence done, as to the power
That dwelt within, whose presence had infused
Into the plant sciential sap, derived
From nectar, drink of Gods. Adam the while,
Waiting desirous her return, had wove
Of choicest flow'rs a garland to adorn
Her tresses, and her rural labors crown,
As reapers oft are wont their harvest queen.
Great joy he promised to his thoughts, and new
Solace in her return, so long delay'd;
Yet oft his heart, divine of something ill,
Misgave him; he the faltering measure felt;
And forth to meet her went, the way she took

[1] The serpent.

That morn when first they parted. By the Tree
Of Knowledge he must pass, there he her met,
Scarce from the tree returning; in her hand
A bough of fairest fruit that downy smiled,
New gather'd, and ambrosial smell diffused.
To him she hasted, in her face excuse
Came prologue, and apology too prompt,
Which with bland words at will she thus address'd.

    Hast thou not wonder'd, Adam, at my stay?
Thee I have miss'd, and thought it long, deprived
Thy presence, agony of love till now
Not felt, nor shall be twice, for never more
Mean I to try, what rash untried I sought,
The pain of absence from thy sight. But strange
Hath been the cause, and wonderful to hear:
This tree is not, as we are told, a tree
Of danger tasted, nor to evil unknown
Op'ning the way, but of divine effect
To open eyes, and make them Gods who taste:
And hath been tasted such. The serpent wise,
Or not restrain'd as we, or not obeying,
Hath eaten of the fruit, and is become
Not dead, as we are threaten'd, but thenceforth
Endued with human voice and human sense,
Reasoning to admiration, and with me
Persuasively hath so prevail'd, that I
Have also tasted, and have also found
Th' effects to correspond; opener mine eyes,
Dim erst, dilated spirits, ampler heart,
And growing up to Godhead; which for thee
Chiefly I sought, without thee can despise.
For bliss, as thou hast part, to me is bliss,
Tedious, unshared with thee, and odious soon.
Thou therefore also taste, that equal lot
May join us, equal joy, as equal love;
Lest thou not tasting, different degree
Disjoin us, and I then too late renounce
Deity for thee, when fate will not permit.

    Thus Eve, with countenance blithe, her story told,
But in her cheek distemper flushing glow'd.
On th' other side, Adam, soon as he heard
The fatal trespass done by Eve, amazed,

Astonied stood and blank, while horror chill
Ran through his veins, and all his joints relax'd;
From his slack hand the garland wreath'd for Eve
Down dropp'd, and all the faded roses shed:
Speechless he stood and pale, till thus at length
First to himself he inward silence broke.

    O fairest of creation, last and best
Of all GOD's works, creature in whom excell'd
Whatever can to sight or thought be form'd,
Holy, divine, good, amiable or sweet!
How art thou lost, how on a sudden lost,
Defaced, deflower'd, and now to death devote!
Rather how hast thou yielded to transgress
The strict forbiddance, how to violate
The sacred fruit forbidden! some cursed fraud
Of enemy hath beguiled thee, yet unknown,
And me with thee hath ruin'd, for with thee
Certain my resolution is to die:
How can I live without thee? how forego
Thy sweet converse and love so dearly join'd,
To live again in these wild woods forlorn?
Should GOD create another Eve, and I
Another rib afford, yet loss of thee
Would never from my heart; no, no, I feel
The link of nature draw me; flesh of flesh,
Bone of my bone thou art, and from thy state
Mine never shall be parted, bliss or woe.

    So having said, as one from sad dismay
Recomforted, and other thoughts disturb'd
Submitting to what seem'd remediless,
Thus in calm mood his words to Eve he turn'd.

    Bold deed thou hast presumed, advent'rous Eve,
And peril great provoked, who thus hast dared,
Had it been only coveting to eye
That sacred fruit, sacred to abstinence,
Much more to taste it under ban to touch.
But past who can recall, or done undo?
Not GOD omnipotent, nor Fate, yet so
Perhaps thou shalt not die, perhaps the fact
Is not so heinous now, foretasted fruit,
Profaned first by the serpent, by him first
Made common and unhallow'd ere our taste;

Nor yet on him found deadly, he yet lives,
Lives, as thou said'st, and gains to live as man,
Higher degree of life, inducement strong
To us, as likely tasting to attain
Proportional ascent, which cannot be
But to be Gods, or angels, demigods.
Nor can I think that GOD, Creator wise,
Though threat'ning, will in earnest so destroy
Us His prime creatures, dignified so high,
Set over all His works, which in our fall,
For us created, needs with us must fail,
Dependent made; so GOD shall uncreate,
Be frustrate, do, undo, and labor lose,
Not well conceived of GOD; who, though His power
Creation could repeat, yet would be loth
Us to abolish, lest the adversary
Triumph and say: Fickle their state whom GOD
Most favors, who can please Him long? Me first
He ruin'd, now mankind; whom will he next?
Matter of scorn, not to be given the foe.
However, I with thee have fix'd my lot,
Certain to undergo like doom; if death
Consort with thee, death is to me as life;
So forcible within my heart I feel
The bond of nature draw me to my own,
My own in thee, for what thou art is mine;
Our state cannot be sever'd, we are one,
One flesh; to lose thee were to lose myself.
  So Adam, and thus Eve to him replied.
O glorious trial of exceeding love,
Illustrious evidence, example high,
Engaging me to emulate, but, short
Of thy perfection, how shall I attain,
Adam, from whose dear side I boast me sprung,
And gladly of our union hear thee speak,
One heart, one soul in both; whereof good proof
This day affords, declaring thee resolved,
Rather than death or aught than death more dread
Shall separate us link'd in love so dear,
To undergo with me one guilt, one crime,
If any be, of tasting this fair fruit,
Whose virtue, for of good still good proceeds.

Direct, or by occasion, hath presented
This happy trial of thy love, which else
So eminently never had been known.
Were it I thought death menaced would ensue
This my attempt, I would sustain alone
The worst, and not persuade thee, rather die
Deserted, than oblige thee with a fact
Pernicious to thy peace, chiefly assured
Remarkably so late of thy so true,
So faithful love unequall'd; but I feel
Far otherwise the event, not death but life
Augmented, open'd eyes, new hopes, new joys,
Taste so divine, that what of sweet before
Hath touch'd my sense, flat seems to this and harsh.
On my experience, Adam, freely taste,
And fear of death deliver to the winds.
  So saying, she embraced him, and for joy
Tenderly wept, much won that he his love
Had so ennobled, as of choice to incur
Divine displeasure for her sake, or death.
In recompence, for such compliance bad
Such recompence best merits, from the bough
She gave him of that fair, enticing fruit
With liberal hand; he scrupled not to eat
Against his better knowledge, not deceived,[1]
But fondly overcome with female charm.
Earth trembled from her entrails, as again
In pangs, and Nature gave a second groan,
Sky lour'd, and, mutt'ring thunder, some sad drops
Wept at completing of the mortal sin
Original; while Adam took no thought,
Eating his fill, nor Eve to iterate
Her former trespass fear'd, the more to soothe
Him with her loved society, that now,
As with new wine intoxicated bóth,
They swim in mirth, and fancy that they feel
Divinity within them breeding wings
Wherewith to scorn the earth; but that false fruit
Far other operation first display'd,
Carnal desire inflaming; he on Eve
Began to cast lascivious eyes, she him

[1] 1 Tim. ii. 14.

As wantonly repaid; in lust they burn;
Till Adam thus 'gan Eve to dalliance move.

Eve, now I see thou art exact of taste,
And elegant, of sapience no small part,
Since to each meaning savor we apply,
And palate call judicious; I the praise
Yield thee, so well this day thou hast purvey'd.
Much pleasure we have lost, while we abstain'd
From this delightful fruit, nor known till now
True relish, tasting; if such pleasure be
In things to us forbidden, it might be wish'd,
For this one tree had been forbidden ten.
But come, so well refresh'd, now let us play,
As meet is, after such delicious fare;
For never did thy beauty, since the day
I saw thee first and wedded thee, adorned
With all perfections, so inflame my sense
With ardor to enjoy thee, fairer now
Than ever, bounty of this virtuous tree.

So said he, and forbore not glance or toy
Of amorous intent, well understood
Of Eve, whose eye darted contagious fire.
Her hand he seized, and to a shady bank,
Thick overhead with verdant roof imbower'd,
He led her nothing loth; flowers were the couch,
Pansies, and violets, and asphodel,
And hyacinth, earth's freshest softest lap.
There they their fill of love and love's disport
Took largely, of their mutual guilt the seal,
The solace of their sin, till dewy sleep
Oppress'd them, wearied with their amorous play.
Soon as the force of that fallacious fruit,
That with exhilarating vapor bland
About their spirits had play'd, and inmost powers
Made err, was now exhaled, and grosser sleep
Bred of unkindly fumes, with conscious dreams
Encumber'd now had left them, up they rose
As from unrest, and, each the other viewing,
Soon found their eyes how open'd, and their minds
How darken'd: innocence, that as a veil
Had shadow'd them from knowing ill, was gone,
Just confidence, and native righteousness,

And honor from about them; naked left
To guilty shame; he cover'd, but his robe
Uncover'd more. So rose the Danite strong
Herculean Samson from the harlot-lap
Of Philistean Dalilah, and waked
Shorn of his strength; they destitute and bare
Of all their virtue: silent, and in face
Confounded, long they sate, as strucken mute,
Till Adam, though not less than Eve abash'd,
At length gave uttterance to these words constrain'd.

    O Eve, in evil hour thou did'st give ear
To that false worm, of whomsoever taught
To counterfeit man's voice, true in our fall
False in our promised rising; since our eyes
Open'd we find indeed, and find we know
Both good and evil, good lost, and evil got,
Bad fruit of knowledge, if this be to know,
Which leaves us naked thus, of honor void,
Of innocence, of faith, of purity,
Our wonted ornaments now soil'd and stain'd,
And in our faces evident the signs
Of foul concupiscence; whence evil store,
Ev'n shame, the last of evils; of the first
Be sure then. How shall I behold the face
Henceforth of GOD or angel, erst with joy
And rapture so oft beheld? those heav'nly shapes
Will dazzle now this earthly, with their blaze
Insufferably bright. O might I here
In solitude live savage, in some glade
Obscured, where highest woods, impenetrable
To star or sun-light, spread their umbrage broad,
And brown as evening: cover me, ye pines,
Ye cedars, with innumerable boughs
Hide me, where I may never see them more
But let us now, as in bad plight, devise
What best may for the present serve to hide
The parts of each from other, that seem most
To shame obnoxious, and unseemliest seen;
Some tree, whose broad smooth leaves together sew'd
And girded on our loins, may cover round
Those middle parts, that this new comer, shame,
There sit not, and reproach us as unclean.

   So counsell'd he, and both together went
Into the thickest wood; there soon they chose
The figtree, not that kind for fruit renown'd,
But such as at this day to Indians known
In Malabar or Decan spreads her arms
Branching so broad and long, that in the ground
The bended twigs take root, and daughters grow
About the mother tree, a pillar'd shade[1]
High overarch'd, and echoing walks between;
There oft the Indian herdsman shunning heat
Shelters in cool, and tends his pasturing herds
At loopholes cut through thickest shade. Those leaves
They gather'd, broad as Amazonian targe,
And with what skill they had together sew'd,
To gird their waist, vain covering, if to hide
Their guilt and dreaded shame; O how unlike
To that first naked glory! Such of late
Columbus found the American so girt
With feather'd cincture, naked else and wild
Among the trees on isles and woody shores.
   Thus fenced, and as they thought, their shame in part
Cover'd, but not at rest or ease of mind,
They sat them down to weep, nor only tears
Rain'd at their eyes, but high winds worse within
Began to rise, high passions, anger, hate,
Mistrust, suspicion, discord, and shook sore
Their inward state of mind, calm region once
And full of peace, now tost and turbulent:
For understanding ruled not, and the will
Heard not her lore, both in subjection now
To sensual appetite, who from beneath
Usurping over sov'reign reason claim'd
Superior sway: from thus distemper'd breast
Adam, estranged in look and alter'd style,
Speech intermitted thus to Eve renew'd.
    Would thou hadst hearken'd to my words, and stay'd
With me, as I besought thee, when that strange
Desire of wand'ring this unhappy morn
I know not whence possess'd thee; we had then

---

[1] The Indian fig, called Ficus Indica by botanists, or Banyan. The largest known nearly covers an island on the Nerbudda. It is 2,000 feet round, and has 1,300 trunks.

Remain'd still happy, not, as now, despoil'd
Of all our good, shamed, naked, miserable.
Let none henceforth seek needless cause to approve
The faith they owe; when earnestly they seek
Such proof, conclude, they then begin to fail.
    To whom soon moved with touch of blame thus Eve.
What words have pass'd thy lips, Adam severe?
Imput'st thou that to my default, or will
Of wand'ring, as thou call'st it, which who knows
But might as ill have happen'd thou being by,
Or to thyself perhaps: hadst thou been there,
Or here th' attempt, thou couldst not have discern'd
Fraud in the serpent, speaking as he spake;
No ground of enmity between us known,
Why he should mean me ill, or seek to harm.
Was I to have never parted from thy side?
As good have grown there still a lifeless rib.
Being as I am, why didst not thou, the head,
Command me absolutely not to go,
Going into such danger, as thou saidst?
Too facile, then thou didst not much gainsay,
Nay, didst permit, approve, and fair dismiss.
Hadst thou been firm and fix'd in thy dissent,
Neither had I transgress'd, nor thou with me.
    To whom then first incensed Adam replied.
Is this the love, is this the recompense
Of mine to thee, ungrateful Eve, express'd
Immutable when thou wert lost, not I,
Who might have lived and joy'd immortal bliss,
Yet willingly chose rather death with thee?
And am I now upbraided, as the cause
Of thy transgressing? not enough severe,
It seems, in thy restraint: what could I more?
I warn'd thee, I admonish'd thee, foretold
The danger, and the lurking enemy
That lay in wait: beyond this had been force,
And force upon free will hath here no place.
But confidence then bore thee on, secure
Either to meet no danger, or to find
Matter of glorious trial; and perhaps
I also err'd in overmuch admiring
What seem'd in thee so perfect, that I thought

No evil durst attempt thee; but I rue
The error now, which is become my crime,
And thou the accuser. Thus it shall befall
Him who to worth in woman overtrusting
Lets her will rule; restraint she will not brook,
And left to herself, if evil thence ensue,
She first his weak indulgence will accuse.
    Thus they in mutual accusation spent
The fruitless hours, but neither self-condemning.
And of their vain contest appear'd no end.

BOOK X

THE ARGUMENT

Man's transgression known, the guardian angels forsake paradise, and return up to heaven to approve their vigilance, and are approved, God declaring that the entrance of Satan could not be by them prevented. He sends his Son to judge the transgressors; who descends, and gives sentence accordingly; then in pity clothes them both and reascends. Sin and Death, sitting till then at the gates of hell, by wondrous sympathy, feeling the success of Satan in this new world, and the sin by man there committed, resolve to sit no longer confined in hell, but to follow Satan their sire up to the place of man: to make the way easier from hell to this world to and fro, they pave a broad highway, or bridge, over Chaos, according to the track that Satan first made; then, preparing for earth, they meet him, proud of his success, returning to hell; their mutual gratulation. Satan arrives at Pandemonium, in full assembly relates with boasting his success against man; instead of applause, is entertained with a general hiss by all his audience, transformed, with himself also, suddenly into serpents, according to his doom, given in Paradise; then, deluded with a show of the forbidden tree springing up before them, they greedily reaching to take of the fruit, chew dust and bitter ashes. The proceedings of Sin and Death; God foretells the final victory of his Son over them, and the renewing of all things; but for the present commands his angels to make several alterations in the heavens and elements. Adam, more and more perceiving his fallen condition, heavily bewails, rejects the condolement of Eve, she persists, and at length appeases him: then, to evade the curse likely to fall on their offspring, proposes to Adam violent ways, which he approves not; but conceiving ˌbetter hope, puts her in mind of the late promise made them, that her seed should be revenged on the serpent, and exhorts her with him to seek peace of the offended Deity, by repentance and supplication.

MEANWHILE the heinous and despiteful act
Of Satan done in paradise, and how
He in the serpent had perverted Eve,

Her husband she, to taste the fatal fruit,
Was known in heav'n; for what can scape the eye
Of God all seeing, or deceive His heart
Omniscient, who, in all things wise and just,
Hinder'd not Satan to attempt the mind
Of man, with strength entire, and freewill arm'd,
Complete to have discover'd and repulsed
Whatever wiles of foe or seeming friend!
For still they knew, and ought to have still remember'd
The high injunction not to taste that fruit,
Whoever tempted; which they not obeying
Incurr'd, what could they less? the penalty,
And, manifold in sin, deserved to fall.

    Up into heav'n from paradise in haste
Th' angelic guards ascended, mute and sad
For man; for of his state by this they knew.
Much wondering how the subtle fiend had stol'n
Entrance unseen. Soon as the unwelcome news
From earth arrived at heaven gate, displeased
All were who heard; dim sadness did not spare
That time celestial visages, yet mix'd
With pity violated not their bliss.
About the new-arrived in multitudes
Th' ethereal people ran, to hear and know
How all befell: they towards the throne supreme
Accountable made haste to make appear
With righteous plea their utmost vigilance,
And easily approved; when the most high
Eternal Father from his secret cloud
Amidst in thunder utter'd thus his voice.

    Assembled angels, and ye powers return'd
From unsuccessful charge, be not dismay'd,
Nor troubled at these tidings from the earth,
Which your sincerest care could not prevent,
Foretold so lately what would come to pass,
When first this tempter cross'd the gulf from hell.
I told ye then he should prevail and speed
On his bad errand; man should be seduced
And flatter'd out of all, believing lies
Against his Maker; no decree of mine
Concurring to necessitate his fall,
Or touch with lightest moment of impulse

His free will, to her own inclining left
In even scale. But fall'n he is, and now
What rests, but that the mortal sentence pass
On his transgression, death denounced that day,
Which he presumes already vain and void,
Because not yet inflicted, as he fear'd,
By some immediate stroke; but soon shall find
Forbearance no acquittance ere day end.
Justice shall not return as bounty scorn'd.
But whom send I to judge them? whom but thee
Vicegerent Son; to thee I have transferr'd [1]
All judgment, whether in heav'n, or earth, or hell.
Easy it may be seen that I intend
Mercy colleague with justice,[2] sending thee
Man's friend, his Mediator, his design'd
Both Ransom and Redeemer voluntary,
And destined Man himself to judge man fall'n.

So spake the Father, and, unfolding bright
Toward the right hand His glory, on the Son
Blazed forth unclouded Deity; He full
Resplendent all His Father manifest
Express'd, and thus divinely answer'd mild.

Father eternal, thine is to decree,
Mine both in heav'n and earth to do thy will
Supreme, that thou in me thy Son belov'd
May'st ever rest well pleased. I go to judge
On earth these thy transgressors, but thou know'st,
Whoever judged, the worst on me must light,
When time shall be; for so I undertook
Before thee, and not repenting this obtain
Of right, that I may mitigate their doom.
On me derived; yet I shall temper so
Justice with mercy, as may illustrate most
Them fully satisfied, and thee appease.
Attendance none shall need, nor train, where none
Are to behold the judgment, but the judged,
Those two; the third best absent is condemn'd,
Convict by flight, and rebel to all law,
Conviction to the serpent none belongs.

Thus saying, from His radiant seat He rose

[1] St. John v. 22.
[2] Psalm lxxxv. 10.

Of high collateral glory: Him thrones and powers,
Princedoms and dominations ministrant
Accompanied to heaven gate, from whence
Eden and all the coast in prospect lay.
Down He descended straight; the speed of gods
Time counts not, tho' with swiftest minutes wing'd.
Now was the sun in western cadence low[1]
From noon, and gentle airs due at their hour
To fan the earth now waked, and usher in
The ev'ning cool, when He from wrath more cool
Came, the mild Judge and Intercessor both,
To sentence man: the voice of GOD they heard
Now walking in the garden, by soft winds
Brought to their ears, while day declined, they heard,
And from His presence hid themselves among
The thickest trees, both man and wife, till GOD
Approaching thus to Adam call'd aloud.

Where art thou Adam,[2] wont with joy to meet
My coming seen far off? I miss thee here;
Not pleased, thus entertain'd with solitude,
Where obvious duty erewhile appear'd unsought:
Or come I less conspicuous, or what change
Absents thee, or what chance detains? Come forth.

He came, and with him Eve, more loth, though first
To offend, discountenanced both, and discomposed.
Love was not in their looks, either to GOD
Or to each other, but apparent guilt,
And shame, and perturbation, and despair,
Anger, and obstinacy, and hate, and guile,
Whence Adam, falt'ring long, thus answer'd brief.

I heard thee in the garden, and of thy voice
Afraid, being naked, hid myself. To whom
The gracious Judge without revile replied.

My voice thou oft hast heard, and hast not fear'd,
But still rejoiced; how is it now become
So dreadful to thee? that thou art naked, who
Hath told thee? hast thou eaten of the tree
Whereof I gave thee charge thou shouldst not eat?

To whom thus Adam sore beset replied.
O heav'n! in evil strait this day I stand

[1] Gen. iii. 8.
[2] Gen. iii. 9 and following verses.

Before my Judge, either to undergo
Myself the total crime, or to accuse
My other self, the partner of my life;
Whose failing, while her faith to me remains,
I should conceal, and not expose to blame
By my complaint; but strict necessity
Subdues me, and calamitous constraint,
Lest on my head both sin and punishment,
However insupportable, be all
Devolved: though should I hold my peace, yet thou
Wouldst easily detect what I conceal.
This woman whom thou madest to be my help,
And gav'st me as thy perfect gift, so good,
So fit, so acceptable, so divine,
That from her hand I could suspect no ill,
And what she did, whatever in itself,
Her doing seem'd to justify the deed;
She gave me of the tree, and I did eat.

    To whom the sov'reign Presence thus replied.
Was she thy GOD, that her thou didst obey
Before His voice? or was she made thy guide,
Superior, or but equal, that to her
Thou didst resign thy manhood, and the place
Wherein GOD set thee above her, made of thee
And for thee, whose perfection far excell'd
Hers in all real dignity? adorn'd
She was indeed, and lovely to attract
Thy love, not thy subjection; and her gifts
Were such as under government well seem'd,
Unseemly to bear rule, which was thy part
And person, hadst thou known thyself aright.

    So having said, He thus to Eve in few:
Say, woman, what is this which thou hast done?

    To whom sad Eve with shame nigh overwhelm'd
Confessing soon, yet not before her Judge
Bold or loquacious, thus abash'd replied.
The serpent me beguiled, and I did eat.

    Which when the Lord GOD heard, without delay
To judgment He proceeded on th' accused
Serpent though brute, unable to transfer
The guilt on him who made him instrument

Of mischief, and polluted from the end
Of his creation; justly then accursed,
As vitiated in nature: more to know
Concern'd not man, since he no further knew,
Nor alter'd his offence: yet GOD at last
To Satan first in sin his doom applied,
Though in mysterious terms, judged as then best:
And on the serpent thus His curse let fall.

 Because thou hast done this, thou art accursed
Above all cattle, each beast of the field;
Upon thy belly grovelling thou shalt go,
And dust shalt eat all the days of thy life.
Between thee and the woman I will put
Enmity, and between thine and her seed;
Her seed shall bruise thy head, thou bruise his heel.

 So spake this oracle, then verified
When Jesus, Son of Mary, second Eve,
Saw Satan fall like lightning down from heav'n,[1]
Prince of the air;[2] then rising from His grave
Spoil'd principalities and powers, triumph'd
In open show, and with ascension bright
Captivity led captive through the air,
The realm itself of Satan long usurp'd,
Whom He shall tread at last under our feet;
Ev'n He who now foretold His fatal bruise;
And to the woman thus His sentence turn'd.

 Thy sorrow I will greatly multiply
By thy conception; children thou shalt bring
In sorrow forth, and to thy husband's will
Thine shall submit; he over thee shall rule.

 On Adam last thus judgment He pronounced.
Because thou hast hearken'd to the voice of thy wife,
And eaten of the tree concerning which
I charged thee, saying: Thou shalt not eat thereof,
Cursed is the ground for thy sake, thou in sorrow
Shalt eat thereof all the days of thy life;
Thorns also and thistles it shall bring thee forth
Unbid, and thou shalt eat the herb of the field;
In the sweat of thy face shalt thou eat bread,

[1] Luke x. 18.
[2] Ephes. ii. 2; iv. 8. Colos. ii. 15.

Till thou return unto the ground, for thou
Out of the ground wast taken; know thy birth,
For dust thou art, and shalt to dust return.

So judged he man, both Judge and Saviour sent;
And th' instant stroke of death denounced that day
Removed far off; then pitying how they stood
Before him naked to the air, that now
Must suffer change, disdain'd not to begin
Thenceforth the form of servant[1] to assume,
As when he wash'd his servants' feet,[2] so now
As father of his family he clad
Their nakedness with skins of beasts, or slain,
Or as the snake with youthful coat repaid;
And thought not much to clothe His enemies.
Nor He their outward only with the skins
Of beasts, but inward nakedness, much more
Opprobrious, with His robe of righteousness,
Arraying, cover'd from his Father's sight.
To Him with swift ascent He up return'd,
Into His blissful bosom reassumed
In glory as of old; to Him appeased
All, though all-knowing, what had past with man
Recounted, mixing intercession sweet.

Meanwhile, ere thus was sinn'd and judged on earth,
Within the gates of hell sat Sin and Death,
In counterview within the gates, that now
Stood open wide, belching outrageous flame
Far into Chaos, since the fiend pass'd through,
Sin opening, who thus now to Death began.

O son, why sit we here, each other viewing
Idly, while Satan our great author thrives
In other worlds, and happier seat provides
For us his offspring dear? It cannot be
But that success attends him; if mishap,
Ere this he had return'd, with fury driven
By his avengers, since no place like this
Can fit his punishment, or their revenge.
Methinks I feel new strength within me rise,
Wings growing, and dominion giv'n me large

[1] Philip. ii. 7.
[2] John xiii. 5.

Beyond this deep; whatever draws me on,
Or sympathy, or some connatural force,
Powerful at greatest distance to unite
With secret amity things of like kind
By secretest conveyance. Thou my shade
Inseparable must with me along;
For Death from Sin no power can separate.
But lest the difficulty of passing back
Stay his return perhaps over this gulf
Impassable, impervious, let us try
Advent'rous work, yet to thy power and mine
Not unagreeable, to found a path
Over this main from hell to that new world
Where Satan now prevails, a monument
Of merit high to all th' infernal host,
Easing their passage hence, for intercourse,
Or transmigration, as their lot shall lead.
Nor can I miss the way so strongly drawn
By this new felt attraction and instinct.
  Whom thus the meagre Shadow answer'd soon.
Go whither fate and inclination strong
Leads thee; I shall not lag behind, nor err,
The way thou leading, such a scent I draw
Of carnage, prey innumerable, and taste
The savor of death from all things there that live:
Nor shall I to the work thou enterprisest
Be wanting, but afford thee equal aid.
  So saying, with delight he snuff'd the smell
Of mortal change on earth. As when a flock
Of ravenous fowl, though many a league remote,
Against the day of battle, to a field,
Where armies lie encamp'd, come flying, lured
With scent of living carcasses design'd
For death, the following day, in bloody fight:
So scented the grim feature, and upturn'd
His nostril wide into the murky air,
Sagacious of his quarry from so far.
Then both from out hell gates into the waste
Wide anarchy of Chaos damp and dark
Flew diverse; and with power, their power was great,
Hovering upon the waters; what they met

Solid or slimy, as in raging sea
Tost up and down, together crowded drove
From each side shoaling towards the mouth of hell.
As when the two polar winds, blowing adverse
Upon the Cronian sea,[1] together drive
Mountains of ice, that stop th' imagined way[2]
Beyond Petsora eastward, to the rich
Cathaian coast. The aggregated soil
Death with his mace petrific, cold and dry,
As with a trident smote, and fix'd as firm
As Delos floating once; the rest his look
Bound with Gorgonian rigor[3] not to move,
And with Asphaltic slime, broad as the gate,
Deep to the roots of hell the gather'd beach
They fasten'd, and the mole immense wrought on
Over the foaming deep high arch'd, a bridge
Of length prodigious joining to the wall
Immovable of this now fenceless world
Forfeit to death: from hence a passage broad,
Smooth, easy, inoffensive, down to hell.
So, if great things to small may be compared,
Xerxes, the liberty of Greece to yoke,
From Susa his Memnonian palace high
Came to the Sea, and over Hellespont
Bridging his way, Europe with Asia join'd,
And scourged with many a stroke th' indignant waves.
Now had they brought the work by wond'rous art
Pontifical,[4] a ridge of pendent rock
Over the vex'd abyss, following the track
Of Satan, to the self-same place where he
First lighted from his wing, and landed safe
From out of Chaos, to the outside bare
Of this round world: with pins of adamant

---

[1] Northern frozen sea.—NEWTON.
[2] The north-east passage to China, *i.e.*, Cathay.
[3] Alluding to Medusa's power of turning people into stone.
[4] Pontifical, *i.e.*, the art of making bridges. The high priest of Rome derived his title, *Pontifex*, from *pons*, a bridge, and *facere*, to make; perhaps because religious rites of great importance inaugurated these highly-valued works, which he always superintended.

And chains they made all fast, too fast they made
And durable; and now in little space
The confines met of empyrean heav'n
And of this world, and on the left hand hell
With long reach interposed; three sev'ral ways
In sight to each of these three places led.
And now their way to earth they had descried;
To paradise first tending, when behold
Satan in likeness of an angel bright
Betwixt the Centaur and the Scorpion steering[1]
His zenith, while the sun in Aries rose:
Disguised he came, but those his children dear
Their parents soon discern'd, though in disguise.
He, after Eve seduced unminded slunk
Into the wood fast by, and, changing shape
To observe the sequel, saw his guileful act
By Eve, though all unweeting, seconded
Upon her husband, saw their shame that sought
Vain covertures: but when he saw descend
The Son of God to judge them, terrified
He fled; not hoping to escape, but shun
The present, fearing, guilty, what His wrath
Might suddenly inflict: that past, return'd,
By night, and listening where the hapless pair
Sat in their sad discourse and various plaint,
Thence gather'd his own doom, which understood
Not instant, but of future time with joy
And tidings fraught, to hell he now return'd,
And at the brink of Chaos, near the foot
Of this new wondrous pontfice,[2] unhoped
Met who to meet him came, his offspring dear.
Great joy was at their meeting, and at sight
Of that stupendous bridge his joy increased.
Long he admiring stood, till Sin, his fair
Enchanting daughter, thus the silence broke.

    O parent, these are thy magnific deeds,
Thy trophies, which thou view'st as not thine own;

[1] To avoid being seen by Uriel. Centaur and Scorpion are con-
stellations in a different part of the heavens to Aries on the equa-
tor.—NEWTON.
[2] Bridge.

Thou art their author and prime architect:
For I no sooner in my heart divined,
My heart which by a secret harmony
Still moves with thine, join'd in connexion sweet
That thou on earth hadst prosper'd, which thy looks
Now also evidence, but straight I felt,
Though distant from thee worlds between, yet felt
That I must after thee with this thy son,
Such fatal consequence unites us three.
Hell could no longer hold us in her bounds,
Nor this unvoyageable gulf obscure
Detain from following thy illustrious track.
Thou hast achieved our liberty, confined
Within hell gates till now; thou us empower'd
To fortify thus far, and overlay
With this portentous bridge the dark abyss.
Thine now is all this world, thy virtue hath won
What thy hands builded not, thy wisdom gain'd
With odds what war hath lost, and fully avenged
Our foil in heav'n; here thou shalt monarch reign,
There didst not; there let Him still victor sway,
As battle hath adjudged, from this new world
Retiring, by His own doom alienated,
And henceforth monarchy with thee divide
Of all things, parted by th' empyreal bounds,
His quadrature, from thy orbicular world,
Or try thee now more dang'rous to his throne.
  Whom thus the prince of darkness answer'd glad.
Fair daughter, and thou son and grandchild both,
High proof ye now have giv'n to be the race
Of Satan, for I glory in the name,
Antagonist of heav'n's almighty King,
Amply have merited of me, of all
Th' infernal empire, that so near heav'n's door
Triumphal with triumphal act have met,
Mine with this glorious work, and made one realm
Hell and this world, one realm, one continent
Of easy thoroughfare. Therefore, while I
Descend through darkness on your road with ease
To my associate powers, them to acquaint
With these successes, and with them rejoice,

You two this way, among these numerous orbs
All yours, right down to Paradise descend;
There dwell and reign in bliss, thence on the earth
Dominion exercise and in the air,
Chiefly on man, sole lord of all declared;
Him first make sure your thrall, and lastly kill.
My substitutes I send ye, and create
Plenipotent on earth, of matchless might
Issuing from me: on your joint vigor now
My hold of this new kingdom all depends,
Through Sin to Death exposed by my exploit.
If your joint power prevail, th' affairs of hell
No detriment need fear; go and be strong.

   So saying he dismiss'd them, they with speed
Their course through thickest constellations held
Spreading their bane; the blasted stars look'd wan,
And planets, planet-struck, real eclipse
Then suffer'd. Th' other way Satan went down
The causey to hell gate: on either side
Disparted Chaos over built exclaim'd,
And with rebounding surge the bars assail'd,
That scorn'd his indignation. Through the gate,
Wide open and unguarded, Satan pass'd,
And all about found desolate; for those
Appointed to sit there had left their charge,
Flown to the upper world; the rest were all
Far to the inland retired, about the walls
Of Pandæmonium, city and proud seat
Of Lucifer, so by allusion call'd,
Of that bright star to Satan paragon'd.
There kept their watch the legions, while the grand
In council sat, solicitous what chance
Might intercept their emperor sent; so he
Departing gave command, and they observed.
As when the Tartar from his Russian foe
By Astracan over the snowy plains
Retires, or Bactrian Sophy[1] from the horns
Of Turkish crescent[2] leaves all waste beyond

  [1] The Persian monarch, thus named from Bactria, one of the
greatest provinces of Persia.
  [2] The ensign or emblem of Turkey.

The realm of Aladule[1] in his retreat
To Tauris or Casbeen: so these, the late
Heav'n-banish'd host, left desert utmost hell
Many a dark league, reduced in careful watch
Round their metropolis, and now expecting
Each hour their great adventurer from the search
Of foreign worlds: he through the midst unmark'd,
In show plebeian angel militant
Of lowest order, pass'd; and from the door
Of that Plutonian hall invisible
Ascended his high throne, which, under state
Of richest texture spread, at th' upper end
Was placed in regal lustre. Down awhile
He sat, and round about him saw unseen:
At last as from a cloud his fulgent head
And shape star-bright appear'd, or brighter, clad
With what permissive glory since his fall
Was left him, or false glitter. All amazed
At that so sudden blaze the Stygian throng
Bent their aspect, and whom they wish'd beheld,
Their mighty chief return'd: loud was th' acclaim.
Forth rush'd in haste the great consulting peers,
Raised from their dark divan, and with like joy,
Congratulant approach'd him, who with hand
Silence, and with these words attention, won.

   Thrones, dominations, princedoms, virtues, powers,
For in possessions such, not only of right,
I call ye and declare ye now, return'd
Successful beyond hope, to lead ye forth
Triumphant out of this infernal pit
Abominable, accursed, the house of woe,
And dungeon of our tyrant: now possess,
As lords, a spacious world, to our native heav'n
Little inferior, by my adventure hard
With peril great achieved. Long were to tell

   [1] "Aladule," the greater Armenia, called by the Turks (under
whom the greatest part of it is) Aladule, of its last King, Aladule,
slain by Selymus I.; "in his retreat to Tauris," a great city in the
kingdom of Persia, now called Ecbatana, sometime in the hands of
the Turks, but in 1603 retaken by Abas, King of Persia; "or Cas-
been," one of the greatest cities in Persia, where the Persian
monarchs made their residence after the loss of Tauris.—HUME.

What I have done, what suffer'd, with what pain
Voyaged th' unreal, vast, unbounded deep
Of horrible confusion, over which
By Sin and Death a broad way now is paved
To expedite your glorious march: but I
Toil'd out my uncouth passage, forced to ride
Th' untractable abyss, plunged in the womb
Of unoriginal Night and Chaos wild,
That jealous of their secrets fiercely opposed
My journey strange, with clamorous uproar
Protesting fate supreme; thence how I found
The new created world, which fame in heav'n
Long had foretold, a fabric wonderful
Of absolute perfection, therein man
Placed in a paradise, by our exile
Made happy: him by fraud I have seduced
From his Creator, and, the more to increase
Your wonder, with an apple; He thereat
Offended, worth your laughter! hath giv'n up
Both His belovèd man and all His world
To Sin and Death a prey, and so to us,
Without our hazard, labor, or alarm,
To range in, and to dwell, and over man
To rule, as over all He should have ruled.
True is, me also he hath judged, or rather
Me not, but the brute serpent, in whose shape
Man I deceived: that which to me belongs
Is enmity, which he will put between
Me and mankind: I am to bruise his heel;
His seed (when is not set)[1] shall bruise my head.
A world who would not purchase with a bruise,
Or much more grievous pain? Ye have th' account
Of my performance: what remains, ye gods,
But up and enter now into full bliss?
   So having said, awhile he stood, expecting
Their universal shout and high applause
To fill his ear, when contrary he hears
On all sides, from innumerable tongues,
A dismal universal hiss, the sound
Of public scorn; he wonder'd, but not long

[1] The time (when) is not declared.

Had leisure, wond'ring at himself now more:
His visage drawn he felt to sharp and spare,
His arms clung to his ribs, his legs entwining
Each other, till supplanted down he fell
A monstrous serpent on his belly prone,
Reluctant, but in vain, a greater power
Now ruled him, punish'd in the shape he sinn'd,
According to his doom. He would have spoke,
But hiss for hiss return'd with forkèd tongue
To forkèd tongue, for now were all transform'd
Alike, to serpents all as accessories
To his bold riot: dreadful was the din
Of hissing through the hall, thick swarming now
With complicated monsters head and tail,
Scorpion, and asp, and amphisbæna[1] dire,
Cerastes[2] horn'd, hydrus,[3] and elop[4] drear,
And dipsas,[5] not so thick swarm'd once the soil
Bedropp'd with blood of Gorgon[6] or the isle
Ophiusa;[7] but still greatest he the midst,
Now dragon grown, larger than whom the sun
Ingender'd in the Pythian vale on slime,
Huge Python,[8] and his power no less he seem'd
Above the rest still to retain. They all
Him follow'd issuing forth to th' open field,
Where all yet left of that revolted rout
Heav'n-fall'n in station stood or just array,
Sublime with expectation when to see,
In triumph issuing forth their glorious chief:
They saw, but other sight instead, a crowd
Of ugly serpents; horror on them fell,
And horrid sympathy; for what they saw,
They felt themselves now changing: down their arms,

[1] A serpent said to have a head at both ends of its body.
[2] A horned snake.
[3] A water snake.
[4] A water serpent.
[5] A snake the bite of which produces feverish thirst.
[6] Lybia, where the blood which dropped from Medusa's head produced serpents.
[7] An island in the Mediterranean, which was deserted on account of its serpents, from which it derived its name.—NEWTON.
[8] A huge serpent, sprung from the slime left after the Deucalion deluge. It was slain by Apollo.

Down fell both spear and shield, down they as fast,
And the dire hiss renew'd, and the dire form
Catch'd by contagion, like in punishment,
As in their crime. Thus was th' applause they meant
Turn'd to exploding hiss, triumph to shame,
Cast on themselves from their own mouths. There stood
A grove hard by, sprung up with this their change,
His will who reigns above, to aggravate
Their penance, laden with fair fruit, like that
Which grew in Paradise, the bait of Eve
Used by the tempter: on that prospect strange
Their earnest eyes they fix'd, imagining
For one forbidden tree a multitude
Now ris'n, to work them further woe or shame:
Yet parch'd with scalding thirst and hunger fierce,
Though to delude them sent, could not abstain,
But on they roll'd in heaps, and up the trees
Climbing sat thicker than the snaky locks
That curl'd Megæra:[1] greedily they pluck'd
The fruitage fair to sight, like that which grew
Near that bituminous lake[2] where Sodom flamed;
This more delusive, not the touch, but taste
Deceived; they, fondly thinking to allay
Their appetite with gust, instead of fruit
Chew'd bitter ashes, which th' offended taste
With spattering noise rejected: oft they assay'd,
Hunger and thirst constraining, drugg'd as oft,
With hatefullest disrelish writhed their jaws
With soot and cinders fill'd; so oft they fell
Into the same illusion, not as man
Whom they triumph'd once lapsed. Thus were they plagued
And worn with famine long and ceaseless hiss,
Till their lost shape, permitted, they resumed;
Yearly enjoin'd, some say, to undergo
This annual humbling certain number'd days
To dash their pride and joy for man seduced.
However, some tradition they dispersed

[1] One of the Furies.
[2] Lake Asphaltites, or Dead Sea. Milton alludes to Josephus's
account of the apples of Sodom, said to have a lovely exterior,
but within to be full of ashes. It is not true.

Among the heathen of their purchase got,
And fabled how the serpent, whom they call'd
Ophion with Eurynome, (the wide
Encroaching Eve perhaps,) had first the rule
Of high Olympus, thence by Saturn driv'n
And Ops, ere yet Dictæan Jove was born.

   Meanwhile in paradise the hellish pair
Too soon arrived, Sin there in power before,
Once actual, now in body, and to dwell
Habitual habitant; behind her Death
Close following pace for pace, not mounted yet
On his pale horse; to whom Sin thus began.

   Second of Satan sprung, all conquering Death,
What think'st thou of our empire now, though earn'd
With travail difficult, not better far
Than still at hell's dark threshold to have sate watch,
Unnamed, undreaded, and thyself half starved?

   Whom thus the sin-born monster answer'd soon.
To me, who with eternal famine pine,
Alike is hell, or paradise, or heaven,
There best, where most with ravine I may meet;
Which here, though plenteous, all too little seems[1]
To stuff this maw, this vast unhide-bound corps.

   To whom th' incestuous mother thus replied.
Thou therefore on these herbs, and fruits, and flowers
Feed first; on each beast next, and fish, and fowl;
No homely morsels; and whatever thing
The scythe of Time mows down, devour unspared,
Till I in man residing through the race,
His thoughts, his looks, words, actions, all infect;
And season him thy last and sweetest prey.

   This said, they both betook them several ways,
Both to destroy, or unimmortal make
All kinds, and for destruction to mature
Sooner or later; which th' Almighty seeing,
From his transcendent seat the saints among,
To those bright orders utter'd thus his voice.

   See with what heat these dogs of hell advance
To waste and havoc yonder world, which I
So fair and good created, and had still
Kept in that state, had not the folly of man

[1] Prov. xxvii. 20.

Let in these wasteful furies, who impute
Folly to me; so doth the prince of hell
And his adherents, that with so much ease
I suffer them to enter and possess
A place so heavenly, and conniving seem
To gratify my scornful enemies,
That laugh, as if, transported with some fit
Of passion, I to them had quitted all,
At random yielded up to their misrule;
And know not that I called and drew them thither
My hell-hounds, to lick up the draff and filth,
Which man's polluting sin with taint hath shed
On what was pure; till cramm'd and gorged, nigh burst
With suck'd and glutted offal, at one sling
Of thy victorious arm, well-pleasing Son,
Both Sin and Death, and yawning Grave, at last
Through Chaos hurl'd, obstruct the mouth of hell
For ever, and seal up his ravenous jaws.[1]
Then heav'n and earth renew'd shall be made pure
To sanctify that shall receive no stain:
Till then the curse pronounced on both precedes.

   He ended, and the heav'nly audience loud
Sung Hallelujah, as the sound of seas,
Through multitude that sung: Just are thy ways,[2]
Righteous are thy decrees on all thy works;
Who can extenuate thee? Next, to the Son,
Destined restorer of mankind, by whom
New heav'n and earth shall to the ages rise,
Or down from heav'n descend. Such was their song,
While the Creator calling forth by name
His mighty angels gave them several charge,
As sorted best with present things. The sun
Had first his precept so to move, so shine,
As might affect the earth with cold and heat
Scarce tolerable, and from the north to call
Decrepit winter; from the south to bring
Solstitial summer's heat. To the blank moon[3]
Her office they prescribed, to th' other five
Their planetary motions and aspects

[1] See Dante's *Inferno*, cant. xxiii.
[2] Rev. xv. 3; xvi. 7.
[3] Some editions printed blanc moon, *i.e., white.*

In Sextile, Square, and Trine, and Opposite,[1]
Of noxious efficacy, and when to join
In synod unbenign, and taught the fix'd
Their influence malignant when to show'r,
Which of them rising with the sun, or falling,
Should prove tempestuous. To the winds they set
Their corners, when with bluster to confound
Sea, air, and shore; the thunder when to roll
With terror through the dark aëreal hall.
Some say, he bid his angels turn askance
The poles of earth twice ten degrees and more
From the sun's axle; they with labor push'd
Oblique the centric globe: some say, the sun
Was bid turn reins from th' equinoctial road
Like distant breadth to Taurus with the sev'n
Atlantic sisters,[2] and the Spartan twins,[3]
Up to the Tropic Crab; thence down amain
By Leo, and the Virgin, and the Scales,
As deep as Capricorn, to bring in change
Of seasons to each clime; else had the spring
Perpetual smiled on earth with vernant flow'rs,
Equal in days and nights, except to those
Beyond the polar circles; to them day

[1] Terms made use of by the astrologers, and signifying the positions or aspects of the five (then known) planets. Sextile means a planet situated at a distance of two signs (the sixth of twelve) from another planet. Square, separated by four signs. Trine, separated by three signs. *Opposite* was considered a position of noxious efficacy. The period in which Milton lived explains the fact of his countenancing these superstitions, as they were universally believed. After the great Fire of London, the House of Commons called the astrologer Lilly before them, to examine him as to his foreknowledge of that calamity, and gravely received his explanation of how he obtained his foresight from the art he practised. He had foretold the fire in a hieroglyphic resembling those formerly published in Old Moore's Almanack, which might be interpreted in any manner the reader pleased. "Did you foresee the year?" asked one of the Committee. "I did not," replied Lilly, "nor was desirous; of that I made no scrutiny." The astrologer then told them, very wisely, that the fire was not of man, but of God. It was believed to have been caused by incendiaries.

[2] The Pleiades, daughters of Atlas. This constellation is in the neck of Taurus.

[3] Castor and Pollux, the Gemini.

Had unbenighted shone, while the low sun
To recompense his distance in their sight
Had rounded still th' horizon, and not known
Or east or west, which had forbid the snow
From cold Estotiland,[1] and south as far
Beneath Magellan.[2] At that tasted fruit
The sun, as from Thyestean banquet,[3] turn'd
His course intended; else how had the world
Inhabited, though sinless, more than now
Avoided pinching cold and scorching heat?
These changes in the heav'ns, though slow, produced
Like change on sea and land, sideral blast,
Vapor, and mist, and exhalation hot,
Corrupt and pestilent. Now from the north
Of Norumbega[4] and the Samoed shore,
Bursting their brazen dungeon, arm'd with ice,
And snow, and hail, and stormy gust, and flaw,
Boreas, and Cæcias, and Argestes loud,
And Thrascias[5] rend the woods, and seas upturn;
With adverse blast upturns them from the south
Notus, and Afer black with thund'rous clouds
From Serraliona,[6] thwart of these as fierce
Forth rush the Levant and the Ponent winds,
Eurus and Zephyr[7] with their lateral noise
Sirocco and Libecchio. Thus began
Outrage from lifeless things; but Discord first,
Daughter of Sin, among th' irrational
Death introduced through fierce antipathy:

[1] A tract of land north of America, near the Arctic Ocean and Hudson's Bay.—HUME.

[2] Extreme south of South America.

[3] Atreus, to avenge an injury, invited his brother Thyestes to a banquet, and served up for his food the flesh of his murdered children. This horrid revenge was visited on the family of Atreus for generations.

[4] A province of the northern Armenia. Samoieda, in the north-east of Muscovy, upon the Frozen Sea.—HUME.

[5] Names of the winds. Boreas, the north; Cæcias, northwest; Argestes, northeast. Thrascias, from Threce. Notus, the south wind. Afer, from Africa.—*From* RICHARDSON.

[6] The Lion Mountains, southwest of Africa, famous for storms.

[7] Levant and Ponent are Italian names for the east and west winds, called by the Greeks Eurus and Zephyr. Sirocco and Libecchio are the southeast and southwest winds.

Beast now with beast gan war, and fowl with fowl,
And fish with fish; to graze the herb all leaving
Devour'd each other; nor stood much in awe
Of man, but fled him, or with count'nance grim
Glared on him passing. These were from without
The growing miseries, which Adam saw
Already in part, though hid in gloomiest shade,
To sorrow abandon'd, but worse felt within,
And, in a troubled sea of passion tost,
Thus to disburden sought with sad complaint.

O miserable of happy! is this the end
Of this new glorious world, and me so late
The glory of that glory, who now become
Accursed of blessèd? Hide me from the face
Of GOD, whom to behold was then my highth
Of happiness: yet well, if here would end
The misery; I deserved it, and would bear
My own deservings; but this will not serve;
All that I eat, or drink, or shall beget,
Is propagated curse. O voice once heard
Delightfully, Encrease and multiply;
Now death to hear! for what can I encrease
Or multiply, but curses on my head?
Who of all ages to succeed, but feeling
The evil on him brought by me, will curse
My head? Ill fare our ancestor impure,
For this we may thank Adam; but his thanks
Shall be the execration; so besides
Mine own that bide upon me, all from me
Shall with a fierce reflux on me redound,
On me, as on their natural centre light
Heavy, though in their place. O fleeting joys
Of paradise, dear bought with lasting woes!
Did I request thee, Maker, from my clay
To mould me man? Did I solicit thee
From darkness to promote me, or here place
In this delicious garden? As my will
Concurr'd not to my being, it were but right
And equal to reduce me to my dust,
Desirous to resign, and render back
All I received, unable to perform
Thy terms too hard, by which I was to hold

The good I sought not. To the loss of that
Sufficient penalty, why hast thou added
The sense of endless woes? Inexplicable
Thy justice seems; yet, to say truth, too late
I thus contest: then should have been refused
These terms, whatever, when they were proposed.
Thou didst accept them; wilt thou enjoy the good,
Then cavil the conditions?[1] and though GOD
Made thee without thy leave, what if thy son
Prove disobedient, and reproved retort,
Wherefore didst thou beget me? I sought it not:
Wouldst thou admit for his contempt of thee
That proud excuse? yet him not thy election,
But natural necessity begot.
GOD made thee of choice his own, and of his own
To serve him, thy reward was of his grace,
Thy punishment then justly is at his will.
Be it so, for I submit, his doom is fair,
That dust I am, and shall to dust return:
O welcome hour whenever! why delays
His hand to execute what His decree
Fix'd on this day? why do I overlive?
Why am I mock'd with death, and lengthen'd out
To deathless pain? how gladly would I meet
Mortality my sentence, and be earth
Insensible! how glad would lay me down
As in my mother's lap? there I should rest
And sleep secure; His dreadful voice no more
Would thunder in my ears; no fear of worse
To me and to my offspring would torment me
With cruel expectation. Yet one doubt
Pursues me still, lest all I cannot die,
Lest that pure breath of life, the spirit of man[2]
Which GOD inspired, cannot together perish
With this corporeal clod; then in the grave,
Or in some other dismal place, who knows
But I shall die a living death? O thought
Horrid, if true! yet why? it was but breath
Of life that sinn'd; what dies but what had life
And sin? the body properly hath neither.

[1] Job ii. 10.
[2] Gen. ii. 7.

All of me then shall die; let this appease
The doubt, since human reach no further knows.
For though the Lord of all be infinite,
Is His wrath also? be it, man is not so,
But mortal doom'd. How can He exercise
Wrath without end on man whom death must end?
Can He make deathless death? that were to make
Strange contradiction, which to God Himself
Impossible is held, as argument
Of weakness, not of power. Will He draw out,
For anger's sake, finite to infinite
In punish'd man, to satisfy his rigor,
Satisfied never? that were to extend
His sentence beyond dust and nature's law,
By which all causes else, according still
To the reception of their matter, act,
Not to th' extent of their own sphere. But say,
That death be not one stroke as I supposed,
Bereaving sense, but endless misery
From this day onward, which I feel begun
Both in me, and without me, and so last
To perpetuity:—ay me! that fear
Comes thund'ring back with dreadful revolution
On my defenceless head; both death and I
Are found eternal, and incorporate both;
Nor I on my part single, in me all
Posterity stands cursed; fair patrimony
That I must leave ye sons! O were I able
To waste it all myself, and leave ye none!
So disinherited, how would ye bless
Me, now your curse! Ah! why should all mankind
For one man's fault, thus guiltless be condemn'd,
If guiltless? But from me what can proceed,
But all corrupt, both mind and will depraved,
Not to do only, but to will the same
With me? how can they then acquitted stand
In sight of God? Him, after all disputes,
Forced I absolve: all my evasions vain,
And reasonings, though through mazes, lead me still
But to my own conviction: first and last
On me, me only, as the source and spring
Of all corruption, all the blame lights due;

So might the wrath! Fond wish! couldst thou support
That burden heavier than the earth to bear,
Than all the world much heavier, though divided
With that bad woman? Thus what thou desir'st,
And what thou fear'st, alike destroys all hope
Of refuge, and concludes thee miserable
Beyond all past example and future:
To Satan only like both crime and doom.
O Conscience, into what abyss of fears
And horrors hast thou driv'n me, out of which
I find no way from deep to deeper plunged!

 Thus Adam to himself lamented loud
Through the still night; not now, as ere man fell
Wholesome, and cool, and mild, but with black air
Accompanied, with damps and dreadful gloom,
Which to his evil conscience represented
All things with double terror. On the ground
Outstretch'd he lay, on the cold ground, and oft
Cursed his creation, death as oft accused
Of tardy execution, since denounced
The day of his offence. Why comes not death,
Said he, with one thrice acceptable stroke
To end me? Shall truth fail to keep her word,
Justice divine not hasten to be just?
But death comes not at call, justice divine
Mends not her slowest pace for prayers or cries.
O woods, O fountains, hillocks, dales, and bow'rs,
With other echo late I taught your shades
To answer, and resound far other song.
Whom thus afflicted when sad Eve beheld,
Desolate where she sat, approaching nigh,
Soft words to his fierce passion she assay'd:
But her with stern regard he thus repell'd.

 Out of my sight, thou serpent! that name best
Befits thee with him leagued, thyself as false
And hateful; nothing wants, but that thy shape,
Like his, and color serpentine may show
Thy inward fraud, to warn all creatures from thee
Henceforth; lest that too heav'nly form, pretended
To hellish falsehood, snare them. But for thee
I had persisted happy, had not thy pride
And wand'ring vanity, when least was safe,

Rejected my forewarning, and disdain'd
Not to be trusted, longing to be seen
Though by the devil himself, him overweening
To over-reach; but with the serpent meeting,
Fool'd and beguiled, by him thou, I by thee,
To trust thee from my side, imagined wise,
Constant, mature, proof against all assaults,
And understood not all was but a show
Rather than solid virtue, all but a rib
Crooked by nature, bent, as now appears,
More to the part sinister from me drawn;
Well if thrown out, as supernumerary
To my just number found. Oh! why did God,
Creator wise, that peopled highest heav'n
With spirits masculine, create at last
This novelty on earth, this fair defect
Of nature, and not fill the world at once
With men as angels without feminine,
Or find some other way to generate
Mankind? This mischief had not then befall'n,
And more that shall befall; innumerable
Disturbances on earth through female snares,
And straight conjunction with this sex: for either
He never shall find out fit mate, but such
As some misfortune brings him, or mistake;
Or whom he wishes most shall seldom gain
Through her perverseness, but shall see her gain'd
By a far worse; or if she love, withheld
By parents; or his happiest choice too late
Shall meet, already link'd and wedlock-bound
To a fell adversary, his hate or shame;
Which infinite calamity shall cause
To human life, and household peace confound.

He added not, and from her turn'd; but Eve
Not so repulsed, with tears that ceased not flowing,
And tresses all disorder'd, at his feet
Fell humble, and, embracing them, besought
His peace, and thus proceeded in her plaint.

Forsake me not thus, Adam, witness heav'n
What love sincere and reverence in my heart
I bear thee, and unweeting have offended,
Unhappily deceived; thy suppliant

I beg, and clasp thy knees; bereave me not
Whereon I live, thy gentle looks, thy aid,
Thy counsel in this uttermost distress,
My only strength and stay: forlorn of thee,
Whither shall I betake me, where subsist?
While yet we live, scarce one short hour perhaps,
Between us two let there be peace, both joining,
As join'd in injuries, one enmity
Against a foe by doom express assign'd us,
That cruel serpent. On me exercise not
Thy hatred for this misery befall'n,
On me already lost, me than thyself
More miserable; both have sinn'd, but thou
Against God only, I against God and thee,
And to the place of judgment will return,
There with my cries importune heaven, that all
The sentence from thy head removed, may light
On me, soul cause to thee of all this woe,
Me, me only, just object of his ire.

      She ended weeping, and her lowly plight,
Immoveable till peace obtain'd from fault
Acknowledged and deplored, in Adam wrought
Commiseration; soon his heart relented
Towards her, his life so late and sole delight,
Now at his feet submissive in distress;
Creature so fair his reconcilement seeking,
His counsel, whom she had displeased, his aid;
As one disarm'd, his anger all he lost,
And thus with peaceful words upraised her soon.

      Unwary and too desirous as before,
So now of what thou know'st not, who desir'st
The punishment all on thyself; alas,
Bear thine own first, ill able to sustain
His full wrath, whose thou feel'st as yet least part,
And my displeasure bear'st so ill. If prayers
Could alter high decrees, I to that place
Would speed before thee, and be louder heard,
That on my head all might be visited,
Thy frailty and infirmer sex forgiv'n,
To me committed, and by me exposed.
But rise, let us no more contend, nor blame
Each other, blamed enough elsewhere, but strive

In offices of love how we may lighten
Each other's burden in our share of woe;
Since this day's death denounced, if aught I see,
Will prove no sudden, but a slow-paced evil,
A long day's dying to augment our pain,
And to our seed, O hapless seed! derived.
    To whom thus Eve, recovering heart, replied.
Adam, by sad experiment I know
How little weight my words with thee can find,
Found so erroneous, thence by just event
Found so unfortunate; nevertheless,
Restored by thee, vile as I am, to place
Of new acceptance, hopeful to regain
Thy love, the sole contentment of my heart
Living or dying, from thee I will not hide
What thoughts in my unquiet breast are ris'n,
Tending to some relief of our extremes,
Or end, though sharp and sad, yet tolerable,
As in our evils, and of easier choice.
If care of our descent perplex us most,
Which must be born to certain woe, devour'd
By Death at last, and miserable it is
To be to others cause of misery,
Our own begotten, and of our loins to bring,
Into this cursed world a woful race,
That after wretched life must be at last
Food for so foul a monster, in thy power
It lies, yet ere conception to prevent
The race unblest, to being yet unbegot.
Childless thou art, childless remain: so Death
Shall be deceived his glut, and with us two
Be forced to satisfy his rav'nous maw.
But if thou judge it hard and difficult,
Conversing, looking, loving, to abstain
From love's due rites, nuptial embraces sweet,
And with desire to languish without hope,
Before the present object languishing
With like desire, which would be misery,
And torment less than none of what we dread,
Then both ourselves and seed at once to free
From what we fear for both, let us make short;
Let us seek Death, or, he not found, supply

With our own hands his office on ourselves:
Why stand we longer shivering under fears,
That show no end but death, and have the power,
Of many ways to die the shortest choosing,
Destruction with destruction to destroy?

   She ended here, or vehement despair
Broke off the rest; so much of death her thoughts
Had entertain'd, as dyed her cheeks with pale.
But Adam, with such counsel nothing sway'd,
To better hopes his more attentive mind
Laboring had raised, and thus to Eve replied.

   Eve, thy contempt of life and pleasure seems
To argue in thee something more sublime
And excellent than what thy mind contemns;
But self-destruction therefore sought refutes
That excellence thought in thee, and implies,
Not thy contempt, but anguish and regret
For loss of life and pleasure overloved.
Or if thou covet death, as utmost end
Of misery, so thinking to evade
The penalty pronounced, doubt not but God
Hath wiselier arm'd his vengeful ire than so
To be forestall'd: much more I fear lest death
So snatch'd will not exempt us from the pain
We are by doom to pay: rather such acts
Of contumacy will provoke the Highest
To make death in us live: then let us seek
Some safer resolution, which methinks
I have in view, calling to mind with heed
Part of our sentence, that thy seed shall bruise
The serpent's head: piteous amends, unless
Be meant, whom I conjecture, our grand foe
Satan, who in the serpent hath contrived
Against us this deceit. To crush his head
Would be revenge indeed; which will be lost
By death brought on ourselves, or childless days
Resolved, as thou proposest; so our foe
Shall scape his punishment ordain'd, and we
Instead shall double ours upon our heads.
No more be mention'd then of violence
Against ourselves, and wilful barrenness,
That cuts us off from hope, and savors only

Rancor and pride, impatience and despite,
Reluctance against God and His just yoke
Laid on our necks. Remember with what mild
And gracious temper He both heard and judged
Without wrath or reviling; we expected
Immediate dissolution, which we thought
Was meant by death that day, when, lo! to thee
Pains only in child-bearing were foretold,
And bringing forth; soon recompensed with joy,
Fruit of thy womb: on me the curse aslope
Glanced on the ground, with labor I must earn
My bread; what harm? idleness had been worse;
My labor will sustain me; and lest cold
Or heat should injure us, His timely care
Hath unbesought provided, and His hands
Clothed us unworthy, pitying while He judged.
How much more, if we pray Him, will His ear
Be open, and His heart to pity incline,
And teach us further by what means to shun
Th' inclement seasons, rain, ice, hail, and snow,
Which now the sky with various face begins
To show us in this mountain, while the winds
Blow moist and keen, shattering the graceful locks
Of these fair spreading trees, which bids us seek
Some better shroud, some better warmth to cherish
Our limbs benumb'd, ere this diurnal star
Leave cold the night; how we his gather'd beams
Reflected may with matter sere foment,
Or by collision of two bodies grind
The air attrite[1] to fire, as late the clouds
Justling or push'd with winds rude in their shock
Tine[2] the slant lightning whose thwart flame driv'n down
Kindles the gummy bark of fir or pine,
And sends a comfortable heat from far,
Which might supply the sun. Such fire to use,
And what may else be remedy or cure
To evils which our own misdeeds have wrought;
He will instruct us praying, and of grace
Beseeching Him, so as we need not fear
To pass commodiously this life, sustain'd

[1] Worn by rubbing or friction.
[2] To kindle.

By Him with many comforts, till we end
In dust, our final rest and native home.
What better can we do, than, to the place
Repairing where He judged us, prostrate fall
Before Him reverent, and there confess
Humbly our faults, and pardon beg, with tears
Watering the ground, and with our sighs the air
Frequenting, sent from hearts contrite, in sign
Of sorrow unfeign'd and humiliation meek?
Undoubtedly He will relent and turn
From His displeasure, in whose look serene,
When angry most He seem'd and most severe,
What else but favor, grace, and mercy shone?

   So spake our father penitent, nor Eve
Felt less remorse: they forthwith to the place
Repairing where He judged them prostrate fell
Before Him reverent, and both confess'd
Humbly their faults, and pardon begg'd, with tears
Watering the ground, and with their sighs the air
Frequenting,[1] sent from hearts contrite, in sign
Of sorrow unfeign'd and humiliation meek.

[1] Beating the air.

BOOK XI

The Argument

The Son of God presents to his Father the prayers of our first parents now repenting, and intercedes for them: God accepts them, but declares that they must no longer abide in paradise; sends Michael with a band of cherubim to dispossess them; but first to reveal to Adam future things: Michael's coming down. Adam shows to Eve certain ominous signs; he discerns Michael's approach; goes out to meet him: the angel denounces their approaching departure. Eve's lamentation. Adam pleads, but submits: the angel leads him up to a high hill; sets before him in vision what shall happen till the Flood.

Thus they in lowliest plight repentant stood,
Praying, for from the mercy-seat above
Prevenient grace descending had removed
The stony from their hearts, and made new flesh
Regenerate grow instead, that sighs now breathed
Unutterable,[1] which the spirit of prayer
Inspired, and wing'd for heav'n with speedier flight
Than loudest oratory: yet their port
Not of mean suitors, nor important less
Seem'd their petition, than when the ancient pair
In fables old, less ancient yet than these,
Deucalion and chaste Pyrrha to restore
The race of mankind drown'd, before the shrine
Of Themis stood devout.[2] To heav'n their prayers
Flew up, nor miss'd the way, by envious winds
Blown vagabond or frustrate: in they pass'd
Dimensionless through heav'nly doors; then clad
With incense,[3] where the golden altar fumed,
By their great Intercessor, came in sight

---

[1] Romans viii. 26.
[2] Thémis, the goddess of justice. The fable of Deucalion and Pyrrha, evidently founded on a heathen tradition of Noah's flood, is told by Ovid, *Met.* I. fab. 8.
[3] Psalm cxli. 2.

Before the Father's throne; them the glad Son
Presenting, thus to intercede began.

    See, Father, what first fruits on earth are sprung
From thy implanted grace in man, these sighs
And prayers, which in this golden censer mix'd
With incense, I thy priest before thee bring,
Fruits of more pleasing savor from thy seed
Sown with contrition in his heart, than those
Which his own hand manuring all the trees
Of paradise could have produced, ere fall'n
From innocence. Now therefore bend thine ear
To supplication, hear his sighs though mute;
Unskilful with what words to pray, let me
Interpret for him, me his advocate[1]
And propitiation; all his works on me
Good or not good ingraft, my merit those
Shall perfect, and for these my death shall pay.
Accept me, and in me from these receive
The smell of peace toward mankind, let him live
Before thee reconciled, at least his days
Number'd, though sad, till death his doom, (which I
To mitigate thus plead, not to reverse,)
To better life shall yield him, where with me
All my redeem'd may dwell in joy and bliss;
Made one with me as I with thee am one.[2]

    To whom the Father, without cloud, serene;
All thy request for man, accepted Son,
Obtain; all thy request was my decree:
But longer in that Paradise to dwell
The law I gave to nature him forbids:
Those pure immortal elements, that know
No gross, no unharmonious mixture foul,
Eject him tainted now, and purge him off
As a distemper gross, to air as gross,
And mortal food, as may dispose him best
For dissolution wrought by sin, that first
Distemper'd all things, and of incorrupt
Corrupted. I, at first, with two fair gifts
Created him endow'd, with happiness
And immortality: that fondly lost,

[1] 1 John ii. 1, 2.
[2] John xvii. 21, 22.

This other served but to eternize woe,
Till I provided death; so death becomes
His final remedy, and after life
Tried in sharp tribulation, and refined
By faith and faithful works, to second life,
Waked in the renovation of the just,
Resigns him up with heav'n and earth renew'd.
But let us call to synod all the blest
Through heav'n's wide bounds; from them I will not hide
My judgment; how with mankind I proceed,
As how with peccant angels late they saw;
And in their state, though firm, stood more confirm'd.
 He ended, and the Son gave signal high
To the bright minister that watch'd; he blew
His trumpet, heard in Oreb since perhaps
When God descended, and perhaps once more
To sound at general doom. The angelic blast
Fill'd all the regions: from their blissful bow'rs
Of Amaranthine shade, fountain or spring,
By the waters of life, where e'er they sat
In fellowships of joy, the sons of light
Hasted, resorting to the summons high,
And took their seats; till from His throne supreme
The Almighty thus pronounced His sov'reign will.
 O Sons, like one of us man is become
To know both good and evil, since his taste
Of that defended [1] fruit; but let him boast
His knowledge of good lost, and evil got;
Happier, had it sufficed him to have known
Good by itself, and evil not at all.
He sorrows now, repents and prays contrite,
My motions in him, longer than they move,
His heart I know how variable and vain
Self-left. Lest therefore his now bolder hand
Reach also of the Tree of Life, and eat,
And live for ever, dream at least to live
For ever, to remove him I decree,
And send him from the garden forth to till
The ground whence he was taken, fitter soil.
Michael, this my behest have thou in charge,
Take to thee from among the Cherubim

[1] Forbidden.

Thy choice of flaming warriors, lest the fiend,
Or in behalf of man, or to invade
Vacant possession, some new trouble raise:
Haste thee, and from the Paradise of GOD
Without remorse drive out the sinful pair,
From hallow'd ground the unholy nd denounce
To them and to their progeny from thence
Perpetual banishment. Yet lest they faint
At the sad sentence rigorously urged,
For I behold them soften'd and with tears
Bewailing their excess, all terror hide.
If patiently thy bidding they obey,
Dismiss them not disconsolate; reveal
To Adam what shall come in future days,
As I shall thee enlighten; intermix
My cov'nant in the woman's seed renew'd;
So send them forth, though sorrowing, yet in peace:
And on the east side of the garden place,
Where entrance up from Eden easiest climbs,
Cherubic watch, and of a sword the flame
Wide waving, all approach far off to fright,
And guard all passage to the Tree of Life:
Lest paradise a receptacle prove
To spirits foul, and all my trees their prey,
With whose stol'n fruit man once more to delude.

   He ceased; and the archangelic pow'r prepared
For swift descent, with him the cohort bright
Of watchful Cherubim; four faces each
Had, like a double Janus;[1] all their shape
Spangled with eyes more numerous than those
Of Argus,[2] and more wakeful than to drowse,
Charm'd with Arcadian Pipe, the pastoral reed
Of Hermes, or his opiate rod. Meanwhile,
To resalute the world with sacred light
Leucothea[3] waked, and with fresh dews imbalm'd

[1] Ezek. x. 12, 14.
[2] Argus, the spy of Juno, who had a hundred eyes, was lulled
to sleep and killed by Mercury (or Hermes), by the command
of Jupiter. The Caduceus of Mercury is called an "opiate rod,"
because with it he could charm sleep on any eyelids he pleased.
[3] "The white goddess," or Dawn. The same with Matuta, or
early morning, in Latin. She preceded Aurora.—NEWTON.

The earth, when Adam and first matron Eve
Had ended now their orisons, and found
Strength added from above, new hope to spring
Out of despair, joy, but with fear yet link'd;
Which thus to Eve his welcome words renew'd.

    Eve, easily may faith admit, that all
The good which we enjoy from heav'n descends;
But that from us aught should ascend to heav'n
So prevalent as to concern the mind
Of GOD high-bless'd, or to incline His will,
Hard to belief may seem; yet this will prayer,
Or one short sigh of human breath, upborne
Ev'n to the seat of GOD. For since I sought
By prayer th' offended Deity to appease,
Kneel'd and before Him humbled all my heart,
Methought I saw Him placable and mild,
Bending His ear: persuasion in me grew
That I was heard with favor; peace return'd
Home to my breast, and to my memory
His promise, that thy seed shall bruise our foe;
Which, then not minded in dismay, yet now
Assures me that the bitterness of death
Is past, and we shall live. Whence hail to thee,
Eve [1] rightly call'd, mother of all mankind,
Mother of all things living, since by thee
Man is to live, and all things live for man.

    To whom thus Eve with sad demeanor meek.
Ill worthy I such title should belong
To me transgressor, who, for thee ordain'd
A help, became thy snare: to me reproach
Rather belongs, distrust and all dispraise:
But infinite in pardon was my Judge,
That I, who first brought death on all, am graced
The source of life; next favorable thou,
Who highly thus to entitle me vouchsaf'st,
Far other name deserving. But the field
To labor calls us now with sweat imposed,
Though after sleepless night; for see, the morn,
All unconcern'd, with our unrest, begins
Her rosy progress smiling; let us forth,
I never from thy side henceforth to stray,

    [1] Eve signifies Life.

Where'er our day's work lies, though now enjoin'd
Laborious, till day droop; while here we dwell,
What can be toilsome in these pleasant walks?
Here let us live, though in fall'n state, content.

So spake, so wish'd much-humbled Eve; but fate
Subscribed not; nature first gave signs, impress'd
On bird, beast, air; air suddenly eclipsed
After short blush of morn: nigh in her sight
The bird of Jove, stoop'd from his aery tow'r,
Two birds of gayest plume before him drove:
Down from a hill the beast that reigns in woods,
First hunter then, pursued a gentle brace,
Goodliest of all the forest, hart and hind;
Direct to th' eastern gate was bent their flight.
Adam observed, and, with his eye the chase
Pursuing, not unmoved to Eve thus spake.

O Eve, some further change awaits us nigh,
Which heav'n by these mute signs in nature shows
Forerunners of his purpose, or to warn
Us haply too secure of our discharge
From penalty, because from death released
Some days; how long, and what till then our life,
Who knows, or more than this, that we are dust,
And thither must return and be no more?
Why else this double object in our sight
Of flight pursued in the air, and o'er the ground,
One way the selfsame hour? Why in the east
Darkness ere day's mid-course, and morning light
More orient in yon western cloud, that draws
O'er the blue firmament a radiant white,
And slow descends, with something heav'nly fraught.

He err'd not, for by this the heav'nly bands
Down from a sky of jasper lighted now
In Paradise, and on a hill made halt,
A glorious apparition, had not doubt
And carnal fear that day dimm'd Adam's eye.
Not that more glorious, when the angels met
Jacob in Mahanaim,[1] where he saw
The field pavilion'd with his guardians bright;
Nor that which on the flaming mount appear'd

[1] Gen. xxxii. 1, 2.

In Dothan, cover'd with a camp fire,[1]
Against the Syrian king, who to surprise
One man assassin-like had levy'd war,
War unproclaim'd. The princely hierarch
In their bright stand there left his powers to seize
Possession of the garden; he alone,
To find where Adam shelter'd, took his way,
Not unperceived of Adam, who to Eve,
While the great visitant approach'd, thus spake.

    Eve, now expect great tidings, which perhaps
Of us will soon determine, or impose
New laws to be observed; for I descry
From yonder blazing cloud that veils the hill
One of the heav'nly host, and by his gait
None of the meanest: some great potentate,
Or of the thrones above, such majesty
Invests him coming; yet not terrible,
That I should fear, nor sociably mild,
As Raphael, that I should much confide;
But solemn and sublime, whom not to offend
With reverence I must meet, and thou retire.

    He ended; and th' archangel soon drew nigh,
Not in his shape celestial, but as man
Clad to meet man; over his lucid arms
A military vest of purple flow'd,
Livelier than Melibœan,[2] or the grain
Of Sarra, worn by kings and heroes old
In time of truce; Iris[3] had dipp'd the woof;
His starry helm unbuckled show'd him prime
In manhood where youth ended; by his side
As in a glistering zodiac hung the sword,
Satan's dire dread, and in his hand the spear
Adam bow'd low, he kingly from his state
Inclined not, but his coming thus declared.

---

[1] Alluding to the King of Syria's attempt to take the prophet Elisha captive, and to the vision the prophet vouchsafed to obtain for his servant of the angel-guards which defended him. 2 Kings vi. 17.

[2] Melibea, a city of Thessaly, was famous for dyeing the noblest purple. Sarra, the dye of Tyre.—HUME. Sar was the name of the fish from which the Tyrian purple dye was extracted.

[3] The rainbow hues are meant.

Adam, heav'n's high behest no preface needs.
Sufficient that thy prayers are heard, and death,
Then due by sentence when thou didst transgress,
Defeated of his seizure many days
Giv'n thee of grace, wherein thou may'st repent
And one bad act with many deeds well done
May'st cover: well may then thy Lord appeased
Redeem thee quite from death's rapacious claim;
But longer in this Paradise to dwell
Permits not: to remove thee I am come,
And send thee from the garden forth to till
The ground whence thou wast taken, fitter soil.

He added not, for Adam at the news
Heart-struck with chilling gripe of sorrow stood,
That all his senses bound; Eve, who unseen
Yet all had heard, with audible lament
Discover'd soon the place of her retire.
O unexpected stroke, worse than of death!
Must I thus leave thee, paradise? thus leave
Thee, native soil, these happy walks and shades,
Fit haunt of Gods? where I had hope to spend,
Quiet though sad, the respite of that day
That must be mortal to us both. O flow'rs,
That never will in other climate grow,
My early visitation, and my last
At ev'n, which I bred up with tender hand
From the first op'ning bud, and gave ye names,
Who now shall rear ye to the sun, or rank
Your tribes, and water from th' ambrosial fount?
Thee lastly, nuptial bow'r! by me adorn'd
With what to sight or smell was sweet; from thee
How shall I part, and whither wander down
Into a lower world, to this obscure
And wild? how shall we breathe in other air
Less pure, accustom'd to immortal fruits?

Whom thus the angel interrupted mild.
Lament not, Eve, but patiently resign
What justly thou hast lost; nor set thy heart,
Thus over fond, on that which is not thine:
Thy going is not lonely, with thee goes
Thy husband, him to follow thou art bound;
Where he abides, think there thy native soil.

Adam, by this from the cold sudden damp
Recovering, and his scatter'd spirits return'd,
To Michael thus his humble words address'd.
        Celestial, whether among the thrones, or named
Of them the highest, for such of shape may seem
Prince above princes, gently hast thou told
Thy message, which might else in telling wound.
And in performing end us; what besides
Of sorrow, and dejection, and despair,
Our frailty can sustain, thy tidings bring;
Departure from this happy place, our sweet
Recess, and only consolation left
Familiar to our eyes, all places else
Inhospitable appear and desolate,
Nor knowing us nor known; and if by prayer
Incessant I could hope to change the will
Of Him who all things can, I would not cease
To weary him with my assiduous cries.
But prayer against His absolute decree
No more avails than breath against the wind,
Blown stifling back on him that breathes it forth:
Therefore to His great bidding I submit.
This most afflicts me, that departing hence
As from His face I shall be hid, deprived
His blessed count'nance; here I could frequent,
With worship, place by place, where he vouchsafed
Presence divine, and to my sons relate,
On this mount he appear'd, under this tree
Stood visible, among these pines His voice
I heard, here with Him at this fountain talk'd:
So many grateful altars I would rear
Of grassy turf, and pile up every stone
Of lustre from the brook, in memory,
Or monument to ages, and thereon
Offer sweet-smelling gums, and fruits, and flow'rs:
In yonder nether world where shall I seek
His bright appearances, or footstep trace?
For though I fled him angry, yet, recall'd
To life prolong'd and promised race, I now
Gladly behold though but His utmost skirts
Of glory, and far off His steps adore.
        To whom thus Michael with regard benign.

Adam, thou know'st heav'n His, and all the earth,
Not this rock only; His omnipresence fills
Land, sea and air, and every kind that lives,[1]
Fomented by His virtual power and warm'd:
All the earth He gave thee to possess and rule,
No despicable gift; surmise not then
His presence to these narrow bounds confined
Of Paradise or Eden: this had been
Perhaps thy capital seat, from whence had spread
All generations, and had hither come
From all the ends of the earth, to celebrate
And reverence thee, their great progenitor.
But this pre-eminence thou hast lost, brought down
To dwell on even ground now with thy sons:
Yet doubt not but in valley and in plain
GOD is as here, and will be found alike
Present, and of His presence many a sign
Still following thee, still compassing thee round
With goodness and paternal love, His face
Express, and of His steps the track divine.
Which that thou may'st believe and be confirm'd
Ere thou from hence depart, know, I am sent
To show thee what shall come in future days
To thee and to thy off-spring; good with bad
Expect to hear, supernal grace contending
With sinfulness of men; thereby to learn
True patience, and to temper joy with fear
And pious sorrow, equally inured
By moderation either state to bear,
Prosperous or adverse: so shalt thou lead
Safest thy life, and best prepared endure
Thy mortal passage when it comes. Ascend
This hill; let Eve, for I have drench'd her eyes,
Here sleep below, while thou to foresight wak'st,
As once thou slept'st, while she to life was form'd.
    To whom thus Adam gratefully replied.
Ascend, I follow thee, safe guide, the path
Thou lead'st me, and to the hand of heav'n submit,
However chast'ning, to the evil turn
My obvious breast, arming to overcome

[1] Jeremiah xxiii. 24.

By suffering, and earn rest from labor won,
If so I may attain. So both ascend
In the visions of GOD. It was a hill
Of Paradise the highest, from whose top
The hemisphere of earth in clearest ken
Stretch'd out to the amplest reach of prospect lay.
Not higher that hill nor wider looking round,
Whereon for different cause the tempter set
Our second Adam [1] in the wilderness,
To show him all earth's kingdoms and their glory.
His eye might there command wherever stood
City of old or modern fame, the seat
Of mightiest empire, from the destined walls
Of Cambalu, [2] seat of Cathaian Can,
And Samarchand by Oxus, Temir's throne, [3]
To Paquin of Sinæan kings, [4] and thence
To Agra and Lahor of great Mogul,
Down to the golden Chersonese, [5] or where
The Persian in Ecbatan sat, or since
In Hispahan, or where the Russian Czar
In Mosco, or the Sultan in Bizance, [6]
Turchestan-born; nor could his eye not ken
The empire of Negus [7] to his utmost port
Ercoco, and the less maritime kings
Mombaza, and Quiloa, and Melind, [8]
And Sofala thought Ophir, to the realm
Of Congo, and Angola farthest south;
Or thence from Niger flood to Atlas mount
The kingdoms of Almansor, [9] Fez, and Sus,
Marocco, and Algiers, and Tremisen;

---

[1] 1 Cor. xv. 45. Matt. iv. 8.

[2] The principal city of Cathay.

[3] The chief city of Zagathian Tartary. It was the royal residence of the great conqueror Tamerlane, or "Temir."

[4] Paquin, or Pekin, in China, the country of the ancient Sinæ.— NEWTON.

[5] The golden Chersonese is Malacca.

[6] Byzantium, or Constantinople. The Turks came from Turkestan, in Tartary.

[7] Upper Ethiopia, or Abyssinia, whose king is still styled the *Negus*. Ercoco, or Erquièo, on the Red Sea.

[8] All on the eastern coast of Africa.

[9] Almansor was King of Barbary, where these states lie.

Or Europe thence, and where Rome was to sway
The world: in spirit perhaps he also saw
Rich Mexico the seat of Motezume,
And Cusco in Peru, the richer seat
Of Atabalipa,[1] and yet unspoil'd
Guiana, whose great city Geryon's sons[2]
Call El Dorado; but to nobler sights
Michael from Adam's eyes the film removed,
Which that false fruit that promised clearer sight
Had bred; then purged with euphrasy[3] and rue
The visual nerve, for he had much to see;
And from the well of life three drops instill'd.
So deep the power of these ingredients pierced,
Ev'n to the inmost seat of mental sight,
That Adam, now enforced to close his eyes,
Sunk down, and all his spirits became intranced:
But him the gentle angel by the hand
Soon raised, and his attention thus recall'd.

Adam, now ope thine eyes, and first behold
Th' effects which thy original crime hath wrought
In some to spring from thee, who never touch'd
The expected tree, nor with the snake conspired,
Nor sinn'd thy sin; yet from that sin derive
Corruption to bring forth more violent deeds.

His eyes he open'd, and beheld a field,
Part arable and tilth, whereon were sheaves
New reap'd, the other part sheep-walks and folds:
I' th' midst an altar as the land-mark stood,
Rustic, of grassy sord;[4] thither anon
A sweaty reaper[5] from his tillage brought
First fruits, the green ear, and the yellow sheaf,

---

[1] Atahuallpa, the last native Emperor or Inca, subdued by Pizarro.

[2] The Spaniards, so called from Geryon, an ancient King of Spain. El Dorado revives the memory of the explorers and navigators of Elizabeth's days. The whole inhabited world is summed up in this sweeping and glorious description of the vision of our Lord on the Mount.

[3] The herb called in English eyebright. Both it and rue were thought to have great medicinal power.

[4] Sward. See green-sord for green-sward in early editions of Shakespeare.

[5] Gen. iv. 2.

Uncull'd as came to hand; a shepherd next
More meek came with the firstlings of his flock
Choicest and best; then sacrificing laid
The inwards and their fat, with incense strew'd,
On the cleft wood, and all due rites perform'd.
His off'ring soon propitious fire from heav'n
Consumed with nimble glance, and grateful steam;
The other's not, for his was not sincere:
Whereat he inly raged, and, as they talk'd,
Smote him into the midriff with a stone
That beat out life; he fell, and deadly pale
Groan'd out his soul with gushing blood effused.
Much at that sight was Adam in his heart
Dismay'd, and thus in haste to the angel cried.

    O teacher, some great mischief hath befall'n
To that meek man, who well had sacrificed;
Is piety thus and pure devotion paid?

    To whom Michael thus, he also moved, replied.
These two are brethren, Adam, and to come
Out of thy loins; the unjust the just hath slain,
For envy that his brother's offering found
From heav'n acceptance; but the bloody fact
Will be avenged, and the other's faith approved
Lose no reward, though here thou see him die,
Rolling in dust and gore. To which our sire:

    Alas, both for the deed and for the cause!
But have I now seen death? is this the way
I must return to native dust? O sight
Of terror, foul and ugly to behold,
Horrid to think, how horrible to feel!

    To whom thus Michael. Death thou hast seen
In his first shape on man; but many shapes
Of Death, and many are the ways that lead
To his grim cave, all dismal; yet to sense
More terrible at the entrance than within.
Some, as thou saw'st, by violent stroke shall die,
By fire, flood, famine, by intemperance more
In meats and drinks, which on the earth shall bring
Diseases dire, of which a monstrous crew
Before thee shall appear; that thou may'st know
What misery th' inabstinence of Eve
Shall bring on men. Immediately a place

Before his eyes appear'd, sad, noisome, dark,
A lazar-house it seem'd, wherein were laid
Numbers of all diseased, all maladies
Of ghastly spasm, or racking torture, qualms
Of heart-sick agony, all feverous kinds,
Convulsions, epilepsies, fierce catarrhs,
Intestine stone, and ulcer, colic pangs,
Dæmoniac frenzy, moping melancholy,
And moon-struck madness, pining atrophy,
Marasmus, and wide-wasting pestilence,
Dropsies, and asthmas, and joint-racking rheums.
Dire was the tossing, deep the groans; despair
Tended the sick, busiest from couch to couch;
And over them triumphant Death his dart
Shook, but delay'd to strike, though oft invoked
With vows, as their chief good, and final hope.
Sight so deform, what heart of rock could long
Dry-ey'd behold? Adam could not, but wept,
Though not of woman born; compassion quell'd
His best of man, and gave him up to tears
A space, till firmer thoughts restrain'd excess,
And scarce recovering words his plaint renew'd.

    O miserable mankind, to what fall
Degraded, to what wretched state reserved!
Better end here unborn. Why is life giv'n
To be thus wrested from us? rather why
Obtruded on us thus? who, if we knew
What we receive, would either not accept
Life offer'd, or soon beg to lay it down,
Glad to be so dismiss'd in peace. Can thus
The image of God in man, created once
So goodly and erect, though faulty since,
To such unsightly sufferings be debased
Under inhuman pains? Why should not man,
Retaining still divine similitude
In part, from such deformities be free,
And for his Maker's image sake exempt?

    Their Maker's image, answer'd Michael, then
Forsook them, when themselves they villified
To serve ungovern'd appetite, and took
His image whom they served, a brutish vice,
Inductive mainly to the sin of Eve.

Therefore so abject is their punishment,
Disfiguring not GOD's likeness, but their own,
Or if His likeness, by themselves defaced,
While they pervert pure nature's healthful rules
To loathesome sickness, worthily, since they
GOD's image did not reverence in themselves.

    I yield it just, said Adam, and submit.
But is there yet no other way, besides
These painful passages, how we may come
To death, and mix with our connatural dust?

    There is, said Michael, if thou well observe
The rule of not too much, by temperance taught
In what thou eat'st and drink'st, seeking from thence
Due nourishment, not gluttonous delight;
Till many years over thy head return,
So may'st thou live, till like ripe fruit thou drop
Into thy mother's lap, or be with ease
Gather'd, not harshly pluck'd, for death mature.
This is old age; but then thou must outlive
Thy youth, thy strength, thy beauty, which will change
To wither'd, weak, and gray: thy senses then
Obtuse all taste of pleasure must forego
To what thou hast, and for the air of youth,
Hopeful and cheerful, in thy blood will reign
A melancholy damp of cold and dry
To weigh thy spirits down, and last consume
The balm of life. To whom our ancestor:

    Henceforth I fly not death, nor would prolong
Life much, bent rather how I may be quit
Fairest and easiest of this cumbrous charge,
Which I must keep till my appointed day
Of rend'ring up, and patiently attend
My dissolution. Michael replied.

    Nor love thy life, nor hate; but what thou liv'st
Live well, how long or short permit to Heav'n:
And now prepare thee for another sight.
He look'd, and saw a spacious plain, whereon
Were tents of various hue; by some were herds
Of cattle grazing:[1] others, whence the sound
Of instruments that made melodious chime

---

[1] Jabal. See Gen. iv. 20.

Was heard, of harp and organ; and who moved
Their stops and chords was seen: his volant touch
Instinct through all proportions low and high
Fled and pursued transverse the resonant fugue,[1]
In other part stood one who, at the forge[2]
Laboring, two massy clods of iron and brass
Had melted, whether found where casual fire
Had wasted woods on mountain or in vale,
Down to the veins of earth, thence gliding hot
To some cave's mouth, or whether wash'd by stream
From underground; the liquid ore he drain'd
Into fit moulds prepared; from which he form'd
First his own tools; then, what might else be wrought
Fusil or grav'n in metal. After these,
But on the hither side, a different sort
From the high neighboring hills, which was their seat,
Down to the plain descended: by their guise
Just men they seem'd,[3] and all their study bent
To worship God aright, and know His works
Not hid, nor those things last, which might preserve
Freedom and peace to men: they on the plain
Long had not walk'd, when from the tents behold
A bevy of fair women, richly gay
In gems and wanton dress; to the harp they sung
Soft amorous ditties, and in dance came on:
The men, though grave, eyed them, and let their eyes
Rove without rein, till, in the amorous net
Fast caught, they liked, and each his liking chose:
And now of love they treat, till the ev'ning star,
Love's harbinger, appear'd; then all in heat
They light the nuptial torch, and bid invoke
Hymen, then first to marriage rites invoked;
With feast and music all the tents resound.
Such happy interview and fair event
Of love and youth not lost, songs, garlands, flow'rs,
And charming symphonies attach'd the heart
Of Adam, soon inclined to admit delight,
The bent of nature, which he thus express'd.
    True opener of mine eyes, prime angel bless'd,

[1] Jubal. See Gen. iv. 21.
[2] Tubal-cain. Gen. iv. 22.
[3] The descendants of Seth.

Much better seems this vision, and more hope
Of peaceful days portends, than those two past;
Those were of hate and death, or pain much worse,
Here nature seems fulfill'd in all her ends.
　　To whom thus Michael. Judge not what is best
By pleasure, though to nature seeming meet,
Created, as thou art, to nobler ends
Holy and pure, conformity divine.
Those tents, thou saw'st so pleasant, were the tent
Of wickedness, wherein shall dwell his race
Who slew his brother; studious they appear
Of arts that polish life, inventors rare,
Unmindful of their Maker, though his Spirit
Taught them, but they his gifts acknowledged none.
Yet they a beauteous offspring shall beget;
For that fair female troup thou saw'st, that seem'd
Of Goddesses, so blithe, so smooth, so gay,
Yet empty of all good wherein consists
Woman's domestic honor and chief praise;
Bred only and completed to the taste
Of lustful appetence, to sing, to dance,
To dress, and troll the tongue, and roll the eye.
To these that sober race of men, whose lives
Religious titled them the sons of GOD,
Shall yield up all their virtue, all their fame
Ignobly, to the trains and to the smiles
Of these fair atheists; and now swim in joy
(Erelong to swim at large) and laugh; for which
The world erelong a world of tears must weep.
　　To whom thus Adam of short joy bereft;
O pity and shame, that they, who to live well
Enter'd so fair, should turn aside to tread
Paths indirect, or in the midway faint!
But still I see the tenor of man's woe
Holds on the same, from woman to begin.
　　From man's effeminate slackness it begins,
Said the angel, who should better hold his place
By wisdom and superior gifts received.
But now prepare thee for another scene.
　　He look'd, and saw wide territory spread
Before him, towns, and rural works between,
Cities of men with lofty gates and tow'rs,

Concourse in arms, fierce faces threat'ning war,
Giants of mighty bone, and bold emprise;
Part wield their arms, part curb the foaming steed,
Single, or in array of battle ranged
Both horse and foot, nor idly must'ring stood:
One way a band select from forage drives
A herd of beeves, fair oxen and fair kine,
From a fat meadow ground; or fleecy flock,
Ewes and their bleating lambs, over the plain,
Their booty; scarce with life the shepherds fly,
But call in aid, which makes a bloody fray.
With cruel tournament the squadrons join;
Where cattle pastured late, now scatter'd lies
With carcasses and arms th' ensanguin'd field,
Deserted. Others to a city strong
Lay siege, encamp'd, by battery, scale, and mine,
Assaulting; others from the wall defend
With dart and javelin, stones and sulphurous fire;
On each hand slaughter and gigantic deeds.
In other part the sceptered heralds call
To council in the city gates: anon
Gray-headed men and grave, with warriors mix'd,
Assemble, and harangues are heard; but soon
In factious opposition; till at last
Of middle age one rising,[1] eminent
In wise-deport, spake much of right and wrong,
Of justice, of religion, truth and peace,
And judgment from above: him old and young
Exploded, and had seized with violent hands,
Had not a cloud descending snatch'd him thence
Unseen amid the throng: so violence
Proceeded, and oppression, and sword-law,
Through all the plain, and refuge none was found.
Adam was all in tears, and to his guide
Lamenting turn'd full sad; O! what are these,
Death's ministers, not men, who thus deal death
Inhumanly to men, and multiply
Ten thousand-fold the sin of him who slew
His brother; for of whom such massacre

---

[1] Enoch, said to be of middle age, because he was translated
when he was only 365 years old, a middle age then. Gen. v. 23.—
RICHARDSON.

Make they but of their brethren, men of men?
But who was that just man, whom had not heav'n
Rescued, had in his righteousness been lost?
  To whom thus Michael. These are the product
Of those ill-mated marriages thou saw'st;
Where good with bad were match'd, who of themselves
Abhor to join; and by imprudence mix'd
Produce prodigious births of body or mind.
Such were these giants, men of high renown;
For in those days might only shall be admired,
And valor and heroic virtue call'd:
To overcome in battle, and subdue
Nations, and bring home spoils with infinite
Manslaughter, shall be held the highest pitch
Of human glory, and for glory done
Of triumph, to be styled great conquerors,
Patrons of mankind, Gods, and sons of Gods,
Destroyers rightlier call'd and plagues of men.
Thus fame shall be achieved, renown on earth,
And what most merits fame in silence hid.
But he, the seventh from thee, whom thou beheld'st
The only righteous in a world perverse,
And therefore hated, therefore so beset
With foes for daring single to be just,
And utter odious truth, that God would come
To judge them with his saints; him the most High
Wrapt in a balmy cloud with wingèd steeds
Did, as thou saw'st, receive, to walk with God
High in salvation and the climes of bliss,
Exempt from death: to show thee what reward
Awaits the good, the rest what punishment:
Which now direct thine eyes and soon behold:
  He look'd, and saw the face of things quite changed,
The brazen throat of war had ceased to roar;
All now was turn'd to jollity and game,
To luxury and riot, feast and dance,
Marrying or prostituting as befell,
Rape or adultery, where passing fair
Allured them; thence from cups to civil broils.
At length a reverend sire[1] among them came,

---

[1] Noah. See 1 Peter iii. 19.

And of their doings great dislike declared,
And testified against their ways; he oft
Frequented their assemblies, whereso met
Triumphs, or festivals, and to them preach'd
Conversion and repentance, as to souls
In prison under judgments imminent:
But all in vain: which when he saw, he ceased
Contending, and removed his tents far off:[1]
Then from the mountain hewing timber tall,
Began to build a vessel of huge bulk,
Measured by cubit, length, and breadth, and highth,
Smear'd round with pitch, and in the side a door
Contrived, and of provisions laid in large
For man and beast: when lo, a wonder strange!
Of every beast, and bird, and insect small,
Came sevens, and pairs, and enter'd in, as taught
Their order: last the sire and his three sons
With their four wives; and God made fast the door.
Meanwhile the south wind rose, and, with black wings
Wide hovering, all the clouds together drove
From under heav'n; the hills to their supply
Vapor, and exhalation dusk and moist
Sent up amain: and now the thicken'd sky
Like a dark ceiling stood; down rush'd the rain
Impetuous, and continued till the earth
No more was seen; the floating vessel swum
Uplifted; and secure with beakèd prow
Rode tilting o'er the waves, all dwellings else
Flood overwhelm'd, and them with all their pomp
Deep under water roll'd; sea cover'd sea,
Sea without shore, and in their palaces,
Where luxury late reign'd, sea-monsters whelp'd
And stabled; of mankind, so numerous late,
All left in one small bottom swum embark'd.
How didst thou grieve then, Adam, to behold
The end of all thy offspring, end so sad,
Depopulation! thee another flood,
Of tears and sorrow a flood thee also drown'd,
And sunk thee as thy sons; till gently rear'd
By the angel, on thy feet thou stood'st at last,

[1] Noah's removal to another land is taken from Josephus. *Antiq.
Fud.* lib. i. c. 3.

Though comfortless, as when a father mourns
His children, all in view destroy'd at once;
And scarce to the angel utter'dst thus thy plaint.
   O visions ill foreseen! better had I
Lived ignorant of future, so had borne
My part of evil only, each day's lot
Enough to bear; those now, that were dispensed
The burden of many ages, on me light
At once, by my foreknowledge gaining birth
Abortive, to torment me ere their being,
With thought that they must be. Let no man seek
Henceforth to be foretold what shall befall
Him or his children; evil he may be sure,
Which neither his foreknowing can prevent;
And he the future evil shall no less
In apprehension than in substance feel,
Grievous to bear: but that care now is past,
Man is not whom to warn; those few escaped
Famine and anguish will at last consume
Wand'ring that wat'ry desert. I had hope
When violence was ceased, and war on earth,
All would have then gone well; peace would have crown'd
With length of happy days the race of man;
But I was far deceived; for now I see
Peace to corrupt no less than war to waste.
How comes it thus? unfold, celestial guide,
And whether here the race of man will end.
   To whom thus Michael. Those whom last thou saw'st
In triumph and luxurious wealth, are they
First seen in acts of prowess eminent
And great exploits, but of true virtue void;
Who having spill'd much blood, and done much waste,
Subduing nations, and achieved thereby
Fame in the world, high titles, and rich prey,
Shall change their course to pleasure, ease, and sloth,
Surfeit, and lust, till wantonness and pride
Raise out of friendship hostile deeds in peace.
The conquered also and enslaved by war
Shall with their freedom lost all virtue lose
And fear of God, from whom their piety feign'd
In sharp contest of battle found no aid
Against invaders; therefore cool'd in zeal

Thenceforth shall practice how to live secure,
Worldly, or dissolute, on what their lords
Shall leave them to enjoy, for the earth shall bear
More than enough, that temperance may be tried:
So all shall turn degenerate, all depraved,
Justice and temperance, truth and faith forgot;
One man except, the only son of light
In a dark age, against example good,
Against allurement, custom, and a world
Offended; fearless of reproach and scorn,
Or violence, he of their wicked ways
Shall them admonish, and before them set
The paths of righteousness, how much more safe
And full of peace, denouncing wrath to come
On their impenitence; and shall return
Of them derided, but of God observed
The one just man alive; by his command
Shall build a wondrous ark, as thou beheld'st,
To save himself and household from amidst
A world devote to universal wreck.
No sooner he with them of man and beast
Select for life shall in the ark be lodged
And sheltered round, but all the cataracts
Of heav'n set open on the earth shall pour
Rain day and night, all fountains of the deep
Broke up shall heave the ocean to usurp
Beyond all bounds, till inundation rise
Above the highest hills: then shall this mount
Of Paradise by might of waves be moved
Out of his place, push'd by the hornèd flood,
With all his verdure spoil'd, and trees adrift,
Down the great river to the op'ning gulf,
And there take root, an island salt and bare,
The haunt of seals, and orcs, and sea-mews' clang;
To teach thee that God attributes to place
No sanctity, if none be thither brought
By men who there frequent, or therein dwell.
And now what further shall ensue, behold.
    He look'd, and saw the ark hull on the flood,
Which now abated, for the clouds were fled,
Driv'n by a keen north-wind, that blowing dry
Wrinkled the face of deluge, as decay'd;

And the clear sun on his wide wat'ry glass
Gazed hot, and of the fresh wave largely drew,
As after thirst, which made their flowing shrink
From standing lake to tripping ebb, that stole
With soft foot towards the deep, who now had stopp'd
His sluices, as the heav'n his windows shut.
The ark no more now floats, but seems on ground
Fast on the top of some high mountain fix'd.
And now the tops of hills as rocks appear;
With clamor thence the rapid currents drive
Towards the retreating sea their furious tide.
Forthwith from out the ark a raven flies,
And after him the surer messenger,
A dove, sent forth once and again to spy
Green tree or ground whereon his foot may light;
The second time returning, in his bill
An olive leaf he brings, pacific sign:
Anon dry ground appears, and from his ark
The ancient sire descends with all his train;
Then with uplifted hands, and eyes devout,
Grateful to heav'n, over his head beholds
A dewy cloud, and in the cloud a bow
Conspicuous with three listed colors gay,
Betok'ning peace from GOD, and cov'nant new.
Whereat the heart of Adam erst so sad
Greatly rejoiced, and thus his joy broke forth.
   O thou, who future things canst represent
As present, heav'nly instructor, I revive
At this last sight, assured that man shall live
With all the creatures, and their seed preserve.
Far less I now lament for one whole world
Of wicked sons destroy'd, than I rejoice
For one man found so perfect and so just,
That GOD vouchsafes to raise another world
From him, and all his anger to forget.
But say, what mean those color'd streaks in heav'n,
Distended as the brow of GOD appeased?
Or serve they as a flow'ry verge to bind
The fluid skirts of that same wat'ry cloud
Lest it again dissolve and show'r the earth?
   To whom the archangel. Dext'rously thou aim'st;
So willingly doth GOD remit His ire,

Though late repenting Him of man depraved,
Grieved at His heart, when looking down He saw
The whole earth fill'd with violence, and all flesh
Corrupting each their way; yet, those removed,
Such grace shall one just man find in His sight,
That He relents, not to blot out mankind,
And makes a covenant never to destroy
The earth again by flood, nor let the sea
Surpass his bounds, nor rain to drown the world
With man therein or beast; but when he brings
Over the earth a cloud, will therein set
His triple-color'd bow, whereon to look,
And call to mind his cov'nant: day and night,
Seed-time and harvest, heat and hoary frost,
Shall hold their course, till fire purge all things new,
Both heav'n and earth, wherein the just shall dwell.

BOOK XII

The Argument

The angel Michael continues from the flood to relate what shall succeed; then, in the mention of Abraham, comes by degrees to explain, who that seed of the woman shall be which was promised Adam and Eve in the fall; his incarnation, death, resurrection, and ascension; the state of the church till his second coming. Adam, greatly satisfied, and recomforted by these relations and promises, descends the hill with Michael; wakens Eve, who all this while had slept, but with gentle dreams composed to quietness of mind and submission. Michael in either hand leads them out of paradise, the fiery sword waving behind them, and the Cherubim taking their stations to guard the place.

As one who in his journey bates at noon,
Though bent on speed, so here th' archangel paused
Betwixt the world destroy'd and world restored;
If Adam aught perhaps might interpose;
Then with transition sweet new speech resumes.
    Thus thou hast seen one world begin and end;
And man as from a second stock proceed.
Much thou hast yet to see, but I perceive
Thy mortal sight to fail: objects divine
Must needs impair and weary human sense:
Henceforth what is to come I will relate,
Thou therefore give due audience, and attend.
    This second source of men, while yet but few,
And while the dread of judgment past remains
Fresh in their minds, fearing the Deity,
With some regard to what is just and right
Shall lead their lives, and multiply apace,
Laboring the soil, and reaping plenteous crop,
Corn, wine, and oil; and from the herd, or flock,
Oft sacrificing bullock, lamb, or kid,
With large wine-offerings pour'd, and sacred feast,
Shall spend their days in joy unblamed, and dwell
Long time in peace by families and tribes

Under paternal rule; till one shall rise
Of proud ambitious heart, who not content
With fair equality, fraternal state,
Will arrogate dominion undeserved
Over his brethren, and quite dispossess
Concord and law of nature from the earth;
Hunting, and men not beasts shall be his game,
With war and hostile snare such as refuse
Subjection to his empire tyrannous.
A mighty hunter thence he shall be styled [1]
Before the Lord, as in despite of heav'n,
Or from heav'n claiming second sov'reignty;
And from rebellion shall derive his name, [2]
Though of rebellion others he accuse.
He with a crew, whom like ambition joins
With him or under him to tyrannize,
Marching from Eden towards the west, [3] shall find
The plain, wherein a black bituminous gurge
Boils out from under ground, the mouth of hell:
Of brick and of that stuff they cast to build
A city and tow'r, whose top may reach to heav'n,
And get themselves a name, lest far disperst
In foreign lands their memory be lost,
Regardless whether good or evil fame.
But GOD, who oft descends to visit men
Unseen, and through their habitations walks,
To mark their doings, them beholding soon,
Comes down to see their city, ere the tower
Obstruct Heav'n-tow'rs, and in derision sets
Upon their tongues a various spirit, to rase
Quite out their native language, and instead
To sow a jangling noise of words unknown.
Forthwith a hideous gabble rises loud
Among the builders, each to other calls
Not understood, till hoarse, and all in rage,

[1] Nimrod, who is supposed to have been the first who assumed kingly power. See Gen. x. 9.
[2] The name Nimrod is derived from a Hebrew word that signifies to rebel.
[3] "And it came to pass, as they journeyed from the east, that they found a plain in the land of Shinar. And they had brick for stone, and slime had they for mortar." Gen. xi. 2, &c.

As mock'd they storm; great laughter was in heav'n,
And looking down, to see the hubbub strange
And hear the din; thus was the building left
Ridiculous, and the work Confusion[1] named.

    Whereto thus Adam fatherly displeased.
O execrable son! so to aspire
Above his brethren, to himself assuming
Authority usurp'd, from GOD not giv'n.
He gave us only over beast, fish, fowl,
Dominion absolute; that right we hold
By His donation; such title to Himself
Reserving, human left from human free.
But this usurper his encroachment proud
Stays not on man; to GOD his tower intends
Siege and defiance. Wretched man! what food
Will he convey up thither to sustain
Himself and his rash army, where thin air
Above the clouds will pine his entrails gross,
And famish him of breath, if not of bread?

    To whom thus Michael. Justly thou abhorr'st
That son, who on the quiet state of men
Such trouble brought, affecting to subdue
Rational liberty; yet know withal,
Since thy original lapse, true liberty
Is lost, which always with right reason dwells
Twinn'd, and from her hath no dividual being:
Reason in man obscured, or not obey'd,
Immediately inordinate desires
And upstart passions catch the government
From reason, and to servitude reduce
Man till then free. Therefore, since he permits
Within himself unworthy powers to reign
Over free reason, GOD in judgment just
Subjects him from without to violent lords
Who oft as undeservedly enthral
His outward freedom. Tyranny must be,
Though to the tyrant thereby no excuse.
Yet sometimes nations will decline so low
From virtue, which is reason, that no wrong,
But justice, and some fatal curse annex'd,

---

[1] Babel signifies *confusion*, in Hebrew.

Deprives them of their outward liberty,
Their inward lost: witness the irreverent son
Of him who built the ark, who for the shame
Done to his father, heard this heavy curse,
Servant of servants, on his vicious race,[1]
Thus will this latter, as the former world,
Still tend from bad to worse, till GOD at last,
Wearied with their iniquities, withdraw
His presence from among them, and avert
His holy eyes; resolving from thenceforth
To leave them to their own polluted ways;
And one peculiar nation to select
From all the rest, of whom to be invoked,
A nation from one faithful man[2] to spring:
Him on this side Euphrates yet residing
Bred up in idol-worship:[3] O that men,
(Canst thou believe?) should be so stupid grown,
While yet the patriarch lived, who scaped the flood,
As to forsake the living GOD, and fall
To worship their own work in wood and stone
For Gods; yet him GOD the most high vouchsafes
To call by vision from his father's house,
His kindred, and false Gods. into a land
Which He will show him, and from him will raise
A mighty nation, and upon him show'r
His benediction so, that in his seed
All nations shall be bless'd; he straight obeys,
Not knowing to what land, yet firm believes.
I see him, but thou canst not, with what faith
He leaves his Gods, his friends, and native soil,
Ur of Chaldæa, passing now the ford
To Haran, after him a cumbrous train
Of herds, and flocks, and numerous servitude;
Not wand'ring poor, but trusting all his wealth
With GOD, who call'd him, in a land unknown.
Canaan he now attains, I see his tents
Pitch'd about Sechem, and the neighboring plain

---

[1] Gen. ix. 22–25.
[2] Abraham.
[3] Terah, Abraham's father, was an idolater. See Josh. xxiv. 2.
Jewish tradition represents the father and grandfather of Abraham
to have been carvers of idols. Terah was born in Noah's lifetime.

Of Moreh; there by promise he receives
Gift to his progeny of all that land;
From Hamath northward to the desert south,
Things by their names I call, though yet unnamed,
From Hermon east to the great western sea,
Mount Hermon, yonder sea, each place behold
In prospect, as I point them; on the shore
Mount Carmel; here the double-founted stream
Jordan, true limit eastward; but his sons
Shall dwell to Senir, that long ridge of hills.
This ponder, that all nations of the earth
Shall in his seed be blessed; by that seed
Is meant thy great Deliverer, who shall bruise
The serpent's head; whereof to thee anon
Plainlier shall be reveal'd. This patriarch bless'd,
Whom faithful Abraham due time shall call,
A son, and of his son a grandchild, leaves,
Like him in faith, in wisdom, and renown.
The grandchild, with twelve sons increased departs
From Canaan, to a land hereafter call'd
Egypt, divided by the river Nile;
See where it flows, disgorging at seven mouths
Into the sea. To sojourn in that land
He comes, invited by a younger son
In time of dearth; a son whose worthy deeds
Raise him to be the second in that realm
Of Pharaoh: there he dies, and leaves his race
Growing into a nation; and now grown
Suspected to a sequent king, who seeks
To stop their overgrowth, as inmate guests
Too numerous; whence of guests he makes them slaves
Inhospitably, and kills their infant males:
Till by two brethren (those two brethren call
Moses and Aaron), sent from GOD to claim
His people from enthralment, they return
With glory and spoil back to their promised land.
But first the lawless tyrant, who denies
To know their GOD, or message to regard,
Must be compell'd by signs and judgments dire;
To blood unshed the rivers must be turn'd;
Frogs, lice, and flies, must all his palace fill
With loath'd intrusion, and fill all the land;

His cattle must of rot and murrain die;
Blotches and blains must all his flesh imboss,
And all his people; thunder mix'd with hail,
Hail mix'd with fire, must rend the Egyptian sky,
And wheel on the earth, devouring where it rolls;
What it devours not, herb, or fruit, or grain,
A darksome cloud of locusts swarming down
Must eat, and on the ground leave nothing green:
Darkness must overshadow all his bounds,
Palpable darkness, and blot out three days;
Last with one midnight stroke all the first-born
Of Egypt must lie dead. Thus with ten wounds
This river-dragon[1] tamed at length submits
To let his sojourners depart, and oft
Humbles his stubborn heart; but still as ice
More harden'd after thaw, till, in his rage
Pursuing whom he late dismiss'd, the sea
Swallows him with his host, but them lets pass
As on dry land between two crystal walls,
Awed by the rod of Moses so to stand
Divided, till his rescued gain their shore:
Such wondrous power God to his saint will lend,
Though present in His angel, who shall go
Before them in a cloud, and pillar of fire,
By day a cloud, by night a pillar of fire,
To guide them in their journey, and remove
Behind them, while the obdurate king pursues:
All night he will pursue, but his approach
Darkness defends between till morning watch;
Then through the fiery pillar and the cloud
God looking forth will trouble all his host,
And craze their chariot wheels: when by command
Moses once more his potent rod extends
Over the sea; the sea his rod obeys;
On their imbattled ranks the waves return,
And overwhelm their war. The race elect
Safe towards Canaan from the shore advance
Through the wild Desert; not the readiest way,
Lest ent'ring on the Canaanite alarm'd

[1] An allusion to the crocodile, the Egyptian animal. Ezekiel also styles Pharaoh "the great dragon that lieth in the midst of his rivers."

War terrify them inexpert, and fear
Return them back to Egypt, choosing rather
Inglorious life with servitude; for life
To noble and ignoble is more sweet
Untrain'd in arms, where rashness leads not on.
This also shall they gain by their delay
In the wide wilderness, there they shall found
Their government, and their great senate choose
Through the twelve tribes, to rule by laws ordain'd.
GOD from the mount of Sinai, whose gray top
Shall tremble, He descending, will Himself
In thunder, lightning, and loud trumpets' sound
Ordain them laws; part, such as appertain
To civil justice; part, religious rites
Of sacrifice, informing them by types
And shadows of that destined seed to bruise
The serpent, by what means He shall achieve
Mankind's deliverance. But the voice of GOD
To mortal ear is dreadful: they beseech
That Moses might report to them His will
And terror cease; He grants what they besought,
Instructed that to God is no access
Without mediator, whose high office now
Moses in figure bears, to introduce
One greater, of whose day he shall foretell;
And all the prophets in their age the times
Of great Messiah shall sing. Thus laws and rites
Establish'd, such delight hath God in men
Obedient to His will, that He vouchsafes
Among them to set up His tabernacle,
The Holy One with mortal men to dwell.
By His prescript a sanctuary is framed
Of cedar, overlaid with gold, therein
An ark, and in the ark His testimony,
The records of His cov'nant, over these
A mercy-seat of gold between the wings
Of two bright Cherubim; before Him burn
Seven lamps, as in a zodiac representing
The heav'nly fires; over the tent a cloud
Shall rest by day, a fiery gleam by night,
Save when they journey, and at length they come
Conducted by His angel to the land

Promised to Abraham and his seed. The rest
Were long to tell, how many battles fought,
How many kings destroy'd, and kingdoms won;
Or how the sun shall in mid heav'n stand still
A day entire, and night's due course adjourn,
Man's voice commanding,—Sun in Gibeon stand,
And thou moon in the vale of Aialon,
Till Israel overcome;—so call the third
From Abraham, son of Isaac, and from him
His whole descent, who thus shall Canaan win.

 Here Adam interposed. O sent from heav'n,
Enlightener of my darkness, gracious things
Thou hast reveal'd, those chiefly which concern
Just Abraham and his seed: now first I find
Mine eyes true op'ning, and my heart much eased,
Erewhile perplex'd with thoughts what would become
Of me and all mankind; but now I see
His day, in whom all nations shall be bless'd;
Favor unmerited by me, who sought
Forbidden knowledge by forbidden means.
This yet I apprehend not, why to those
Among whom GOD will deign to dwell on earth
So many and so various laws are giv'n:
So many laws argue so many sins
Among them; how can GOD with such reside?

 To whom thus Michael. Doubt not but that sin
Will reign among them, as of thee begot;
And therefore was law given them to evince
Their natural pravity, by stirring up
Sin against law to fight; that when they see
Law can discover sin, but not remove,
Save by those shadowy expiations weak,
The blood of bulls and goats, they may conclude
Some blood more precious must be paid for man,
Just for unjust, that in such righteousness
To them by faith imputed they may find
Justification towards GOD, and peace
Of conscience, which the law by ceremonies
Cannot appease, nor man the moral part
Perform, and not performing cannot live.
So law appears imperfect, and but giv'n
With purpose to resign them in full time

Up to a better covenant, disciplined
From shadowy types to truth, from flesh to spirit,
From imposition of strict laws to free
Acceptance of large grace, from servile fear
To filial, works of law to works of faith.
And therefore shall not Moses, though of God
Highly beloved, being but the minister
Of law, his people into Canaan led;
But Joshua, whom the Gentiles Jesus call,
His name and office bearing, who shall quell
The adversary serpent, and bring back
Through the world's wilderness long wander'd man
Safe to eternal paradise of rest.
Meanwhile they in their earthly Canaan placed
Long time shall dwell and prosper, but when sins
National interrupt their public peace,
Provoking God to raise them enemies,
From whom as oft He saves them penitent,
By judges first, then under kings; of whom
The second, both for piety renown'd
And puissant deeds, a promise shall receive
Irrevocable, that his regal throne
Forever shall endure; the like shall sing
All prophesy, that of the royal stock
Of David, so I name this king, shall rise
A son, the woman's seed to thee foretold,
Foretold to Abraham, as in whom shall trust
All nations, and to kings foretold, of kings
The last, for of his reign shall be no end.
But first a long succession must ensue,
And his next son, for wealth and wisdom famed,
The clouded ark of God, till then in tents
Wand'ring, shall in a glorious temple enshrine.
Such follow him, as shall be register'd
Part good, part bad, of bad the longer scroll;
Whose foul idolatries, and other faults
Heap'd to the popular sum, will so incense
God, as to leave them, and expose their land,
Their city, His temple, and His Holy ark,
With all His sacred things, a scorn and prey
To that proud city, whose high walls thou saw'st
Left in confusion, Babylon thence call'd.

There in captivity He lets them dwell
The space of seventy years, then brings them back,
Rememb'ring mercy and His cov'nant sworn
To David stablish'd as the days of heav'n.
Return'd from Babylon by leave of kings
Their lords, whom GOD disposed, the house of GOD
They first re-edify, and for awhile
In mean estate live moderate, till grown
In wealth and multitude, factious they grow;
But first among the priests dissension springs,[1]
Men who attend the altar, and should most
Endeavor peace: their strife pollution brings
Upon the temple itself: at last they seize
The sceptre, and regard not David's sons;[2]
Then lose it to a stranger,[3] that the true
Anointed king Messiah might be born
Barr'd of his right; yet at his birth a star
Unseen before in heav'n proclaims him come;
And guides the eastern sages, who inquire
His place, to offer incense, myrrh, and gold:
His place of birth a solemn angel tells
To simple shepherds, keeping watch by night;
They gladly thither haste, and by a choir
Of squadron'd angels hear his carol sung.
A virgin is his mother, but his sire
The power of the Most High; he shall ascend
The throne hereditary, and bound his reign
With earth's wide bounds, his glory with the heav'ns.[4]

---

[1] The murder of Jesus, or Joshua, in the Temple by his brother John, the high priest, is perhaps alluded to here. Bagoas, the general of Artaxerxes' army, had promised to procure Jesus the high priesthood. In confidence of the Persian's support, Jesus insulted his brother in the temple, and so provoked him that the latter slew him. Thus the Temple was polluted by fratricide, committed by the high priest himself. The old commentators suppose, however, that the passage alludes to the quarrels between Jason and Menelaus for the high priesthood, which led to the profanation of the Temple by Antiochus Epiphanes.

[2] Aristobulus, a Maccabee, or Asmonean, erected the theocratic republic of the Jews into a kingdom 481 years after the return from the Babylonian captivity.

[3] Herod, an Idumean or Edomite.

[4] Psalm ii. 8. Isaiah ix. 7. Zech. ix. 9.

He ceased, discerning Adam with such joy
Surcharged, as had like grief been dew'd in tears,
Without the vent of words, which these he breathed.

   O prophet of glad tidings, finisher
Of utmost hope! now clear I understand
What oft my steadiest thoughts have search'd in vain,
Why our great expectation should be call'd
The seed of woman: Virgin Mother, hail,
High in the love of Heav'n, yet from my loins
Thou shalt proceed, and from thy womb the Son
Of GOD most high; so GOD with man unites.
Needs must the serpent now his capital bruise
Expect with mortal pain: say where and when
Their fight, what stroke shall bruise the victor's heel.

   To whom thus Michael. Dream not of their fight,
As of a duel, or the local wounds
Of head or heel: not therefore joins the Son
Manhood to Godhood, with more strength to foil
Thy enemy; nor so is overcome
Satan, whose fall from heav'n, a deadlier bruise,
Disabled not to give thee thy death's wound;
Which He, who comes thy Saviour, shall recure,
Not by destroying Satan, but his works
In thee and in thy seed: nor can this be,
But by fulfilling that which thou didst want,
Obedience to the law of GOD, imposed
On penalty of death, and suffering death,
The penalty to thy transgression due,
And due to theirs which out of thine will grow:
So only can high justice rest appaid.
The law of GOD exact He shall fulfil,
Both by obedience and by love, though love
Alone fulfil the law; thy punishment
He shall endure by coming in the flesh
To a reproachful life and cursèd death,
Proclaiming life to all who shall believe
In his redemption; and that His obedience
Imputed becomes theirs by faith; His merits
To save them, not their own (though legal) works.
For this He shall live hated, be blasphemed,
Seized on by force, judged, and to death condemn'd
A shameful and accursed, nail'd to the cross

By His own nation, slain for bringing life:
But to the cross He nails thy enemies,
The law that is against thee, and the sins
Of all mankind, with Him there crucified,
Never to hurt them more who rightly trust
In this His satisfaction: so He dies,
But soon revives, death over Him no power
Shall long usurp; ere the third dawning light
Return, the stars of morn shall see Him rise
Out of his grave, fresh as the dawning light,
Thy ransom paid, which man from death redeems,
His death for man, as many as offer'd life
Neglect not, and the benefit embrace
By faith not void of works. This godlike act
Annuls thy doom, the death thou shouldst have died,
In sin forever lost from life; this act
Shall bruise the head of Satan, crush his strength
Defeating sin and death, his two main arms,
And fix far deeper in his head their stings,
Than temporal death shall bruise the victor's heel,
Or theirs whom He redeems, a death, like sleep
A gentle wafting to immortal life.
Nor after resurrection shall He stay
Longer on earth than certain times to appear
To His disciples, men who in His life
Still follow'd Him; to them shall leave in charge
To teach all nations what of Him they learn'd
And His salvation; them who shall believe
Baptizing in the profluent stream, the sign
Of washing them from guilt of sin to life
Pure, and in mind prepared, if so befall,
For death, like that which the redeemer died.
All nations they shall teach; for from that day
Not only to the sons of Abraham's loins
Salvation shall be preach'd, but to the sons
Of Abraham's faith wherever through the world:
So in his seed all nations shall be bless'd.
Then to the heav'n of heav'ns He shall ascend
With victory, triumphing through the air
Over His foes and thine; there shall surprise
The serpent, prince of air, and drag in chains
Through all his realm, and there confounded leave;

Then enter into glory, and resume
His seat at God's right hand, exalted high
Above all names in heav'n; and thence shall come,
When this world's dissolution shall be ripe,
With glory and power to judge both quick and dead,
To judge th' unfaithful dead, but to reward
His faithful, and receive them into bliss,
Whether in heav'n or earth; for then the earth
Shall all be paradise, far happier place
Than this of Eden, and far happier days.

So spake the Archangel Michael, then paused,
As at the world's great period; and our sire
Replete with joy and wonder thus replied.

O goodness infinite, goodness immense!
That all this good of evil shall produce,
And evil turn to good; more wonderful
Than that which by creation first brought forth
Light out of darkness! full of doubt I stand,
Whether I should repent me now of sin
By me done and occasion'd, or rejoice
Much more, that much more good thereof shall spring.
To God more glory, more good will to men
From God, and over wrath grace shall abound.
But say, if our Deliverer up to heav'n
Must reascend, what will betide the few
His faithful, left among th' unfaithful herd,
The enemies of truth; who then shall guide
His people, who defend? will they not deal
Worse with His followers than with Him they dealt?

Be sure they will, said the angel; but from heav'n
He to His own a Comforter will send,
The promise of the Father, who shall dwell
His spirit within them, and the law of faith
Working through love upon their hearts shall write,
To guide them in all truth, and also arm
With spiritual armor, able to resist
Satan's assaults, and quench his fiery darts,
What man can do against them, not afraid,
Though to the death, against such cruelties
With inward consolations recompensed,
And oft supported so as shall amaze
Their proudest persecutors: for the Spirit

Pour'd first on his apostles, whom he sends
To evangelize the nations, then on all
Baptized, shall them with wondrous gifts indue,
To speak all tongues, and do all miracles,
As did their Lord before them. Thus they win
Great numbers of each nation to receive
With joy the tidings brought from heav'n: at length
Their ministry perform'd, and race well run,
Their doctrine and their story written left,
They die; but in their room, as they forewarn,
Wolves shall succeed for teachers, grievous wolves,
Who all the sacred mysteries of heav'n
To their own vile advantages shall turn
Of lucre and ambition, and the truth
With superstitions and traditions taint,
Left only in those written records pure,
Though not but by the Spirit understood.
Then shall they seek to avail themselves of names,
Places, and titles, and with these to join
Secular power, though feigning still to act
By spiritual, to themselves appropriating
The Spirit of GOD, promised alike and giv'n
To all believers; and from that pretence
Spiritual laws by carnal powers shall force
On every conscience; laws which none shall find
Left them inroll'd, or what the Spirit within
Shall on the heart engrave. What will they then
But force the Spirit of Grace itself, and bind
His consort Liberty? what, but unbuild
His living temples, built by faith to stand,
Their own faith, not another's? for on earth
Who against faith and conscience can be heard
Infallible? yet many will presume:
Whence heavy persecution shall arise
On all who in the worship persevere
Of spirit and truth; the rest, far greater part,
Will deem in outward rites and specious forms
Religion satisfied; truth shall retire
Bestruck with slanderous darts, and works of faith
Rarely be found: so shall the world go on,
To good malignant, to bad men benign,
Under her own weight groaning till the day

Appear of restoration to the just,
And vengeance to the wicked, at return
Of Him so lately promised to thy aid,
The woman's seed, obscurely then foretold,
Now amplier known thy Saviour and thy Lord,
Last in the clouds from heav'n to be reveal'd
In glory of the Father, to dissolve
Satan with his perverted world, then raise
From the conflagrant mass, purged and refined,
New heav'ns, new earth, ages of endless date
Founded in righteousness, and peace, and love,
To bring forth fruits joy and eternal bliss.

    He ended; and thus Adam last replied.
How soon hath thy prediction, Seer bless'd,
Measured this transient world, the race of time
Till time stand fix'd! beyond is all abyss,
Eternity, whose end no eye can reach:
Greatly instructed I shall hence depart,
Greatly in peace of thought, and have my fill
Of knowledge, what this vessel can contain;
Beyond which was my folly to aspire.
Henceforth I learn that to obey is best,
And love with fear the only GOD, to walk
As in His presence, ever to observe
His providence, and on Him sole depend,
Merciful over all His works, with good
Still overcoming evil; and by small
Accomplishing great things, by things deem'd weak
Subverting worldly strong, and worldly wise
By simply meek; that suffering for truth's sake
Is fortitude to highest victory,
And to the faithful death the gate of life;
Taught this by his example, whom I now
Acknowledge my Redeemer ever bless'd.

    To whom thus also th' angel last replied.
This having learn'd, thou hast attain'd the sum
Of wisdom; hope no higher, though all the stars
Thou knew'st by name, and all th' ethereal powers,
All secrets of the deep, all nature's works,
Or works of GOD in heav'n, air, earth, or sea,
And all the riches of this world enjoy'dst,
And all the rule, one empire; only add

Deeds to thy knowledge answerable, add faith,
Add virtue, patience, temperance, add love,
By name to come call'd charity, the soul
Of all the rest; then wilt thou not be loth
To leave this paradise, but shalt possess
A paradise within thee, happier far.
Let us descend now, therefore, from this top
Of speculation; for the hour precise
Exacts our parting hence; and see the guards,
By me encamp'd on yonder hill, expect
Their motion, at whose front a flaming sword,
In signal of remove, waves fiercely round;
We may no longer stay: go, waken Eve;
Her also I with gentle dreams have calm'd
Portending good, and all her spirits composed
To meek submission: thou at season fit
Let her with thee partake what thou hast heard.
Chiefly what may concern her faith to know,
The great deliverance by her seed to come,
For by the woman's seed, on all mankind.
That ye may live, which will be many days,
Both in one faith unanimous, though sad
With cause for evils past; yet much more cheer'd
With meditation on the happy end.

 He ended, and they both descend the hill:
Descended, Adam to the bower, where Eve
Lay sleeping, ran before, but found her waked;
And thus with words not sad she him received.

 Whence thou return'st, and whither went'st, I know;
For GOD is also in sleep, and dreams advise,
Which He hath sent propitious, some great good
Presaging, since with sorrow and heart's distress
Wearied I fell asleep: but now lead on;
In me is no delay; with thee to go
Is to stay here; without thee here to stay
Is to go hence unwilling; thou to me
Art all things under heav'n, all places thou,
Who for my wilful crime art banish'd hence.
This further consolation yet secure
I carry hence; though all by me is lost,
Such favor I unworthy am vouchsafed,
By me the Promised Seed shall all restore.

So spake our mother Eve, and Adam heard
Well pleased, but answer'd not; for now too nigh
Th' Archangel stood, and from the other hill
To their fix'd station all in bright array
The Cherubim descended; on the ground
Gliding meteorous, as ev'ning mist
Ris'n from a river o'er the marish[1] glides,
And gathers ground fast at the laborer's heel
Homeward returning. High in front advanced
The brandish'd sword of God before them blazed
Fierce as a comet; which with torrid heat,
And vapor as the Libyan air adust,
Began to parch that temperate clime: whereat
In either hand the hast'ning angel caught
Our ling'ring parents, and to the eastern gate
Led them direct, and down the cliff as fast
To the subjected plain; then disappear'd.
They looking back all the eastern side beheld
Of Paradise, so late their happy seat,
Waved over by that flaming brand; the gate
With dreadful faces throng'd and fiery arms:
Some natural tears they dropp'd, but wiped them soon;
The world was all before them, where to choose
Their place of rest, and Providence their guide.
They, hand in hand with wand'ring steps and slow,
Through Eden took their solitary way.

[1] An old word for marsh.

Paradise Regained

BOOK I

I, WHO erewhile the happy garden sung,
By one man's disobedience lost, now sing
Recover'd Paradise to all mankind,
By one man's firm obedience fully tried
Through all temptation, and the tempter foil'd
In all his wiles, defeated, and repulsed,
And Eden raised in the waste wilderness.
Thou Spirit, who led'st this glorious Eremite
Into the desert, His victorious field,
Against the spiritual foe, and brought'st Him thence
By proof the undoubted Son of GOD, inspire,
As thou art wont, my prompted song, else mute,
And bear through highth or depth of nature's bounds
With prosperous wing full summ'd [1] to tell of deeds
Above heroic, though in secret done,
And unrecorded left through many an age,
Worthy t' have not remain'd so long unsung.
　Now had the great Proclaimer,[2] with a voice
More awful than the sound of trumpet, cried
Repentance, and heaven's kingdom nigh at hand
To all baptized: to his great baptism flock'd
With awe the regions round, and with them came
From Nazareth the Son of Joseph deem'd
To the flood Jordan, came, as then obscure,
Unmark'd, unknown; but Him the Baptist soon
Descried, divinely warn'd, and witness bore

---

[1] Full feathered, a term used in falconry.
[2] John the Baptist.

As to his worthier, and would have resign'd
To him his heavenly office, nor was long
His witness unconfirm'd: on Him baptized
Heav'n open'd, and in likeness of a dove
The Spirit descended, while the Father's voice
From heav'n pronounced Him His belovèd Son.
That heard the adversary, who, roving still
About the world, at that assembly famed
Would not be last, and, with the voice divine
Nigh thunder-struck, th' exalted Man, to whom
Such high attest was giv'n, a while survey'd
With wonder, then, with envy fraught and rage,
Flies to his place, nor rests, but in mid air
To council summons all his mighty peers,
Within thick clouds and dark ten-fold involved,
A gloomy consistory; and then amidst
With looks aghast and sad he thus bespake.
　　O ancient Powers of air[1] and this wide world,
For much more willingly I mention air,
This our old conquest, than remember Hell,
Our hated habitation; well we know
How many ages, as the years of men,
This universe we have possest, and ruled
In manner at our will th' affairs of earth,
Since Adam and his facile consort Eve
Lost Paradise deceived by me, though since
With dread attending when that fatal wound
Shall be inflicted by the seed of Eve
Upon my head; long the decrees of heav'n
Delay, for longest time to Him is short;
And now too soon for us the circling hours
This dreaded time have compast, wherein we
Must bide the stroke of that long threaten'd wound,
At least if so we can, and by the head
Broken be not intended all our power
To be infringed, our freedom, and our being,
In this fair empire won of earth and air:
For this ill news I bring, the woman's seed,
Destined to this, is late of woman born;
His birth to our just fear gave no small cause,

[1] See Ephes. ii. 2; vi. 12.

But his growth now to youth's full flow'r, displaying
All virtue, grace, and wisdom to achieve
Things highest, greatest, multiplies my fear.
Before him a great prophet to proclaim
His coming is sent harbinger, who all
Invites, and in the consecrated stream
Pretends to wash off sin, and fit them so
Purified to receive Him pure, or rather
To do Him honor as their king: all come,
And He Himself among them was baptized,
Not thence to be more pure, but to receive
The testimony of heav'n, that who He is
Thenceforth the nations may not doubt. I saw
The prophet do him reverence, on Him, rising
Out of the water, heav'n above the clouds
Unfold her crystal doors, thence on His head
A perfect dove descend, whate'er it meant,
And out of heav'n the sovereign voice I hear,
—This is my Son beloved, in Him am pleased.
His mother then is mortal, but His sire
He who obtains the monarchy of heav'n;
And what will He not do to advance His Son?
His first-begot we know, and sore have felt,
When His fierce thunder drove us to the deep;
Who this is we must learn,[1] for man He seems
In all His lineaments, though in His face
The glimpses of His Father's glory shine.
Ye see our danger on the utmost edge
Of hazard, which admits no long debate,
But must with something sudden be opposed,
Not force, but well-couch'd fraud, well-woven snares,
Ere in the head of nations He appear
Their king, their leader, and supreme on earth.
I, when no other durst, sole undertook
The dismal expedition to find out
And ruin Adam, and the exploit perform'd
Successfully; a calmer voyage now
Will waft me; and the way found prosp'rous once

---

[1] Milton's idea that Satan did not know that the wondrous Man
baptized was the Messiah, originated probably by the opinions of
Ignatius, Bezu, etc., who believed that the devil did not recognize
in mortal form the Son of God.—*From* NEWTON.

Induces best to hope of like success.
  He ended, and his words impression left
Of much amazement to th' infernal crew,
Distracted and surprised with deep dismay
At these sad tidings; but no time was then
For long indulgence to their fears or grief.
Unanimous they all commit the care
And management of this main enterprise
To him their great dictator, whose attempt
At first against mankind so well had thrived
In Adam's overthrow, and led their march
From hell's deep-vaulted den to dwell in light,
Regents, and potentates, and kings, yea gods
Of many a pleasant realm and province wide.
So to the coast of Jordan he directs
His easy steps, girded with snaky wiles,[1]
Where he might likeliest find this new-declared,
This man of men, attested Son of GOD,
Temptation and all guile on Him to try;
So to subvert whom he suspected raised
To end his reign on earth so long enjoy'd:
But contrary unweeting he fulfill'd
The purposed counsel pre-ordain'd and fixt
Of the most High, who, in full frequence bright
Of angels, thus to Gabriel [2] smiling spake.
  Gabriel, this day by proof thou shalt behold,
Thou and all angels conversant on earth
With man or men's affairs, how I begin
To verify that solemn message late,
On which I sent thee to the virgin pure
In Galilee, that she should bear a son
Great in renown, and call'd the Son of GOD;
Thou told'st her, doubting how these things could be
To her a virgin, that on her should come
The Holy Ghost, and the power of the Highest
O'ershadow her: this man born, and now up-grown,
To show him worthy of his birth divine

---

  [1] Alluding to the habits of pretended sorcerers, who wore a girdle of snake's skin.—NEWTON. Milton also alluded to the temptation of Eve.
  [2] The rabbis say that Gabriel was the angel of mercy: Michael, of justice.—*From* NEWTON.

And high prediction, henceforth I expose
To Satan; let him tempt and now assay
His utmost subtlety, because he boasts
And vaunts of his great cunning to the throng
Of his apostasy; he might have learnt
Less overweening, since he fail'd in Job,
Whose constant perseverance overcame
Whate'er his cruel malice could invent.
He now shall know I can produce a man
Of female seed, far abler to resist
All his solicitations, and at length
All his vast force, and drive him back to hell,
Winning by conquest what the first man lost
By fallacy surprised. But first I mean
To exercise him in the wilderness;
There he shall first lay down the rudiments
Of his great welfare, ere I send him forth
To conquer sin and death, the two grand foes
By humiliation and strong sufferance.
His weakness shall o'ercome satanic strength,
And all the world, and mass of sinful flesh;
That all the angels and ethereal powers,
They now, and men hereafter, may discern,
From what consummate virtue I have chose
This perfect man, by merit called my son,
To earn salvation for the sons of men.

So spake th' eternal Father, and all heav'n
Admiring stood a space, then into hymns
Burst forth, and in celestial measures moved,
Circling the throne and singing, while the hand
Sung with the voice, and this the argument.

Victory and triumph to the Son of God,
Now ent'ring his great duel, not of arms,
But to vanquish by wisdom hellish wiles.
The Father knows the Son; therefore secure
Ventures His filial virtue, though untried,
Against whate'er may tempt, whate'er seduce,
Allure, or terrify, or undermine.
Be frustrate all ye stratagems of hell,
And devilish machinations come to nought.

So they in heav'n their odes and vigils tuned:
Meanwhile the Son of God, who yet some days

Lodg'd in Bethabara where John baptized,
Musing and much revolving in his breast,
How best the mighty work he might begin
Of Saviour to mankind, and which way first
Publish his god-like office now mature,
One day forth walked alone, the Spirit leading,
And his deep thoughts, the better to converse
With solitude, till far from track of men,
Thought following thought, and step by step led on,
He enter'd now the bordering desert wild,[1]
And, with dark shades and rocks environ'd round,
His holy meditations thus pursued.

  O what a multitude of thoughts at once
Awaken'd in me swarm, while I consider
What from within I feel my self, and hear
What from without comes often to my ears,
Ill sorting with my present state compared.
When I was yet a child, no childish play
To me was pleasing, all my mind was set
Serious to learn and know, and thence to do
What might be public good; myself I thought
Born to that end, born to promote all truth,
All righteous things: therefore, above my years.
The law of God I read, and found it sweet,
Made it my whole delight, and in it grew
To such perfection, that, ere yet my age
Had measured twice six years, at our great feast
I went into the temple, there to hear
The teachers of our law, and to propose
What might improve my knowledge or their own,
And was admired by all; yet this not all
To which my spirit aspired, victorious deeds
Flamed in my heart, heroic acts; one while
To rescue Israel from the Roman yoke,
Then to subdue and quell o'er all the earth
Brute violence and proud tyrannic pow'r,
Till truth were freed, and equity restored:
Yet held it more humane, more heav'nly, first
By winning words to conquer willing hearts,
And make persuasion do the work of fear;

---

[1] The Wilderness of Judea, or Ziph. It extended from the Jordan
along the western side of the Dead Sea.

At least to try, and teach the erring soul,
Not wilfully misdoing, but unware
Misled; the stubborn only to subdue.
These growing thoughts my Mother soon perceiving
By words at times cast forth, inly rejoiced,
And said to me apart. High are thy thoughts
O son, but nourish them, and let them soar
To what highth sacred virtue and true worth
Can raise them, thou above example high;
By matchless deeds express thy matchless Sire.
For know, thou art no son of mortal man,
Though men esteem thee low of parentage,
Thy father is the eternal King who rules
All heav'n and earth, angels and sons of men:
A messenger from GOD foretold thy birth
Conceived in me a virgin;[1] he foretold
Thou should'st be great, and sit on David's throne,
And of thy kingdom there should be no end.
At thy nativity a glorious quire
Of angels in the fields of Bethlehem sung
To shepherds watching at their folds by night,[2]
And told them the Messiah now was born,
Where they might see him; and to thee they came,
Directed to the manger where thou lay'st,
For in the inn was left no better room.
A star, not seen before, in heav'n appearing
Guided the wise men thither from the east,[3]
To honor thee with incense, myrrh, and gold,
By whose bright course led on they found the place,
Affirming it thy star new grav'n in heav'n,
By which they knew the king of Israel born.
Just Simeon and prophetic Anna, warn'd
By vision, found thee in the temple, and spake,
Before the altar and the vested Priest,
Like things of thee to all that present stood.
This having heard, straight I again revolved
The law and prophets, searching what was writ
Concerning the Messiah, to our scribes
Known partly, and soon found of whom they spake

[1] Luke i. 30–35.
[2] Luke ii. 8 and following vs.
[3] Matt. ii.

I am; this chiefly, that my way must lie
Through many a hard assay, even to the death,
Ere I the promised kingdom can attain,
Or work redemption for mankind, whose sins
Full weight must be transferr'd upon my head.
Yet, neither thus dishearten'd or dismay'd,
The time prefixt I waited, when, behold!
The Baptist, of whose birth I oft had heard,
Not knew by sight,[1] now come, who was to come
Before Messiah and his way prepare.
I, as all others, to his baptism came,
Which I believed was from above; but he
Straight knew me, and with loudest voice proclaim'd
Me Him (for it was shown him so from heav'n),
Me Him whose harbinger he was; and first
Refused on me his baptism to confer,
As much his greater, and was hardly won:
But as I rose out of the laving stream,
·Heaven open'd her eternal doors, from whence
The Spirit descended on me like a dove;
And last, the sum of all, my Father's voice,
Audibly heard from heav'n pronounced me His,
Me His belovèd Son, in whom alone
He was well pleased; by which I knew the time
Now full, that I no more should live obscure,
But openly begin, as best becomes
The authority which I derived from heav'n.
And now by some strong motion I am led
Into this wilderness, to what intent
I learn not yet, perhaps, I need not know;
For what concerns my knowledge GOD reveals.

   So spake our Morning Star, then in his rise,
And looking round on every side beheld
A pathless desert, dusk with horrid shades;
The way he came not having mark'd, return
Was difficult, by human steps untrod;
And he still on was led, but with such thoughts
Accompanied of things past and to come
Lodged in his breast, as well might recommend

---

[1] St. John was brought up in a different part of the country from
Jesus, and first saw his divine cousin at his baptism. John i. 31, 32.
"I knew him not."

Such solitude before choicest society.
Full forty days he pass'd, whether on hill
Sometimes, anon in shady vale, each night
Under the cover of some ancient oak
Or cedar, to defend him from the dew,
Or harbor'd in one cave, is not reveal'd;
Nor tasted human food, nor hunger felt
Till those days ended, hunger'd then at last
Among wild beasts: they at his sight grew mild,
Nor sleeping him nor waking harm'd; his walk
The fiery serpent fled and noxious worm,
The lion and fierce tiger glared aloof.
But now an agèd man in rural weeds,
Following, as seem'd, the quest of some stray ewe,
Or wither'd sticks to gather, which might serve
Against a winter's day, when winds blow keen,
To warm him wet return'd from field at eve,
He saw approach, who first with curious eye
Perused him, then with words thus utter'd spake.

   Sir, what ill chance hath brought thee to this place
So far from path or road of men, who pass
In troop or caravan, for single none
Durst ever, who return'd, and dropt not here
His carcass, pined with hunger and with drought.
I ask the rather, and the more admire,
For that to me thou seem'st the man, whom late
Our new baptizing prophet at the ford
Of Jordan honor'd so, and call'd thee Son
Of GOD; I saw and heard, for we sometimes,
Who dwell this wild, constrain'd by want, come forth
To town or village nigh, (nighest is far,)
Where aught we hear, and curious are to hear,
What happens new; fame also finds us out.

   To whom the Son of GOD. Who brought me hither
Will bring me hence; no other guide I seek.

   By miracle he may, replied the swain,
What other way I see not, for we here
Live on tough roots and stubs, to thirst inured
More than the camel, and to drink go far,
Men to much misery and hardship born.
But if thou be the Son of GOD, command
That out of these hard stones be made thee bread,

So shalt thou save thyself and us relieve
With food, whereof we wretched seldom taste.
 He ended, and the Son of God replied.
Think'st thou such force in bread? is it not written,
(For I discern thee other than thou seem'st,)
Man lives not by bread only, but each word
Proceeding from the mouth of God, who fed
Our fathers here with Manna? in the mount
Moses was forty days, nor eat, nor drank;
And forty days Elijah without food
Wander'd this barren waste, the same I now.
Why dost thou then suggest to me distrust,
Knowing who I am, as I know who thou art?
 Whom thus answer'd the arch fiend now undisguised.
'Tis true, I am that spirit unfortunate,
Who leagued with millions more in rash revolt,
Kept not my happy station, but was driv'n
With them from bliss to the bottomless deep;
Yet to that hideous place not so confined
By rigor unconniving, but that oft,
Leaving my dolorous prison, I enjoy
Large liberty, to round this globe of earth,
Or range in the air, nor from the heav'n of heav'ns
Hath he excluded my resort sometimes.
I came among the sons of God, when he
Gave up into my hands Uzzean Job
To prove him, and illustrate his high worth;
And when to all his angels he proposed
To draw the proud king Ahab into fraud,
That he might fall in Ramoth, they demurring,
I undertook that office, and the tongues
Of all his flattering prophets glibb'd with lies[1]
To his destruction, as I had in charge;
For what He bids I do. Though I have lost
Much lustre of my native brightness, lost
To be beloved of God, I have not lost
To love, at least contemplate and admire,
What I see excellent in good, or fair,
Or virtuous; I should so have lost all sense.
What can be then less in me than desire

[1] 1 Kings xxii. 19 and following vs.

To see thee and approach thee, whom I know
Declared the Son of God, to hear attent
Thy wisdom, and behold thy Godlike deeds?
Men generally think me much a foe
To all mankind: why should I? they to me
Never did wrong or violence, by them
I lost not what I lost, rather by them
I gain'd what I have gain'd, and with them dwell,
Copartner in these regions of the world,
If not disposer; lend them oft my aid,
Oft my advice by presages, and signs,
And answers, oracles, portents, and dreams,
Whereby they may direct their future life.[1]
Envy they say excites me thus to gain
Companions of my misery and woe.
At first it may be; but long since with woe.
Nearer acquainted, now I feel by proof,
That fellowship in pain divides not smart,
Nor lightens aught each man's peculiar load.
Small consolation then, were man adjoin'd:
This wounds me most, what can it less? that man,
Man fall'n shall be restored, I never more.

    To whom our Saviour sternly thus replied.
Deservedly thou griev'st, composed of lies
From the beginning, and in lies wilt end,
Who boast release from hell, and leave to come
Into the Heav'n of Heav'ns. Thou com'st indeed,
As a poor miserable captive thrall
Comes to the place where he before had sat
Among the prime in splendor, now deposed,
Ejected, emptied, gazed, unpitied, shunn'd,
A spectacle of ruin or of scorn
To all the host of heav'n. The happy place
Imports to thee no happiness, no joy,

---

[1] The following passage of Cicero reflects so much light on these
lines as would incline one to think that Milton had it in his mind.
"Multa cernunt haruspices; multa augures provident, multa oraculis
declarantur, multa vaticinationibus, multa somniis, multa portentis:
quibus cognitis, multæ sæpe res hominum sententia atque utilitate
partæ" (or, as Lambinus reads, "ex animi sententia atque utilitate
partæ"); "multa etiam pericula depulsa sunt."—*De Nat. Deor.* II.
65.—NEWTON.

Rather inflames thy torment, representing
Lost bliss to thee no more communicable,
So never more in hell than when in heav'n.
But thou art serviceable to heaven's King.
Wilt thou impute t' obedience what thy fear
Extorts, or pleasure to do ill excites?
What but thy malice moved thee to misdeem
Of righteous Job, then cruelly to afflict him
With all inflictions? but his patience won.
The other service was thy chosen task,
To be a liar in four hundred mouths;
For lying is thy sustenance, thy food.
Yet thou pretend'st to truth; all oracles
By thee are giv'n, and what confest more true
Among the nations? that hath been thy craft,
By mixing somewhat true to vent more lies.
But what have been thy answers? what but dark,
Ambiguous, and with double sense deluding,
Which they who asked have seldom understood,
And not well understood as good not known?
Who ever by consulting at thy shrine
Return'd the wiser, or the more instruct
To fly or follow what concern'd him most,
And run not sooner to his fatal snare?
For God hath justly given the nations up
To thy delusions; justly, since they fell
Idolatrous. But when His purpose is
Among them to declare His providence
To thee not known, whence hast thou then thy truth,
But from Him or His angels president
In every province? who, themselves disdaining
T' approach thy temples, give thee in command
What to the smallest tittle thou shalt say
To thy adorers; thou with trembling fear,
Or like a fawning parasite, obey'st;
Then to thyself ascrib'st the truth foretold.
But this thy glory shall be soon retrench'd;
No more shalt thou by oracling abuse
The Gentiles; henceforth oracles are ceased,[1]
And thou no more with pomp and sacrifice

---

[1] Ceased. *Fuv. Sat.* VI. 554. "Delphis oracula cessant."

Shalt be inquired at Delphos or elsewhere,
At least in vain, for they shall find thee mute.[1]
GOD hath now sent His living oracle
Into the world to teach His final will,
And sends His Spirit of Truth henceforth to dwell
In pious hearts, and inward oracle
To all truth requisite for men to know.

    So spake our Saviour; but the subtle fiend,
Though inly stung with anger and disdain,
Dissembled, and this answer smooth return'd.

    Sharply thou hast insisted on rebuke,
And urged me hard with doings, which not will
But misery, hath wrested from me; where
Easily canst thou find one miserable,
And not enforced ofttimes to part from truth;
If it may stand him more in stead to lie,
Say and unsay, feign, flatter, or abjure?
But thou art placed above me, thou art Lord;
From thee I can, and must, submiss endure
Check or reproof, and glad to escape so quit.
Hard are the ways of truth, and rough to walk,
Smooth on the tongue discoursed, pleasing to th' ear,
And tuneable as sylvan pipe or song;
What wonder then if I delight to hear
Her dictates from thy mouth? most men admire
Virtue, who follow not her lore: permit me
To hear thee when I come, since no man comes,
And talk at least, though I despair to attain.
Thy Father, who is holy, wise, and pure,
Suffers the hypocrite or atheous priest
To tread his sacred courts, and minister
About his altar, handling holy things,
Praying or vowing, and vouchsafed his voice
To Balaam reprobate, a prophet yet
Inspired; disdain not such access to me.

    To whom our Saviour with unalter'd brow.

---

[1] Thus the priestess tells Appius when he wishes to consult the oracle at Delphi, and finds it dumb:

> "Muto Parnassus hiatu
> Conticuit pressitque Deum; seu spiritus istas
> Destituit fauces mundique in devia versum.
> Duxit iter."—   LUCAN, quoted by DUNSTER.

Thy coming hither, though I know thy scope,
I bid not or forbid; do as thou find'st
Permission from above; thou canst not more.
   He added not; and Satan, bowing low
His gray dissimulation, disappear'd
Into thin air diffused:[1] for now began
Night with her sullen wings to double-shade
The desert; fowls in their clay nests were couch'd;
And now wild beasts come forth the woods to roam.

[1] "These our actors,
As I foretold you, were all spirits, and
Are melted into air, into *thin air*."—
        SHAKESPEARE, *Tempest*, Act IV. Sc. 2.

BOOK II

MEANWHILE the new-baptized, who yet remain'd
At Jordan with the Baptist, and had seen
Him whom they heard so late expressly call'd
Jesus, Messiah, Son of GOD declared,
And on that high authority had believed,
And with him talk'd, and with him lodged,[1] I mean
Andrew and Simon, famous after known,
With others though in holy writ not named,
Now missing him their joy so lately found,
So lately found, and so abruptly gone,
Began to doubt, and doubted many days,
And, as the days increased, increased their doubt:
Sometimes they thought he might be only shown,
And for a time caught up to GOD, as once
Moses was in the Mount, and missing long;
And the great Thisbite,[2] who on fiery wheels
Rode up to heav'n, yet once again to come.
Therefore as those young prophets then with care
Sought lost Elijah,[3] so in each place these
Nigh to Bethabara; in Jericho
The city of palms,[4] Ænon, and Salem old.
Machærus,[5] and each town or city wall'd
On this side the broad lake Genezaret,
Or in Peræa; but return'd in vain.
Then on the bank of Jordan, by a creek,
Where winds with reeds and osiers whisp'ring play,
Plain fishermen, no greater men them call,
Close in a cottage low together got,
Their unexpected loss and plaints outbreathed.
Alas, from what high hope to what relapse
Unlook'd for are we fall'n! our eyes beheld
Messiah certainly now come, so long

[1] See John i. 35–40.
[2] Elijah.
[3] 2 Kings ii. 17.
[4] Jericho is called the city of palm trees in Deut. xxxiv. 3.
[5] A stronghold fortified by Herod Antipas.

Expected of our fathers; we have heard
His words, his wisdom full of grace and truth:
Now, now, for sure, deliverance is at hand,
The kingdom shall to Israel be restored:
Thus we rejoiced, but soon our joy is turn'd
Into perplexity and new amaze:
For whither is he gone, what accident
Hath wrapt him from us? will he now retire
After appearance, and again prolong
Our expectation? God of Israel,
Send thy Messiah forth, the time is come,
Behold the kings of the earth how they oppress
Thy chosen, to what highth their power unjust
They have exalted, and behind them cast
All fear of thee. Arise and vindicate
Thy glory, free thy people from their yoke.
But let us wait; thus far He hath perform'd,
Sent His Anointed, and to us reveal'd him,
By His great prophet pointed at and shown
In public, and with him we have conversed;
Let us be glad of this, and all our fears
Lay on His providence; He will not fail,
Nor will withdraw him now, nor will recall;
Mock us with his blest sight, then snatch him hence;
Soon we shall see our hope, our joy return.

　　Thus they out of their plaints new hope resume
To find whom at the first they found unsought:
But to his mother Mary, when she saw
Others return'd from baptism, not her Son,
Nor left at Jordan, tidings of him none,
Within her breast though calm, her breast though pure,
Motherly cares and fears got head, and raised
Some troubled thoughts, which she in sighs thus clad.

　　O what avails me now that honor high
To have conceived of GOD, or that salute,
Hail, highly favor'd, among women blest!
While I to sorrows am no less advanced,
And fears as eminent, above the lot
Of other women, by the birth I bore,
In such a season born, when scarce a shed
Could be obtain'd to shelter him or me
From the bleak air! a stable was our warmth,

A manger his: yet soon enforced to fly
Thence into Egypt, till the murd'rous king
Were dead, who sought his life, and missing fill'd
With infant blood the streets of Bethlehem.
From Egypt home return'd, in Nazareth
Hath been our dwelling many years; his life
Private, unactive, calm, contemplative,
Little suspicious to any king; but now
Full grown to man, acknowledged, as I hear,
By John the Baptist, and in public shown,
Son own'd from heav'n by his Father's voice;
I look'd for some great change: to honor? no,
But trouble, as old Simeon plain foretold,
That to the fall and rising he should be
Of many in Israel, and to a sign
Spoken against, that through my very soul
A sword shall pierce. This is my favor'd lot,
My exaltation to afflictions high;
Afflicted I may be, it seems, and blest;
I will not argue that, nor will repine.
But where delays he now? some great intent
Conceals him. When twelve years he scarce had seen,
I lost him, but so found, as well I saw
He could not lose himself; but went about
His father's business. What he meant I mused,
Since understand. Much more his absence now
Thus long to some great purpose he obscures.
But I to wait with patience am inured;
My heart hath been a store-house long of things
And sayings laid up, portending strange events.

　　Thus Mary pond'ring oft, and oft to mind
Recalling what remarkably had pass'd
Since first her salutation heard, with thoughts
Meekly composed awaited the fulfilling:
The while her Son, tracing the desert wild,
Sole but with holiest meditations fed,
Into himself descended, and at once
All his great work to come before him set;
How to begin, how to accomplish best
His end of being on earth, and mission high:
For Satan, with sly preface to return,
Had left him vacant, and with speed was gone

Up to the middle region of thick air,
Where all his potentates in council sat;
There, without sign of boast, or sign of joy,
Solicitous and blank he thus began.

   Princes, heav'n's ancient sons, ethereal thrones,
Demonian spirits now from the element
Each of his reign allotted, rightlier call'd
Pow'rs of fire, air, water, and earth beneath,
So may we hold our place, and these mild seats
Without new trouble; such an enemy
Is risen to invade us, who no less
Threatens, than our expulsion down to hell;
I, as I undertook, and with the vote
Consenting in full frequence was impower'd,
Have found him, view'd him, tasted him,[1] but find
Far other labor to be undergone
Than when I dealt with Adam first of men,
Though Adam by his wife's allurement fell,
However, to this man inferior far,
If he be man by mother's side at least,
With more than human gifts from heav'n adorn'd,
Perfections absolute, graces divine,
And amplitude of mind to greatest deeds.
Therefore I am return'd, lest confidence
Of my success with Eve in paradise
Deceive ye to persuasion oversure
Of like succeeding here: I summon all
Rather to be in readiness, with hand
Or counsel to assist, lest I, who erst
Thought none my equal, now be overmatch'd.

   So spake the old Serpent doubting, and from all
With clamor was assured their utmost aid
At his command; when from amidst them rose
Belial, the dissolutest spirit that fell,
The sensualest, and after Asmodai[2]
The fleshliest Incubus, and thus advised.

   Set women in his eye, and in his walk,
Among daughters of men the fairest found;

---

[1] A Grecism. See also Psalm xxxiv. 8: "O taste and see how gracious the Lord is!"

[2] Or Asmodeus, the angel who persecuted Sara, the daughter of Raguel, and slew her husbands. See Tobit.

Many are in each region passing fair
As the noon sky; more like to goddesses
Than mortal creatures, graceful and discreet,
Expert in amorous arts, enchanting tongues
Persuasive, virgin majesty with mild
And sweet allay'd, yet terrible to approach,
Skill'd to retire, and in retiring draw
Hearts after them tangled in amorous nets.
Such object hath the power to soften and tame
Severest temper, smooth the rugged'st brow,
Enerve, and with voluptuous hope dissolve,
Draw out with credulous desire, and lead
At will the manliest, resolutest breast,
As the magnetic[1] hardest iron draws.
Women, when nothing else, beguiled the heart
Of wisest Solomon, and made him build,
And made him bow to the gods of his wives.
      To whom quick answer Satan thus return'd.
Belial, in much uneven scale thou weigh'st
All others by thyself; because of old
Thou thyself doat'dst on woman-kind, admiring
Their shape, their color, and attractive grace,
None are, thou think'st, but taken with such toys.
Before the flood thou with thy lusty crew,
False titled sons of god, roaming the earth,
Cast wanton eyes on the daughters of men,
And coupled with them, and begot a race.
Have we not seen, or by relation heard,
In courts and regal chambers how thou lurk'st,
In wood or grove by mossy fountain side,
In valley or green meadow, to way-lay
Some beauty rare, Calisto, Clymene,
Daphne, or Semele, Antiopa,[2]
Or Amymone, Syrinx, many more
Too long, then lay'st thy scapes on names adored,
Apollo, Neptune, Jupiter, or Pan,
Satyr, or fawn, or sylvan? but these haunts
Delight not all; among the sons of men,

[1] The loadstone, or magnet.
[2] Women beloved by the heathen deities. Ovid relates these fables. Calisto, Semele, and Antiopa were the loves of Jupiter; Clymene and Daphne, of Apollo; Syrinx, of Pan.

How many have with a smile made small account
Of beauty and her lures, easily scorn'd
All her assaults, on worthier things intent?
Remember that Pellean conqueror,[1]
A youth, how all the beauties of the east
He slightly view'd, and slightly overpass'd;
How he surnamed of Africa[2] dismiss'd
In his prime youth the fair Iberian maid.
For Solomon, he lived at ease, and full
Of honor, wealth, high fare, aim'd not beyond
Higher design than to enjoy his state;
Thence to the bait of women lay exposed:
But He whom we attempt is wiser far
Than Solomon, of more exalted mind,
Made and set wholly on the accomplishment
Of greatest things; what woman will you find,
Though of this age the wonder and the fame,
On whom his leisure will vouchsafe an eye
Of fond desire? or should she confident,
As sitting queen adored on beauty's throne,
Descend with all her winning charms begirt
To enamour, as the zone of Venus once
Wrought that effect on Jove, so fables tell;
How would one look from his majestic brow,
Seated as on the top of virtue's hill,
Discount'nance her despised, and put to rout
All her array; her female pride deject,
Or turn to reverent awe? for beauty stands
In the admiration only of weak minds
Led captive. Cease to admire, and all her plumes
Fall flat and shrink into a trivial toy,
At every sudden slighting quite abash'd:
Therefore with manlier objects we must try
His constancy, with such as have more show
Of worth, of honor, glory, and popular praise;
Rocks whereon greatest men have oftest wreck'd;
Or that which only seems to satisfy
Lawful desires of nature, not beyond;
And now I know he hungers where no food

[1] Alexander the Great. He was born at Pella, in Macedonia.
[2] Scipio Africanus. His generous treatment of his Spanish captive
is well-known.

Is to be found, in the wide wilderness;
The rest commit to me, I shall let pass
No advantage, and his strength as oft assay.

   He ceased, and heard their grant in loud acclaim:
Then forthwith to him takes a chosen band
Of spirits, likest to himself in guile,
To be at hand, and at his beck appear,
If cause were to unfold some active scene
Of various persons each to know his part;
Then to the desert takes with these his flight;
Where still from shade to shade the Son of GOD
After forty days' fasting had remain'd,
Now hung'ring first, and to himself thus said.

   Where will this end? four times ten days I've pass'd
Wand'ring this woody maze, and human food
Nor tasted, nor had appetite: that fast
To virtue I impute not, or count part
Of what I suffer here. If nature need not,
Or GOD support nature without repast
Though needing, what praise is it to endure?
But now I feel I hunger, which declares
Nature hath need of what she asks; yet GOD
Can satisfy that need some other way,
Though hunger still remain: so it remain
Without this body's wasting, I content me,
And from the sting of famine fear no harm,
Nor mind it, fed with better thoughts, that feed
Me hung'ring more to do my Father's will.

   It was the hour of night, when thus the Son
Communed in silent walk, then laid him down
Under the hospitable covert nigh
Of trees thick interwoven; there he slept,
And dream'd, as appetite is wont to dream,
Of meats and drinks, nature's refreshment sweet:
Him thought he by the brook of Cherith stood,
And saw the ravens with their horny beaks[1]
Food to Elijah bringing even and morn,
Though ravenous, taught to abstain from what they
       brought:
He saw the prophet also how he fled

---

[1] 1 Kings xvii. 5, 6.

Into the desert, and how there he slept
Under a juniper: then how, awaked,
He found his supper on the coals prepared,
And by the angel was bid rise and eat,
And eat the second time after repose,
The strength whereof sufficed him forty days;
Sometimes that with Elijah he partook,
Or as a guest with Daniel at his pulse.[1]
Thus wore out night, and now the herald lark
Left his ground-nest, high tow'ring to descry
The morn's approach, and greet her with his song.
As lightly from his grassy couch up rose
Our Saviour, and found all was but a dream,
Fasting he went to sleep, and fasting waked.
Up to a hill anon his steps he rear'd,
From whose high top to ken the prospect round,
If cottage were in view, sheep-cote, or herd;
But cottage, herd, or sheep-cote none he saw,
Only in a bottom saw a pleasant grove,
With chaunt of tuneful birds resounding loud;
Thither he bent his way, determined there
To rest at noon, and enter'd soon the shade
High roof'd, and walks beneath, and alleys brown,
That open'd in the midst a woody scene;
Nature's own work it seem'd, nature taught art,
And to a superstitious eye the haunt
Of wood-gods and wood-nymphs; he view'd it round,
When suddenly a man before him stood,
Not rustic as before, but seemlier clad,
As one in city, or court, or palace bred,
And with fair speech these words to him address'd.

 With granted leave officious I return,
But much more wonder that the Son of GOD
In this wild solitude so long should bide
Of all things destitute, and well I know,
Not without hunger. Others of some note,
As story tells, have trod this wilderness;
The fugitive bond-woman with her son
Out-cast Nebaioth, yet found here relief

---

[1] Daniel i. 12.

By a providing angel;[1] all the race
Of Israel here had famish'd, had not God
Rain'd from heav'n manna; and that prophet bold
Native of Thebez[2] wand'ring here was fed
Twice by a voice inviting him to eat.[3]
Of thee these forty days none hath regard,
Forty and more deserted here indeed.

    To whom thus Jesus. What conclud'st thou hence?
They all had need, I, as thou seest, have none.

    How hast thou hunger then? Satan replied.
Tell me, if food were now before thee set,
Would'st thou not eat? Thereafter as I like
The giver, answer'd Jesus. Why should that
Cause thy refusal? said the subtle fiend.
Hast thou not right to all created things?
Owe not all creatures by just right to thee
Duty and service, nor to stay till bid,
But tender all their power? nor mention I
Meats by the law unclean, or offer'd first
To idols, those young Daniel could refuse;
Nor proffer'd by an enemy, though who
Would scruple that with want opprest? behold
Nature ashamed, or, better to express,
Troubled that thou should'st hunger, hath purvey'd
From all the elements her choicest store
To treat thee as beseems, and as her Lord
With honor, only deign to sit and eat.

    He spake no dream, for as his words had end,
Our Saviour lifting up his eyes beheld
In ample space under the broadest shade
A table richly spread, in regal mode,
With dishes piled, and meats of noblest sort
And savor, beasts of chase, or fowl of game,

[1] Hagar and Ishmael. See Gen. xxi. 14–21. Nebaioth was Ishmael's
eldest son, who gave their name to the nation descended from him,
the Nebatheans.

[2] Thisbe was the birthplace of Elijah.

[3] Hagar, the Israelites, and Elijah did not suffer hunger on the
identical spot where the Lord fasted; but Milton takes in the *whole
desert* at one view, not caring to distinguish different spots in one
wide tract.—*From* NEWTON.

In pastry-built,[1] or from the spit, or boil'd,
Gris-amber[2] steam'd; all fish from sea or shore,
Freshet[3] or purling brook, of shell or fin,
And exquisitest name, for which was drain'd
Pontus, and Lucrine bay,[4] and Afric coast.
Alas how simple, to these cates compared,
Was that crude apple that diverted [5] Eve!
And at a stately side-board by the wine
That fragrant smell diffused, in order stood
Tall stripling youths rich clad, of fairer hue
Than Ganymed or Hylas,[6] distant more
Under the trees now tripp'd, now solemn stood
Nymphs of Diana's train, and Naiades
With fruits and flowers from Amalthea's horn,
And ladies of the Hesperides,[7] that seem'd
Fairer than feign'd of old, or fabled since
Of fairy damsels met in forest wide
By knights of Logres,[8] or of Lyones,[9]
Lancelot, or Pelleas, or Pellenore,[10]
And all the while harmonious airs were heard
Of chiming strings or charming pipes, and winds

[1] Milton alludes to the culinary feats called "subtilities," or "sotilties"—wonderful pastry built in the shape of embattled towers, &c., to a great height.

[2] Ambergris, which was used in Milton's day in cookery.

[3] A stream of fresh water.

[4] Pontus is the Black Sea; the Lucrine bay in Italy.

[5] Diverted here means "turned aside," from the Latin *diverto*, to turn aside.

[6] Ganymede was the cupbearer of Jupiter; Hylas drew water for Hercules.

[7] The "ladies of the Hesperides" were famed for their lovely singing. The nymphs of the chase and of the water (the Naiades) appropriately attend such a feast.

[8] Logres, or Logris, is the same as *Loegria*, an ancient name for England. See Holinshed's "History of England," B. II. 4, 5. Spenser uses this name in his "Faerie Queene":—

> "And Camber did possess the western quart
>   Which Severn now from Logris doth depart."
> —*From* Dunster's Note.

[9] Lyones, or Lionesse, was an ancient name for part of Cornwall —the extreme west, towards the Land's End.

[10] Lancelot's name has again become a "household word," through Tennyson's exquisite "Idylls." It is scarcely necessary to say that he, Pelleas, and Pellenore were three of Arthur's knights

Of gentlest gale Arabian odors fann'd
From their soft wings, and Flora's earliest smells.
Such was the splendor; and the tempter now
His invitation earnestly renew'd.

 What doubts the Son of GOD to sit and eat?
These are not fruits forbidden; no interdict
Defends the touching of these viands pure;
Their taste no knowledge works at least of evil,
But life preserves, destroy's life's enemy,
Hunger, with sweet restorative delight.
All these are spirits of air, and woods, and springs,
Thy gentle ministers, who come to pay
Thee homage, and acknowledge thee their lord:
What doubt'st thou, Son of GOD? sit down and eat.

 To whom thus Jesus temperately replied.
Said'st thou not that to all things I had right?
And who withholds my power that right to use?
Shall I receive by gift what of my own,
When and where likes me best, I can command?
I can at will, doubt not, as soon as thou,
Command a table in this wilderness,
And call swift flights of angels ministrant,
Array'd in glory, on my cup to attend;
Why should'st thou then obtrude this diligence,
In vain, where no acceptance it can find?
And with my hunger what hast thou to do?
Thy pompous delicacies I contemn,
And count thy specious gifts no gifts, but guiles.

 To whom thus answer'd Satan malecontent.
That I have also power to give thou seest.
If of that power I bring thee voluntary
What I might have bestow'd on whom I pleased,
And rather opportunely in this place
Chose to impart to thy apparent need,
Why should'st thou not accept it? but I see
What I can do or offer is suspect;
Of these things others quickly will dispose,
Whose pains have earn'd the far-fet[1] spoil. With that
Both table and provision vanish'd quite
With sounds of Harpies' wings and talons heard;

---

[1] Far-fetched. "Far-fet" is used by Chaucer and Spenser.

Only the importune tempter still remained,
And with these words his temptations pursued.

By hunger, that each other creature tames,
Thou art not to be harm'd, therefore not moved;
Thy temperance invincible besides,
For no allurement yields to appetite,
And all thy heart is set on high designs,
High actions; but wherewith to be achieved?
Great acts require great means of enterprise;
Thou art unknown, unfriended, low of birth,
A carpenter thy father known, thyself
Bred up in poverty and straits at home,
Lost in a desert here and hunger-bit:
Which way, or from what hope, dost thou aspire
To greatness? whence authority deriv'st?
What followers, what retinue can'st thou gain?
Or at thy heels the dizzy multitude,
Longer than thou canst feed them on thy cost?
Money brings honor, friends, conquest, and realms.
What raised Antipater the Edomite,
And his son Herod placed on Judah's throne,[1]
Thy throne, but gold that got him puissant friends?
Therefore, if at great things thou would'st arrive,
Get riches first, get wealth, and treasure heap,
Not difficult, if thou hearken to me;
Riches are mine, fortune is in my hand;
They whom I favor thrive in wealth amain,
While virtue, valor, wisdom, sit in want.

To whom thus Jesus patiently replied.
Yet wealth without these three is impotent
To gain dominion, or to keep it gain'd.
Witness those ancient empires of the earth,
In highth of all their flowing wealth dissolved.
But men endued with these have oft attain'd
In lowest poverty to highest deeds;
Gideon[2] and Jeptha,[3] and the shepherd lad,
Whose offspring on the throne of Judah sat
So many ages, and shall yet regain
That seat, and reign in Israel without end.

[1] See Josephus, B. IV. 26.
[2] Judges vi. 15.
[3] Judges xi. 1.

Among the heathen, for throughout the world
To me is not unknown what hath been done
Worthy of memorial, canst thou not remember
Quintius,[1] Fabricius,[2] Curius,[3] Regulus?[4]
For I esteem those names of men so poor,
Who could do mighty things, and could contemn
Riches though offer'd from the hands of kings.
And what in me seems wanting, but that I
May also in this poverty as soon
Accomplish what they did, perhaps, and more?
Extol not riches then, the toil of fools,
The wise man's cumbrance, if not snare, more apt
To slacken virtue, and abate her edge,
Than prompt her to do aught may merit praise.
What, if with like aversion I reject
Riches and realms? yet not, for that a crown,
Golden in show, is but a wreath of thorns,
Brings dangers, troubles, cares, and sleepless nights,
To him who wears the regal diadem,
When on his shoulders each man's burden lies;
For therein stands the office of a king.
His honor, virtue, merit, and chief praise,
That for the public all this weight he bears.
Yet he who reigns within himself, and rules
Passions, desires, and fears, is more a king;
Which ev'ry wise and virtuous man attains:
And who attains not, ill aspires to rule
Cities of men, or head-strong multitudes,

[1] Quintius Cincinnatus, twice taken from the plough to be Consul and Dictator of Rome. After subduing the enemies of his country, he refused the wealth the people would have lavished on him, and returned to his cottage and humble life.

[2] Fabricius refused to be bribed by all the wealth of Pyrrhus of Epirus to negotiate a peace for that King with the Romans, and died so poor that he was obliged to be buried at the public expense.

[3] Curius Dentatus, when offered a large sum of money by the Samnites, as he sat by the fire roasting turnips with his own hands, refused it, saying that it was not his ambition to be rich, but to command those who were so.

[4] The story of how Regulus kept his word to the Carthaginians, and returned to die in torture rather than break his pledged promise, is well known.

Subject himself to anarchy within,
Or lawless passions in him, which he serves.
But to guide nations in the way of truth,
By saving doctrine, and from error lead
To know, and knowing worship God aright,
Is yet more kingly; this attracts the soul,
Governs the inner man, the nobler part;
That other o'er the body only reigns,
And oft by force, which to a generous mind,
So reigning, can be no sincere delight.
Besides, to give a kingdom hath been thought
Greater and nobler done, and to lay down
Far more magnanimous than to assume.
Riches are needless then, both for themselves,
And for thy reason why they should be sought,
To gain a sceptre, oftest better miss'd.

BOOK III

So spake the Son of God, and Satan stood
Awhile as mute, confounded what to say,
What to reply, confuted and convinced
Of his weak arguing and fallacious drift;
At length, collecting all his serpent wiles,
With soothing words renew'd, him thus accosts.

I see thou know'st what is of use to know,
What best to say canst say, to do canst do;
Thy actions to thy words accord, thy words
To thy large heart give utterance due, thy heart
Contains of good, wise, just, the perfect shape.
Should kings and nations from thy mouth consult,
Thy counsel would be as the oracle
Urim and Thummim, those oraculous gems
On Aaron's breast; or tongue of seers old
Infallible: or wert thou sought to deeds
That might require th' array of war, thy skill
Of conduct would be such, that all the world
Could not sustain thy prowess, or subsist
In battle, though against thy few in arms.
These god-like virtues wherefore dost thou hide,
Affecting private life, or more obscure
In savage wilderness? wherefore deprive
All earth her wonder at thy acts, thyself
The fame and glory, glory the reward
That sole excites to high attempts, the flame
Of most erected spirits, most temper'd pure
Ætherial, who all pleasures else despise,
All treasures and all gain esteem as dross,
And dignities and powers, all but the highest?
Thy years are ripe,[1] and over-ripe; the son
Of Macedonian Philip[2] had ere these
Won Asia, and the throne of Cyrus held

---

[1] Our Saviour was then "about thirty years of age." Luke iii. 23.
[2] Alexander the Great.

At his dispose; young Scipio[1] had brought down
The Carthaginian pride; young Pompey quell'd
The Pontic king, and in triumph had rode.[2]
Yet years, and to ripe years judgment mature,
Quench not the thirst of glory, but augment.
Great Julius, whom now all the world admires,
The more he grew in years, the more inflamed
With glory, wept that he had lived so long
Inglorious,[3] but thou yet art not too late.

To whom our Saviour calmly thus replied.
Thou neither dost persuade me to seek wealth
For empire's sake, nor empire to affect
For glory's sake by all thy argument.
For what is glory but the blaze of fame,
The people's praise, if always praise unmixt?
And what the people but a herd confused,
A miscellaneous rabble, who extol
Things vulgar, and well weigh'd, scarce worth the praise?
They praise and they admire they know not what,
And know not whom, but as one leads the other:
And what delight to be by such extoll'd,
To live upon their tongues and be their talk,
Of whom to be dispraised were no small praise,
His lot who dares be singularly good.
Th' intelligent among them and the wise
Are few, and glory scarce of few is raised.
This is true glory and renown, when God,
Looking on the earth, with approbation marks
The just man, and divulges him through heaven
To all His angels, who with true applause
Recount his praises. Thus He did to Job,
When, to extend his fame through heav'n and earth,
As thou to thy reproach may'st well remember,

[1] Scipio was only twenty-nine years old when he conquered the Carthaginians.

[2] Pompey distinguished himself in his youth; but when he conquered Mithridates he was forty years old.

[3] Julius Cæsar, whilst meditating over a "Life of Alexander," was seen to weep by his friends. On being asked the reason of his tears, he replied, "Do you not think I have just cause to weep, when I consider that Alexander at my age had conquered so many nations, and I in all these years have done nothing memorable?"— PLUTARCH.

He ask'd thee, Hast thou seen my servant Job?
Famous he was in heav'n, on earth less known;
Where glory is false glory, attributed
To things not glorious, men not worthy of fame.
They err who count it glorious to subdue
By conquest far and wide, to overrun
Large countries, and in field great battles win,
Great cities by assault: what do these worthies,
But rob, and spoil, burn, slaughter, and enslave
Peaceable nations, neighboring or remote,
Made captive, yet deserving freedom more
Than those their conquerors, who leave behind
Nothing but ruin whereso'er they rove,
And all the flourishing works of peace destroy,
Then swell with pride, and must be titled gods,
Great benefactors of mankind, deliverers,
Worshipp'd with temple, priest, and sacrifice;
One is the son of Jove, of Mars the other;
Till conqueror death discover them scarce men,
Rolling in brutish vices, and deform'd,
Violent or shameful death their due reward.
But if there be in glory aught of good,
It may by means far different be attain'd
Without ambition, war, or violence;
By deeds of peace, by wisdom eminent,
By patience, temperance. I mention still
Him whom thy wrongs with saintly patience borne
Made famous in a land and times obscure;
Who names not now with honor patient Job?
Poor Socrates, who next more memorable?
By what he taught and suffer'd for so doing,
For truth's sake suffering death unjust, lives now
Equal in fame to proudest conquerors.
Yet if for fame and glory aught be done,
Aught suffer'd; if young African[1] for fame
His wasted country freed from Punic rage,
The deed becomes unpraised, the man at least,
And loses, though but verbal his reward.
Shall I seek glory then, as vain men seek,
Oft not deserved? I seek not mine, but His

[1] Scipio Africanus.

Who sent me, and thereby witness whence I am.
　　To whom the tempter murmuring thus replied.
Think not so slight of glory, therein least
Resembling thy great Father: He seeks glory,
And for His glory all things made, all things
Orders and governs; nor content in heav'n
By all His angels glorified requires
Glory from men, from all men good or bad,
Wise or unwise, no difference, no exemption;
Above all sacrifice or hallow'd gift
Glory He requires, and glory He receives
Promiscuous from all nations, Jew, or Greek,
Or barbarous, nor exception hath declared:
From us, His foes pronounced, glory He exacts.
　　To whom our Saviour fervently replied.
And reason, since His word all things produced,
Though chiefly not for glory as prime end,
But to show forth His goodness, and impart
His good communicable to every soul
Freely; of whom what could He less expect
Than glory and benediction, that is, thanks,
The slightest, easiest, readiest, recompense
From them who could return Him nothing else,
And not returning that would likeliest render
Contempt instead, dishonor, obloquy?
Hard recompense, unsuitable return
For so much good, so much beneficence.
But why should man seek glory, who of his own
Hath nothing, and to whom nothing belongs
But condemnation, ignominy, and shame?
Who for so many benefits received
Turn'd recreant to GOD, ingrate and false,
And so of all true good himself despoil'd,
Yet, sacrilegious, to himself would take
That which to GOD alone of right belongs:
Yet so much bounty is in GOD, such grace,
That who advance His glory, not their own,
Them He Himself to glory will advance.
　　So spake the Son of GOD; and here again
Satan had not to answer, but stood struck
With guilt of his own sin, for he himself
Insatiable of glory had lost all;

Yet of another plea bethought him soon.

  Of glory, as thou wilt, said he, so deem,
Worth or not worth the seeking, let it pass.
But to a kingdom thou art born, ordain'd
To sit upon thy father David's throne,
By mother's side thy father; though thy right
Be now in powerful hands, that will not part
Easily from possession won with arms.
Judæa now and all the promised land,
Reduced a province under Roman yoke,
Obeys Tiberius; nor is always ruled
With temperate sway: oft have they violated
The temple,[1] oft the law with foul affronts,
Abominations rather, as did once
Antiochus:[2] and think'st thou to regain
Thy right by sitting still or thus retiring?
So did not Maccabeus:[3] he indeed
Retired unto the desert, but with arms;
And o'er a mighty king so oft prevail'd,
That by strong hand his family obtain'd,
Though priests, the crown, and David's throne usurp'd,
With Modin and her suburbs once content.
If kingdom move thee not, let move thee zeal
And duty; zeal and duty are not slow;
But on occasion's forelock[4] watchful wait.
They themselves rather are occasion best,
Zeal of thy father's house, duty to free
Thy country from her heathen servitude;
So shalt thou best fulfil, best verify
The prophets old, who sung thy endless reign;
The happier reign the sooner it begins;
Reign then; what canst thou better do the while?

  To whom our Saviour answer thus return'd.
All things are best fulfill'd in their due time,

---

[1] Pompey, with several of his officers, entered the Holy of Holies, where none were allowed to step except the high priest once a year, on the great day of expiation.

[2] 2 Maccab. v.

[3] Judas Maccabeus. Modin was the inheritance of the Maccabees.

[4] The Greek and Latin poets represented Time (or Opportunity) with a single lock of hair in front. The expression of seizing Time by the forelock is proverbial.

And time there is for all things, Truth had said:[1]
If of my reign prophetic writ hath told
That it shall never end, so when begin
The Father in his purpose hath decreed,
He in whose hands all times and seasons roll.[2]
What, if He hath decreed that I shall first
Be tried in humble state and things adverse,
By tribulations, injuries, insults,
Contempts, and scorns, and snares, and violence,
Suffering, abstaining, quietly expecting,
Without distrust or doubt, that he may know
What I can suffer, how obey? Who best
Can suffer, best can do; best reign, who first
Well hath obey'd:[3] just trial, ere I merit
My exaltation without change or end.
But what concerns it thee when I begin
My everlasting kingdom? why art thou
Solicitous? what moves thy inquisition?
Know'st thou not that my rising is thy fall,
And my promotion will be thy destruction?

To whom the tempter, inly rack'd, replied.
Let that come when it comes; all hope is lost
Of my reception into grace: what worse?
For where no hope is left, is left no fear:
If there be worse, the expectation more
Of worse torments me than the feeling can
I would be at the worst, worst is my port,
My harbor, and my ultimate repose;
The end I would attain, my final good.
My error was my error, and my crime
My crime; whatever for itself condemn'd,
And will alike be punish'd, whether thou
Reign or reign not; though to that gentle brow
Willingly I could fly, and hope thy reign,
From that placid aspect and meek regard,
Rather than aggravate my evil state,

[1] Eccles. iii. 1.
[2] Acts i. 7. Mark xii. 32.
[3] "Qui bene imperat, paruerit aliquando necesse est; et qui modeste paret, videtur, qui aliquando imperet, dignus esse."—CICERO, quoted by NEWTON.

Would stand between me and thy Father's ire,
(Whose ire I dread more than the fire of hell,)
A shelter, and a kind of shading cool
Interposition, as a summer's cloud.
If I then to the worst that can be haste,
Why move thy feet so slow to what is best,
Happiest both to thyself and all the world,
That thou who worthiest art should'st be their king?
Perhaps thou linger'st in deep thoughts detain'd
Of the enterprize so hazardous and high:
No wonder, for, though in thee be united
What of perfection can in man be found,
Or human nature can receive, consider,
Thy life hath yet been private, most part spent
At home, scarce view'd the Galilean towns,
And once a year Jerusalem,[1] few days'
Short sojourn; and what thence could'st thou observe?
The world thou hast not seen, much less her glory,
Empires, and monarchs, and their radiant courts,
Best school of best experience, quickest insight
In all things that to greatest actions lead.
The wisest, unexperienced, will be ever
Timorous and loth, with novice modesty,
As he who seeking asses found a kingdom,[2]
Irresolute, unhardy, unadvent'rous:
But I will bring thee where thou soon shall quit
Those rudiments, and see before thine eyes
The monarchies of the earth, their pomp and state,
Sufficient introduction to inform
Thee, of thyself so apt, in regal arts
And regal mysteries, that thou may'st know
How best their opposition to withstand.

    With that (such power was given him then) he took
The Son of GOD up to a mountain high.[3]
It was a mountain at whose verdant feet
A spacious plain outstretch'd in circuit wide

---

[1] At the Passover.
[2] Saul. See 1 Sam. ix. 20, 21.
[3] Milton is supposed to mean Mount Niphates, in the Taurus, which rises immediately above Assyria, and from whence he had made Satan survey Eden in the "Paradise Lost."—*See* DUNSTER.

Lay pleasant; from his side two rivers flow'd,[1]
The one winding, the other straight, and left between
Fair champaign with less rivers intervein'd,
Then meeting join'd their tribute to the sea:
Fertile of corn the glebe, of oil and wine,
With herds the pastures throng'd, with flocks the hills;
Huge cities and high tower'd, that well might seem
The seats of mightiest monarchs, and so large
The prospect was that here and there was room
For barren desert, fountainless and dry.
To this high mountain top the tempter brought
Our Saviour, and new train of words began.

Well have we speeded, and o'er hill and dale,
Forest and field, and flood, temples, and towers,
Cut shorter many a league; here thou behold'st
Assyria, and her empire's ancient bounds,
Araxes, and the Caspian lake, thence on
As far as Indus east, Euphrates west,
And oft beyond; to south the Persian bay,
And inaccessible the Arabian drought:[2]
Here Nineveh, of length within her wall
Several days' journey, built by Ninus old,
Of that first golden monarchy the seat,
And seat of Salmanassar,[3] whose success
Israel in long captivity still mourns;
There Babylon, the wonder of all tongues,
As ancient, but rebuilt by him[4] who twice
Judah and all thy father David's house
Led captive, and Jerusalem laid waste,
Till Cyrus set them free; Persepolis
His city there thou seest, and Bactra there;
Ecbactana her structure vast there shows,
And Hecatompylos[5] her hundred gates;
There Susa by Choaspes, amber stream,

---

[1] The Euphrates—"vagus Euphrates"—and the Tigris, the course
of which was very straight.—TODD.

[2] A figure of speech for the desert.

[3] Shalmansar, in the reign of Hezekiah, King of Judah, carried
away captive to Assyria the ten tribes of Israel.

[4] Nebuchadnezzar.

[5] Capital of Parthia, so called from its hundred gates.

The drink of none but kings;[1] of later fame
Built by Emathian,[2] or by Parthian hands,
The great Seleucia, Nisibis,[3] and there
Artaxata, Teredon, Ctesiphon,
Turning with easy eye thou may'st behold.
All these the Parthian, now some ages past,
By great Arsaces led, who founded first
That empire, under his dominion holds,
From the luxurious kings of Antioch won.
And just in time thou com'st to have a view
Of his great power; for now the Parthian king
In Ctesiphon hath gather'd all his host[4]
Against the Scythian, whose incursions wild
Have wasted Sogdiana; to her aid
He marches now in haste; see, though from far,
His thousands, in what martial equipage
They issue forth, steel bows and shafts their arms,
Of equal dread in flight[5] or in pursuit;
All horsemen, in which fight they most excel:
See how in warlike muster they appear,
In rhombs, and wedges, and half-moons, and wings,
He look'd, and saw what numbers numberless
The city gates outpour'd, light armèd troops
In coats of mail and military pride;
In mail their horses clad, yet fleet and strong,
Prancing their riders bore, the flower and choice
Of many provinces from bound to bound;

---

[1] Modern research confirms this fact in a singular manner. "It is
a fact worthy of remark," says Buckingham, "that at this moment,
while all the inhabitants of Kermanshah drink of the stream of
Aub Dedoong, and of the spring called Aubi-i-Hassan-Khan, the
King's son alone has the water for himself and his harem brought
from the stream of the Kara Soo (the Choaspes). We drank of
it ourselves as we passed, and from its superiority to all the waters
of which we had tasted since leaving the banks of the Tigris, the
draught was delicious enough to be sweet even to the palsied taste
of royalty itself."—*Quoted in Aldine Edition.*

[2] Macedonian.

[3] Also named Antiochus.

[4] Ctesiphon was the place at which the Parthian kings always
assembled their forces.

[5] They discharged their arrows as they fled.

From Arachosia, from Candaor east,
And Margiana to the Hyrcanian cliffs
Of Caucasus, and dark Iberian dales,[1]
From Atropatia and the neighboring plains
Of Adiabene, Media, and the south
Of Susiana, to Balsara's[2] haven.
He saw them in their forms of battle ranged,
How quick they wheel'd, and flying behind them shot
Sharp sleet of arrowy showers against the face
Of their pursuers, and overcame by flight;
The field all iron cast a gleaming brown:
Nor wanted clouds of foot, nor on each horn
Cuirassiers all in steel for standing fight,
Chariots or elephants endorsed with towers
Of archers, nor of laboring pioneers
A multitude with spades and axes arm'd
To lay hills plain, fell woods, or valleys fill,
Or, where plain was raise hill, or overlay
With bridges rivers proud, as with a yoke;
Mules after these, camels, and dromedaries,
And waggons fraught with utensils of war.
Such forces met not, nor so wide a camp,
When Agrican[3] with all his northern powers
Besieged Albracca, as romances tell,
The city of Gallaphrone, from thence to win
The fairest of her sex Angelica
His daughter, sought by many prowest[4] knights
Both Paynim, and the peers of Charlemain.
Such and so numerous was their chivalry;

[1] Said to be "dark" from their thick forests.
[2] The Persian Gulf, so called from Bussora, or Balsera, the port
situated on it.
[3] Agricano, one of the heroes of Boiardo's "Orlando Inamorato."
Angelica, his daughter, was fabled to be the most beautiful woman
of the age, and, like Helen of Troy, a fair mischief, who gave
rise to continual strife. She reappears in Ariosto's "Orlando Fu-
rioso." Orlando goes mad for love of her. We must remember,
when we marvel somewhat at this blending of truth and fiction,
that the poems of Ariosto and Boiardo had probably been the de-
light of Milton's youth; and that he is alluding to the greatest
poets of his own age, not merely to romances.
[4] Prowest is the superlative of prow, from the old French *preux*,
valiant.—DUNSTER.

At sight whereof the fiend yet more presumed,
And to our Savior thus his words renew'd.

   That thou may'st know I seek not to engage
Thy virtue, and not every way secure
On no slight grounds thy safety, hear and mark
To what end I have brought thee hither and shown
All this fair sight; thy kingdom, though foretold
By prophet or by angel, unless thou
Endeavor, as thy father David did,
Thou never shalt obtain; prediction still
In all things, and all men, supposes means,
Without means used, what it predicts revokes.
But say thou wert possess'd of David's throne
By free consent of all, none opposite
Samaritan or Jew; how could'st thou hope
Long to enjoy it quiet and secure,
Between two such enclosing enemies,
Roman and Parthian? therefore one of these
Thou must make sure thy own, the Parthian first
By my advice, as nearer, and of late
Found able by invasion to annoy
Thy country, and captive lead away her kings,
Antigonus, and old Hyrcanus[1] bound,
Maugre the Roman. It shall be my task
To render thee the Parthian at dispose;
Choose which thou wilt, by conquest or by league
By him thou shalt regain, without him not,
That which alone can truly reinstall thee
In David's royal seat, his true successor,
Deliverance of thy brethren, those ten tribes,
Whose offspring in his territory yet serve,
In Habor, and among the Medes dispersed;
Ten sons of Jacob, two of Joseph lost
Thus long from Israel, serving, as of old
Their fathers in the land of Egypt served,
This offer sets before thee to deliver.
These if from servitude thou shalt restore
To their inheritance, then, nor till then,
Thou on the throne of David in full glory,
From Egypt to Euphrates and beyond,

[1] The Parthians led Hyrcanus away captive to Seleucia when he
was seventy years old.—*See* JOSEPHUS.

Shalt reign, and Rome or Cæsar not need fear.
  To whom our Saviour answer'd thus unmoved.
Much ostentation vain of fleshly arm,
And fragile arms, much instrument of war
Long in preparing, soon to nothing brought,
Before mine eyes thou hast set; and in my ear
Vented much policy, and prójects deep
Of enemies, of aids, battles, and leagues,
Plausible to the world, to me worth nought.
Means I must use, thou say'st, prediction else
Will unpredict and fail me of the throne.
My time, I told thee, (and that time for thee
Were better farthest off,) is not yet come;
When that comes, think not thou to find me slack
On my part aught endeavoring, or to need
Thy politic maxims, or that cumbersome
Luggage of war there shown me, argument
Of human weakness rather than of strength.
My brethren, as thou call'st them, those ten tribes
I must deliver, if I mean to reign
David's true heir, and his full sceptre sway
To just extent over all Israel's sons,
But whence to thee this zeal, where was it then
For Israel, or for David, or his throne,
When thou stood'st up his tempter to the pride
Of numb'ring Israel, which cost the lives
Of threescore and ten thousand Israelites
By three days' pestilence? [1] such was thy zeal
To Israel then, the same that now to me.
As for those captive tribes, themselves were they
Who wrought their own captivity, fell off
From God to worship calves, the deities
Egypt, Baal next, and Ashtaroth,
And all th' idolatries of heathen round,
Besides their other worse than heathenish crimes;
Nor in the land of their captivity,
Humbled themselves, or penitent besought
The God of their forefathers; but so died
Impenitent, and left a race behind
Like to themselves, distinguishable scarce

---

[1] 1 Chron. xxi. 1.

From Gentiles, but by circumcision vain,
And GOD with idols in their worship join'd.
Should I of these the liberty regard,
Who freed as to their ancient patrimony,
Unhumbled, unrepentant, unreform'd,
Headlong would follow; and to their gods perhaps
Of Bethel and of Dan? no, let them serve
Their enemies, who serve idols with GOD.
Yet he at length, time to himself best known,
Rememb'ring Abraham, by some wondrous call
May bring them back repentant and sincere,
And at their passing cleave the Assyrian flood,
While to their native land with joy they haste,
As the Red Sea and Jordan once he cleft,
When to the promised land their fathers pass'd;
To his due time and providence I leave them.

So spake Israel's true king, and to the fiend
Made answer meet, that made void all his wiles.
So fares it when with truth falsehood contends.

BOOK IV

PERPLEX'D and troubled at his bad success
The tempter stood, nor had what to reply,
Discover'd in his fraud, thrown from his hope
So oft, and the persuasive rhetoric
That sleek'd his tongue, and won so much on Eve;
So little here, nay lost: but Eve was Eve,
This far his over-match, who self-deceived
And rash before-hand had no better weigh'd
The strength he was to cope with, or his own:
But as a man who had been matchless held
In cunning, over-reach'd where least he thought,
To salve his credit, and for very spite,
Still will be tempting him who foils him still,
And never cease, though to his shame the more;
Or as a swarm of flies in vintage time,
About the wine-press where sweet must is pour'd,
Beat off, returns as oft with humming sound;
Or surging waves against a solid rock,
Though all to shivers dash'd, the assault renew,
Vain batt'ry, and in froth or bubbles end;
So Satan, whom repulse upon repulse
Met ever, and to shameful silence brought,
Yet gives not o'er, though desperate of success,
And his vain importunity pursues.
He brought our Savior to the western side
Of that high mountain, whence he might behold
Another plain,[1] long, but in breadth not wide,
Wash'd by the southern sea, and on the north
To equal length back'd with a ridge of hills,[2]
That screen'd the fruits of the earth and seats of men
From cold Septentrion blasts, thence in the midst
Divided by a river, of whose banks
On each side an imperial city stood,
With towers and temples proudly elevate

---

[1] Italy, washed by the Mediterranean.
[2] The Apennines.

On seven small hills, with palaces adorn'd,
Porches, and theatres, baths, aqueducts,
Statues, and trophies, and triumphal arcs,
Gardens, and groves presented to his eyes,
Above the highth of mountains interposed:
By what strange parallax or optic skill
Of vision, multiplied through air, or glass
Of telescope, were curious to enquire:
And now the tempter thus his silence broke.

   The city which thou seest no other deem
Than great and glorious Rome, queen of the earth
So far renown'd, and with the spoils enrich'd
Of nations; there the Capitol thou seest
Above the rest lifting his stately head
On the Tarpeian rock, her citadel
Impregnable, and there mount Palatine,
Th' imperial palace, compass huge, and high
The structure, skill of noblest architects,
With gilded battlements conspicuous far,
Turrets, and terraces, and glittering spires.
Many a fair edifice besides, more like
Houses of gods, so well I have disposed
My aery microscope, thou mayst behold
Outside and inside both, pillars and roofs,
Carved work, the hand of famed artificers
In cedar, marble, ivory or gold.
Thence to the gates cast round thine eye, and see
What conflux issuing forth, or ent'ring in,
Prætors, proconsuls to their provinces
Hasting, or on return, in robes of state;
Lictors and rods, the ensigns of their power,
Legions and cohorts, turms[1] of horse and wings;
Or embassies from regions far remote
In various habits on the Appian road,
Or on th' Emilian,[2] some from farthest south
Syene,[3] and where the shadow both way falls,
Meroe, Nilotic isle, and more to west.

[1] Troops of horse, a word coined from the Latin *turma.* "Equitum turmæ."—VIRG. *Æn.* V. 360.—NEWTON.
[2] The Appian road led towards the south of Italy, and the Emilian towards the north.
[3] Put for the farthest point of the Roman Empire.

The realm of Bocchus[1] to the Black-moor sea;
From the Asian kings and Parthian, among these,
From India and the golden Chersonese,
And utmost Indian isle Taprobane,
Dusk faces with white silken turbans wreath'd:
From Gallia, Gades,[2] and the British west,
Germans, and Scythians, and Sarmatians north
Beyond Danubius to the Tauric pool.[3]
All nations now to Rome obedience pay,
To Rome's great emperor, whose wide domain
In ample territory, wealth, and power,
Civility of manners, arts, and arms,
And long renown, thou justly may'st prefer
Before the Parthian; these two thrones except,
The rest are barbarous, and scarce worth the sight,
Shared among petty kings too far removed.
These having shown thee, I have shown thee all
The kingdoms of the world, and all their glory.
This emperor[4] hath no son, and now is old,
Old and lascivious, and from Rome retired
To Capreæ, an island small but strong
On the Campanian shore, with purpose there
His horrid lusts in private to enjoy,
Committing to a wicked favorite[5]
All public cares, and yet of him suspicious,
Hated of all and hating: with what ease,
Indued with regal virtues as thou art,
Appearing and beginning noble deeds,
Might'st thou expel this monster from his throne
Now made a sty, and, in his place ascending,
A victor people free from servile yoke?
And with my help thou may'st; to me the power
Is given, and by that right I give it thee.
Aim therefore at no less than all the world,
Aim at the highest without the highest attain'd
Will be for thee no sitting, or not long,
On David's throne, be prophesied what will.

[1] Mauritania.
[2] Cadiz, in Spain, the extreme west of the Roman Empire.
[3] Palus Mæotis, or Black Sea.
[4] Tiberius.
[5] Sejanus.

To whom the Son of God unmoved replied.
Nor doth this grandeur and majestic show
Of luxury, though call'd magnificence,
More than of arms before, allure mine eye.
Much less my mind; though thou should'st add to tell
Their sumptuous gluttonies and gorgeous feasts
On citron tables[1] or Atlantic stone,
For I have also heard, perhaps have read.
Their wines of Setia, Cales, and Falerne,[2]
Chios, and Crete,[3] and how they quaff in gold,
Crystal and myrrhine cups emboss'd with gems
And studs of pearl, to me should'st tell who thirst
And hunger still. Then embassies thou show'st
From nations far and nigh. What honor that,
But tedious waste of time to sit and hear
So many hollow compliments and lies,
Outlandish flatteries? then proceed'st to talk
Of the emperor, how easily subdued,
How gloriously; I shall, thou say'st, expel
A brutish monster: what if I withal
Expel a devil who first made him such?
Let his tormentor conscience find him out;
For him I was not sent, nor yet to free
That people, victor once, now vile and base,
Deservedly made vassal, who, once just,
Frugal, and mild, and temperate, conquer'd well,
But govern ill the nation under yoke,
Peeling their provinces, exhausted all
But lust and rapine; first ambitious grown
Of triumph, that insulting vanity;
Then cruel, by their sports to blood inured
Of fighting beasts, and men to beasts exposed,
Luxurious by their wealth, and greedier still,
And from the daily scene effeminate.
What wise and valiant man would seek to free

[1] Tables of citron-wood were very highly valued by the Romans.
It grew on Mount Atlas. Atlantic stone was probably marble from
Numidia. Pliny, in his *Hist. Nat.* lib. v. c. i., says that the woods
of Atlas were explored for citron-wood.

[2] These were famous Campanian wines. Falerian was the best
wine they possessed.

[3] Greek wines.

These thus degenerate, by themselves enslaved,
Or could of inward slave make outward free?
Know therefore, when my season comes to sit
On David's throne, it shall be like a tree
Spreading and overshadowing all the earth,
Or as a stone that shall to pieces dash
All monarchies besides throughout the world,
And of my kingdom there shall be no end.
Means there shall be to this, but what the means,
Is not for thee to know, nor me to tell.
    To whom the tempter impudent replied.
I see all offers made by me how slight
Thou valu'st, because offer'd, and reject'st;
Nothing will please the difficult and nice,
Or nothing more than still to contradict.
On the other side know also thou, that I
On what I offer set as high esteem,
Nor what I part with mean to give for nought;
All these which in a moment thou behold'st,
The kingdoms of the world to thee I give;
For, giv'n to me, I give to whom I please,
No trifle; yet with this reserve, not else,
On this condition, if thou wilt fall down,
And worship me as thy superior lord,
Easily done, and hold them all of me:
For what can less so great a gift deserve?
    Whom thus our Savior answer'd with disdain.
I never liked thy talk, thy offers less,
Now both abhor, since thou hast dared to utter
The abominable terms, impious condition;
But I endure the time, till which expired,
Thou hast permission on me. It is written
The first of all commandments, Thou shalt worship
The Lord thy GOD, and only him shalt serve;
And dar'st thou to the Son of GOD propound
To worship thee accurst, now more accurst
For this attempt, bolder than that on Eve,
And more blasphemous? which expect to rue.
The kingdoms of the world to thee were giv'n,
Permitted rather, and by thee usurp'd,
Other donation none thou canst produce:
If giv'n, by whom but by the King of kings,

GOD over all Supreme? if given to thee,
By thee how fairly is the giver now
Repaid? but gratitude in thee is lost
Long since. Wert thou so void of fear or shame,
As offer them to me the Son of GOD,
To me my own, on such abhorrèd pact,
That I fall down and worship thee as GOD?
Get thee behind me; plain thou now appear'st
That evil one, Satan for ever damn'd.
  To whom the fiend with fear abash'd replied.
Be not so sore offended, Son of GOD,
Though sons of GOD both angels are and men,
If I, to try whether in higher sort
Than these thou bear'st that title, have proposed
What both from men and angels I receive,
Tetrachs of fire, air, flood, and on the earth
Nations besides from all the quarter'd winds,
GOD of this world invoked and world beneath;
Who then thou art, whose coming is foretold
To me so fatal, me it most concerns.
The trial hath indamaged thee no way,
Rather more honor left and more esteem;
Me nought advantaged, missing what I aim'd.
Therefore let pass, as they are transitory,
The kingdoms of this world; I shall no more
Advise thee; gain them as thou canst, or not.
And thou thyself seem'st otherwise inclined
Than to a worldly crown, addicted more
To contemplation and profound dispute,
As by that early action may be judged,
When slipping from thy mother's eye, thou went'st
Alone into the temple, thou wast found
Amongst the gravest rabbies disputant
On points and questions fitting Moses' chair,
Teaching, not taught. The childhood shows the man,
As morning shows the day. Be famous then
By wisdom; as thy empire must extend,
So let extend thy mind o'er all the world
In knowledge, all things in it comprehend:
All knowledge is not couch'd in Moses' law,
The Pentateuch, or what the prophets wrote;
The Gentiles also know, and write, and teach

To admiration, led by nature's light;
And with the Gentiles much thou must converse,
Ruling them by persuasion as thou mean'st;
Without their learning how wilt thou with them,
Or they with thee, hold conversation meet?
How wilt thou reason with them? how refute
Their idolisms, traditions, paradoxes?
Error by his own arms is best evinced.
Look once more, ere we leave this specular mount,
Westward, much nearer by south-west, behold
Where on the Ægean shore a city stands
Built nobly, pure the air, and light the soil,
Athens the eye of Greece,[1] mother of arts
And eloquence, native to famous wits,
Or hospitable, in her sweet recess,
City or suburban, studious walks and shades;
See there the olive grove of Academe,[2]
Plato's retirement, where the Attic bird [3]
Trills her thick-warbled notes the summer long;
There flow'ry hill Hymettus with the sound
Of bees' industrious murmur oft invites
To studious musing; there Ilissus rolls
His whispering stream; within the walls then view
The schools of ancient sages; his[4] who bred
Great Alexander to sudue the world;
Lyceum there, and painted Stoa next.
There thou shalt hear and learn the secret power
Of harmony, in tones and numbers hit
By voice or hand, and various-measured verse,
Æolian charms[5] and Dorian lyric odes,
And his who gave them breath, but higher sung,

[1] So called by Demosthenes.—NEWTON.
[2] "A gymnasium, or place of exercise," in the suburbs of Athens surrounded by woods. It took its name from Academus, one of the heroes. In this Academe, or Academy, Plato taught.
[3] The nightingale; *i.e.*, Philomela, the daughter of Pandion, King of Athens, was changed into a nightingale.
[4] Aristotle. The Lyceum was the school of Aristotle. Stoa wa the school of Zeno, whose disciples were hence called Stoics. This Stoa, or *portico*, was adorned with a variety of paintings.
[5] Æolian charms. The poems of Alcæus and Sappho; the Dorian lyric odes were those of Pindar.—NEWTON.

Blind Melesigenes,[1] thence Homer call'd,
Whose poem Phœbus challenged for his own.
Thence what the lofty grave tragedians taught
In Chorus or Iambick, teachers best
Of moral prudence, with delight received,
In brief sententious precepts, while they treat
Of fate and chance, and change in human life;
High actions and high passions best describing.
Thence to the famous orators repair,
Those ancient, whose resistless eloquence
Wielded at will that fierce democratic,
Shook the arsenal, and fulmin'd over Greece,
To Macedon, and Artaxerxes' throne:
To sage philosophy next lend thine ear,
From heav'n descended to the low-rooft house
Of Socrates; see there his tenement,
Whom well inspired the oracle pronounced
Wisest of men; from whose mouth issued forth
Mellifluous streams that water'd all the schools
Of Academics[2] old and new, with those
Surnamed Peripatetics,[3] and the sect
Epicurean, and the Stoic severe;
These here revolve, or, as thou lik'st, at home,
Till time mature thee to a kingdom's weight;
These rules will render thee a king complete
Within thyself, much more with empire join'd.

   To whom our Saviour thus sagely replied.
Think not but that I know these things, or think
I know them not; not therefore am I short
Of knowing what I ought: he who receives
Light from above, from the fountain of light,
No other doctrine needs, though granted true:
But these are false, or little else but dreams,
Conjectures, fancies, built on nothing firm.
The first and wisest of them all [4] professed

---

[1] Homer was so called by his mother because he was born near the River Meles.
[2] The old Academic philosophers were those who followed Plato; the new, those who followed Carneades.—*See* DUNSTER.
[3] Pupils of Aristotle, so called because they taught while walking.
[4] Socrates.

To know this only, that he nothing knew;
The next to fabling fell and smooth conceits;[1]
A third sort doubted all things,[2] though plain sense;
Others in virtue placed felicity,
But virtue join'd with riches and long life;
In corporal pleasure he and careless ease;
The Stoic last in philosophic pride,
By him call'd virtue; and his virtuous man,
Wise, perfect in himself, and all possessing,
Equal to GOD, oft shames not to prefer,
As fearing GOD nor man, contemning all
Wealth, pleasure, pain or torment, death and life,
Which when he lists he leaves, or boasts he can,
For all his tedious talk is but vain boast,
Or subtle shifts conviction to evade.
Alas! what can they teach and not mislead,
Ignorant of themselves, of GOD much more,
And how the world began, and how man fell
Degraded by himself, on grace depending?
Much of the soul they talk, but all awry,
And in themselves seek virtue, and to themselves
All glory arrogate, to GOD give none,
Rather accuse him under usual names,
Fortune and fate, as one regardless quite
Of mortal things. Who therefore seeks in these
True wisdom, finds her not, or by delusion
Far worse, her false resemblance only meets,
An empty cloud.[3] However, many books
Wise men have said are wearisome;[4] who reads
Incessantly, and to his reading brings not
A spirit and judgment equal or superior,
(And what he brings what need he elsewhere seek?)
Uncertain and unsettled still remains,
Deep versed in books and shallow in himself,
Crude or intoxicate, collecting toys,
And trifles for choice matters, worth a sponge;

---

[1] Plato.

[2] The Pyrrhonians, or disciples of Pyrrho, who were sceptics.—
NEWTON.

[3] An allusion to the fable of Ixion, who embraced a cloud which
had the form of Juno.—NEWTON.

[4] Eccles. xii. 12.

As children gath'ring pebbles on the shore.
Or if I would delight my private hours
With music or with poem, where so soon
As in our native language can I find
That solace? all our law and story strew'd
With hymns, our psalms with artful terms inscribed,
Our Hebrew songs and harps in Babylon,
That pleased so well our victor's ear, declare
That rather Greece from us these arts derived;
Ill imitated, while they loudest sing
The vices of their deities and their own
In fable, hymn, or song, so personating
Their gods ridiculous, and themselves past shame.
Remove their swelling epithets, thick laid
As varnish on a harlot's cheek, the rest,
Thin sown, with aught of profit or delight,
Will far be found unworthy to compare
With Sion's songs, to all true tastes excelling,
Where God is praised aright, and godlike men,
The Holiest of Holies, and his saints:
Such are from God inspired, not such from thee,
Unless where moral virtue is express'd
By light of nature not in all quite lost.
Their orators thou then extol'st, as those
The top of eloquence, statists indeed,
And lovers of their country, as may seem;
But herein to our prophets far beneath,
As men divinely taught, and better teaching
The solid rules of civil government
In their majestic unaffected style,
Than all the oratory of Greece and Rome.
In them is plainest taught, and easiest learnt,
What makes a nation happy, and keeps it so,
What ruins kingdoms, and lays cities flat;
These only with our law best form a king.
    So spake the Son of God; but Satan, now,
Quite at a loss, for all his darts were spent,
Thus to our Saviour with stern brow replied.
    Since neither wealth, nor honor, arms, nor arts,
Kingdom nor empire pleases thee, nor aught
By me proposed in life contemplative
Or active, tended on by glory or fame,

What dost thou in this world? the wilderness
For thee is fittest place; I found thee there,
And thither will return thee; yet remember
What I foretell thee, soon thou shalt have cause
To wish thou never hadst rejected thus
Nicely or cautiously my offer'd aid,
Which would have set thee in short time with ease
On David's throne, or throne of all the world,
Now at full age, fulness of time, thy season,
When prophecies of thee are best fulfill'd.
Now contrary, if I read aught in heav'n,
Or heav'n write aught of fate, by what the stars,
Voluminous, or single characters,
In their conjunction met, give me to spell,
Sorrows, and labors, opposition, hate,
Attends thee, scorns, reproaches, injuries,
Violence, and stripes, and lastly cruel death;
A kingdom they portend thee, but what kingdom,
Real or allegoric, I discern not,
Nor when, eternal sure, as without end,
Without beginning; for no date prefixt
Directs me in the starry rubric set.
　　So saying he took, for still he knew his pow'r
Not yet expired, and to the wilderness
Brought back the Son of God, and left him there,
Feigning to disappear. Darkness now rose,
As daylight sunk, and brought in low'ring Night,
Her shadowy offspring, unsubstantial both,
Privation mere of light and absent day.
Our Saviour, meek and with untroubled mind
After his aery jaunt, though hurried sore,
Hungry and cold betook him to his rest,
Wherever, under some concourse of shades,
Whose branching arms thick intertwined might shield
From dews and damps of night his shelter'd head,
But shelter'd slept in vain, for at his head
The tempter watch'd, and soon with ugly dreams
Disturbed his sleep: and either tropic now
'Gan thunder, and both ends of heav'n the clouds
From many a horrid rift abortive pour'd
Fierce rain with light'ning mix'd, water with fire
In ruin reconciled: nor slept the winds

Within their stony caves, but rush'd abroad
From the four hinges[1] of the world, and fell
On the vext wilderness, whose tallest pines,
Though rooted deep as high, and sturdiest oaks
Bow'd their stiff necks, loaden with stormy blasts,
Or torn up sheer: ill wast thou shrouded then,
O patient Son of GOD, yet only stood'st
Unshaken; nor yet staid the terror there,
Infernal ghosts and hellish furies round
Environ'd thee; some howl'd, some yell'd, some shriek'd,
Some bent at thee their fiery darts, while thou
Sat'st unappall'd in calm and sinless peace.
Thus pass'd the night so foul, till morning fair
Came forth with pilgrim steps in amice gray,
Who with her radiant finger still'd the roar
Of thunder, chased the clouds, and laid the winds,
And grisly spectres, which the fiend had raised
To tempt the Son of GOD with terrors dire.
And now the sun with more effectual beams
Had cheer'd the face of earth, and dried the wet
From drooping plant or drooping tree; the birds,
Who all things now behold more fresh and green,
After a night of storm so ruinous,
Clear'd up their choicest notes in bush and spray,
To gratulate the sweet return of morn:
Nor yet amidst this joy and brightest morn
Was absent, after all his mischief done,
The prince of darkness, glad would also seem
Of this fair change, and to our Savior came,
Yet with no new device, they all were spent,
Rather by this his last affront resolved,
Desperate of better course, to vent his rage,
And mad despite to be so oft repell'd.
Him walking on a sunny hill he found,
Back'd on the north and west by a thick wood:
Out of the wood he starts in wonted shape,
And in a careless mood thus to him said.

　　Fair morning yet betides thee, Son of GOD,
After a dismal night: I heard the rack
As earth and sky would mingle, but myself

---

[1] The cardinal points—north, south, east, and west. *Cardo*, from
whence the word cardinal is derived, signifies *a hinge*.

Was distant; and these flaws,[1] though mortals fear them
As dangerous to the pillar'd frame of heav'n,
Or to the earth's dark basis underneath,
Are to the main as inconsiderable
And harmless, if not wholesome, as a sneeze
To man's less universe, and soon are gone;
Yet as being ofttimes noxious where they light
On man, beast, plant, wasteful, and turbulent,
Like turbulencies in the affairs of men,
Over whose heads they roar, and seem to point,
They oft fore-signify and threaten ill:
This tempest at this desert most was bent:
Of men at thee, for only thou here dwell'st.
Did I not tell thee, if thou did'st reject
The perfect season offer'd with my aid
To win thy destined seat, but wilt prolong
All to the push of fate, pursue thy way
Of gaining David's throne no man knows when,
For both the when and how is no where told,
Thou shalt be what thou art ordain'd, no doubt;
For angels have proclaim'd it, but concealing
The time and means; each act is rightliest done
Not when it must, but when it may be best.
If thou observe not this, be sure to find,
What I foretold thee, many a hard assay
Of dangers, and adversities, and pains,
Ere thou of Israel's sceptre get fast hold;
Whereof this ominous night that closed thee round,
So many terrors, voices, prodigies,
May warn thee, as a sure fore-going sign.
    So talk'd he, while the Son of GOD went on
And staid not, but in brief him answer'd thus.
    Me worse than wet thou find'st not; other harm
Those terrors, which thou speak'st of, did me none;
I never fear'd they could, though noising loud
And threat'ning nigh; what they can do as signs
Betok'ning, or ill-boding, I contemn
As false portents, not sent from GOD, but thee;
Who, knowing I shall reign past thy preventing,
Obtrud'st thy offer'd aid, that I accepting

---

[1] A sea term for a sudden gust of wind.

At least might seem to hold all pow'r of thee,
Ambitious spirit! and would'st be thought my GOD,
And storm'st refused, thinking to terrify
Me to thy will. Desist, thou art discern'd
And toil'st in vain, nor me in vain molest.
　　To whom the fiend now swoll'n with rage replied.
Then hear, O Son of David, virgin-born;
For Son of GOD to me is yet in doubt:
Of the Messiah I had heard, foretold
By all the prophets; of thy birth at length
Announced by Gabriel with the first I knew,
And of the angelic song in Bethlehem field,
On thy birthnight, that sung thee Saviour born.
From that time seldom have I ceased to eye
Thy infancy, thy childhood, and thy youth,
Thy manhood last, though yet in private bred;
Till at the ford of Jordan, whither all
Flock'd to the Baptist, I among the rest,
Though not to be baptized, by voice from heav'n
Heard thee pronounced the Son of GOD beloved.
Thenceforth I thought thee worth my nearer view
And narrower scrutiny, that I might learn
In what degree or meaning thou art call'd
The Son of GOD, which bears no single sense;
The Son of GOD I also am, or was,
And if I was I am; relation stands;
All men are sons of GOD; yet thee I thought
In some respect far higher so declared.
Therefore I watch'd thy footsteps from that hour,
And follow'd thee still on to this waste wild;
Where by all best conjectures I collect
Thou art to be my fatal enemy.
Good reason then, if I beforehand seek
To understand my adversary, who,
And what he is; his wisdom, power, intent;
By parl, or composition, truce, or league,
To win him, or win from him what I can.
And opportunity I here have had
To try thee, sift thee, and confess have found thee
Proof against all temptation, as a rock
Of adamant, and as a centre firm,
To the utmost of mere man both wise and good,

Not more; for honors, riches, kingdoms, glory,
Have been before contemn'd, and may again:
Therefore to know what more thou art than man,
Worth naming Son of God by voice from heav'n,
Another method I must now begin.

So saying he caught him up, and without wing
Of hippogrif [1] bore through the air sublime
Over the wilderness and o'er the plain;
Till underneath them fair Jerusalem,
The holy city, lifted high her towers,
And higher yet the glorious temple rear'd
Her pile, far off appearing like a mount
Of alabaster, topp'd with golden spires:
There on the highest pinnacle he set
The Son of God, and added thus in scorn.

There stand, if thou wilt stand; to stand upright
Will ask thee skill; I to thy Father's house
Have brought thee, and highest placed; highest is best;
Now show thy progeny; if not to stand,
Cast thyself down; safely, if Son of God;
For it is written, He will give command
Concerning thee to his angels, in their hands
They shall uplift thee, lest at any time
Thou chance to dash thy foot against a stone.

To whom thus Jesus. Also it is written,
Tempt not the Lord thy God: he said and stood:
But Satan smitten with amazement fell.
As when earth's son Antæus,[2] to compare
Small things with greatest, in Irassa strove
With Jove's Alcides, and oft foil'd still rose,
Receiving from his mother earth new strength,
Fresh from his fall, and fiercer grapple join'd,
Throttled at length in th' air, expired and fell;
So after many a foil the tempter proud,
Renewing fresh assaults, amidst his pride

---

[1] A fabulous creature, on which Ariosto's heroes were borne through the air.
[2] A giant of Libya, of Terra (the earth) and Neptune (the sea). Alcides (Hercules) attacked him; and as every time the giant touched the earth he received new strength, Hercules lifted him up into the air, and squeezed him to death in his arms. Irassa was a city in Libya.

Fell whence he stood to see his victor fall.
And as that Theban monster[1] that proposed
Her riddle, and him who solved it not, devour'd,
That once found out and solved, for grief and spite
Cast herself headlong from th' Ismenian steep;
So struck with dread and anguish fell the fiend,
And to his crew that sat consulting, brought
Joyless triumphals of his hoped success,
Ruin, and desperation, and dismay,
Who durst so proudly tempt the Son of GOD.
So Satan fell; and straight a fiery globe
Of angels on full sail of wing flew nigh,
Who on their plumy vans received Him soft
From His uneasy station, and upbore
As on a floating couch through the blithe air,
Then in a flow'ry valley set Him down
On a green bank, and set before Him spread
A table of celestial food, divine,
Ambrosial fruits, fetch'd from the Tree of Life,
And from the Fount of Life ambrosial drink,
That soon refresh'd Him wearied, and repair'd
What hunger, if aught hunger had impair'd
Or thirst; and, as He fed, angelic quires
Sung heav'nly anthems of his victory
Over temptation and the tempter proud.
　　True Image of the Father, whether throned
In the bosom of bliss, and light of light
Conceiving, or remote from heav'n, enshrined
In fleshly tabernacle and human form,
Wand'ring the wilderness, whatever place,
Habit, or state, or motion, still expressing
The Son of GOD, with god-like force indued
Against the attempter of thy Father's throne,
And thief of paradise; him long of old
Thou didst debel,[2] and down from heav'n cast
With all his army, now thou has avenged
Supplanted Adam, and by vanquishing
Temptation, hast regain'd lost Paradise;
And frustrated the conquest fraudulent:
never more henceforth will dare set foot

Sphinx.
quer.

In Paradise to tempt; his snares are broke:
For though that seat of earthly bliss be fail'd,
A fairer paradise is founded now
For Adam and his chosen sons, whom thou
A Savior art come down to re-install
Where they shall dwell secure, when time shall be,
Of tempter and temptation without fear.
But thou infernal serpent, shalt not long
Rule in the clouds; like an autumnal star
Or light'ning thou shalt fall from heav'n, trod down
Under His feet: for proof, ere this thou feel'st
Thy wound, yet not thy last and deadliest wound,
By this repulse received, and hold'st in hell
No triumph. In all her gates Abaddon[1] rues
Thy bold attempt; hereafter learn with awe
To dread the Son of God: he all unarm'd
Shall chase thee with the terror of his voice
From thy demoniac holds, possession foul,
Thee and thy legions; yelling they shall fly,
And beg to hide them in a herd of swine,
Lest he command them down into the deep
Bound, and to torment sent before their time.
Hail Son of the Most High, heir of both worlds,
Queller of Satan, on thy glorious work
Now enter, and begin to save mankind.

　　Thus they the Son of God, our Saviour meek
Sung victor, and from heav'nly feast refresh'd
Brought on his way with joy; he unobserved
Home to his mother's house private return'd.

---

[1] Rev. ix. 11. The name is here applied to hell.

OTHER AIRMONT CLASSICS

Complete and Unabridged with Introductions